P9-DEF-816

WITHDRAWN

ADULT DEPARTMENT

1. Fine Schedule
   1-·5 days overdue . . . . grace period, no fine
   6-10 days overdue . . . . 25¢ per item
   11-19 days overdue . . . . 75¢ per item.
   20th day overdue . . . . $2.00 per item
2. Injury to books beyond reasonable wear and all losses shall be paid for.
3. Each borrower is held responsible for all books drawn on his card and for all fines accruing on the same.

FOND DU LAC PUBLIC LIBRARY
COUNTY EXTENSION DEPARTMENT
FOND DU LAC, WISCONSIN

THE FORGIVING MARRIAGE

THE FORGIVING MARRIAGE

DR. PAUL W. COLEMAN

CONTEMPORARY
BOOKS
CHICAGO · NEW YORK

Library of Congress Cataloging-in-Publication Data

Coleman, Paul W.
    The forgiving marriage : resolving anger and resentment and
rediscovering each other / Paul W. Coleman.
        p.   cm.
    Bibliography: p.
    ISBN 0-8092-4498-5 : $16.95
        1. Marriage—United States—Psychological aspects.
2. Communication in marriage—United States.   3. Forgiveness.
4. Reconciliation.   I. Title.
HQ734.C5965   1989
646.7'8—dc 19   88-36956
                                                                              CIP

Author's Note:
To protect confidentiality, the names and identifying characteristics
of the individuals and couples mentioned in this book have been
changed. Many of the case examples are composites of several
people. Any resemblance to persons living or dead is entirely
coincidental and unintended.
    Since making changes in one's life, even positive changes, can
produce anxiety, readers should consult a qualified mental health
professional if any undue anxiety persists.

Copyright © 1989 by Paul W. Coleman
All rights reserved
Published by Contemporary Books, Inc.
180 North Michigan Avenue, Chicago, Illinois 60601
Manufactured in the United States of America
Library of Congress Catalog Card Number: 88-36956
International Standard Book Number: 0-8092-4498-5

Published simultaneously in Canada by Beaverbooks, Ltd.
195 Allstate Parkway, Valleywood Business Park
Markham, Ontario L3R 4T8 Canada

Lovingly dedicated to Jody,
and to our children,
Luke and Anna

Contents

Acknowledgments

To my wife, Jody, for her love, encouragement, caring, and willingness to make sacrifices for a project that began as a pipe dream;

To my literary agent, Mike Snell, whose expert advice, steady enthusiasm, and comforting faith in a first-time author made this publication a reality;

To my editors at Contemporary Books, most notably Stacy Prince, Deborah Brody, and Karen Schenkenfelder, whose skills in editing and shaping the book were remarkable;

To Sandy Lash, M.S.W., of Harlem Valley Psychiatric Center, a good friend and colleague whose review of the first draft gave me wonderful guidance and direction;

To Joel Gurin of *American Health* magazine, who graciously took time from his busy schedule and offered much-needed advice when the book was in its early stages;

To Herb Pavel, who started it all;

To Minnie and Marty, whose lives have more meaning than they know;

To my close friends near and far, who may never have known how much laughing with them meant to me, especially when I doubted this book might ever be published;

To my entire family, especially my parents, George and Frances Coleman, and to Claire, Ann, Jane, Debby, and John, who've always been there no matter what;

To the people whose stories were the inspiration for this book, who time and again found the courage to face themselves;

I give my love, and my warmest and most heartfelt thanks.

—Wappingers Falls, New York
1989

THE FORGIVING MARRIAGE

PART ONE

PREPARING FOR RECONCILIATION AND FORGIVENESS

Chapter One

The Beckoning: The Call to Reconcile and Forgive

"I just don't think she cares. I've tried; I really have. But maybe I've waited too long. Maybe she won't change. Maybe she doesn't want to change. Well, now it's my turn not to care."

—Barry, age 31

"My husband left me for another woman two years ago. And I still feel so bitter, especially after all I've done for him. It was so unfair! He was wrong to do that! And I can't seem to feel good about anything anymore."

—Matty, age 55

"He was my dad. If I loved him, it was because he told me to. I hated him because I had no choice. But I thought my husband would be different. Now I'm not so sure. Tell me what to do."

—Donna, age 33

"I haven't seen him in five years. I know I hurt him

3

when I walked out on him and his mother, but I can't talk to him now. If I stir up the past, I may lose him completely. He's my son, but sometimes I just wish I could get him, and his mother, out of my mind."

—*Samuel, age 47*

There is a call that you hear from deep inside your spirit.

It is a beckoning within to do something about a long-standing hurt. It is both a felt pain and an urge to let go of the pain. Maybe you find yourself thinking, "I want to forgive him but I can't," or, "How long must I suffer for the pain I've caused?" Still, there is a call, a tugging to go back to someone you have been estranged from and find forgiveness, to complete the unfinished business.

Even if the other person is gone forever from your life and no reunion is possible, there are times when you wish you could finally and thoroughly resolve the pain that has kept you feeling angry or guilty, depressed or ashamed, for so long.

Or perhaps you vow, "I will never forgive!" but the bitterness and preoccupations about what happened stir up and complicate your life every day. You are angry and not really intimate with others. You expect your partner (and maybe the world) to treat you unjustly, so you go through life ready to flee or do battle on a moment's notice. And inside you is an aching emptiness you just can't seem to fill. You want to heal your wounded marriage. This book can help you to do just that.

Your vow to never forgive is your admission that you are still suffering. It is a plea to yourself to do something constructive that will allow you to let go of the hurts and be reconciled in a manner that won't leave you open for more certain pain. And when you are honest with yourself, you know that is what you really want.

You may not fully understand those complicated urges that beckon you. It may seem confusing and against your better judgment to consider forgiving someone who has hurt you so deeply. You may believe that to forgive is to let that other person get away with the acts of abuse or betrayal.

Yet you may also have discovered that by withholding forgiveness, you only keep the pain alive long after it first occurred. You still feel betrayed; you still feel saddened at the loss or fading of a relationship that once was so vital. That can't be fair to you.

And if you caused some of the pain too (and you probably did), you may be uncertain about wanting to be forgiven and reconciled. Perhaps you feel ashamed and unworthy. Maybe you are still too angry to seek a reunion just yet. Maybe more issues remain to be settled. Regardless, amid the confusing ideas and lingering anger, hate, guilt, or depression, is that echoing call that beckons you still.

Pay attention to that urge. It comes from the part of you that yearns to recreate a loving relationship with someone you are distant from now. It has its beginnings in the part of you that knows you do not deserve the hate, the bitterness, or the guilt that interferes with your ability to love more fully.

You can answer that call within you. You can relinquish the pain and live a more honest, free, and fulfilling life. You can reinvent the important relationship that right now leaves you feeling cheated or frightened.

But to be open to the embrace of forgiveness and reconciliation, you must also be open to the truths about yourself. You must be witness to your strengths and to your weaknesses so that the healing can be complete.

YOU ARE ESTRANGED

Being estranged from someone simply means being unable to be your best self when you are with that person. Out of anger or fear, you withhold your feelings and the truest aspects of yourself.

Barbara and Forrest had professional careers and a combined income now into six figures. Married for twenty years, they had no children. One day they sat on opposite ends of a couch and discussed their relationship.

"I don't know. I just feel as if I've missed out on something," Barbara began. "Maybe I'm being selfish. After all, we have enough money, and we both enjoy our jobs. I guess it hit me when we moved into our new house. We just had it built. It looks all pretty and polished inside, but all I've felt like doing is crying. 'So this is it?' I asked Forrest. 'This is what we said was so important all these years?' "

"That's what I don't understand," Forrest interrupted. "Our life is not that house. You make it sound like all we care about is what we can buy next."

"All I'm saying is that I'm not happy, and I don't know why. And I'm beginning to regret that we never had children."

"We certainly had our chances," Forrest shot back. "Five years ago, even ten years ago, I kept saying 'It's time to start a family,' but you always resisted. Now you're forty-one, and you tell me we should have had kids by now. You're something else, you know that?"

Neither one looked at the other. They each sat

staring in opposite directions, unsettled by thoughts and feelings they had never really faced before.

The Faces of Estrangement

Like Barbara and Forrest, you don't have to be enemies to be estranged. You and your spouse are living and sleeping together but still maintain a psychological distance from one another. You know how that is. You spend time together, maybe out of habit, fear, or obligation, but there is little sharing and no real closeness and growth in the relationship. There is instead a constant, gnawing strain that leaves you tired and frustrated. Sex may be a chore, or it still may be somewhat satisfying. Then again, something is probably missing. And you think about many more things than you could ever feel free to say. Maybe you think about how angry you are, how self-sacrificing you have been, or how guilty you feel. But you hold back from being completely open, even with yourself. You are frightened of your honesty and of an honest reaction.

Maybe your anger is veiled by forced laughter; your critical remarks couched in "harmless" teasing. Maybe your rage is directed inward, and you feel depressed. Perhaps your fear of being honest about your feelings shows itself as anxiety that weaves like ivy through many areas of your life. You feel more and more threatened by a broadening band of places, situations, and events. You are estranged.

Or, you may be open about your feelings, but all that you communicate is hostility. You are caught up in a vicious cycle of blaming, hurting, and being hurt. Sometimes the fighting and feelings of contempt are overt and obvious, while at other times they are covert and subtle. But they continue.

If you have perpetuated a relationship that is fueled more by fear and anxiety than by honesty, more by anger than by joy, more by guilt and shame than by the faith to be yourself, then there will only be deeper estrangement. And when you allow this restriction in intimacy to characterize an important relationship without doing something to try and change your role in it, then you have been estranged from your best self as well.

Have you really been honest with yourself about all of your faults, fears, and strengths? Have you really done something constructive with those truths about yourself, or have you hidden them and pretended that they aren't relevant to your current problems?

If you have not answered yes, then you have set yourself up to be less able to manage the kind of hurt that now keeps you separated from someone you've loved. You owe it to yourself and to the people who matter to you to face some of the personal challenges you have avoided until now.

You *can* reunite with your spouse and anyone else you are estranged from. You *can* transform the relationships into much more loving ones. At the very least, you can resolve your own pain enough to be able to get on productively with your life. But to do so, you may need to reunite your feelings with your thoughts and actions instead of continuing to live by pretense, always doing one thing but thinking and feeling another.

Over time you can be forgiving. Forgive yourself for any pain you've caused and for any failure to have done something about the estrangement until now. You can forgive the person who hurt you; you can forgive your partner and come together again in love and friendship.

WHY SHOULD I FORGIVE?

I looked for tenderness between them and could find only torment.

"She simply doesn't know how to love," Dwight stated matter-of-factly. "She never gives. She's afraid of losing control, of losing power." His eyes darted in her direction, then quickly away. She was untouched. He continued. "She never loved our son. And he died never understanding why." This time, his eyes stayed focused on her.

Her lips were drawn tightly, thin and bloodless. She kept her composure. "Michael crashed his motorcycle on the night that you hit him, Dwight. In your drunken stupor, you told him to get the hell out, and he did. Don't speak to me about love. I doubt he ever felt loved by you."

The details went on and on. Twenty-four years filled mostly with anguish and bitterness. They remain together, so they say, for the sake of their fifteen-year-old daughter. What do they hope to accomplish by coming to me? To succeed in staying married until their daughter leaves for college? To try to reconcile? To feel less guilty?

It was a later session, Judy alone. Though she still held contempt for her husband, there was now, at least, a warmth to her.

"You loved your son," I said. "But I'm wondering if there was anger, too."

"Michael was a wonderful boy," she answered. "But as he got older he got . . . reckless. . . ." She shook her head, as if quietly saying no to some memory. "His grades in school were falling. He didn't seem to care. All he cared about was his motorcycle. Dwight was always furious with him. Actually, I think Dwight saw himself in Michael. Dwight lost two businesses out of his own recklessness early in our marriage. That was when he started to drink more heavily."

She paused, about to come to terms with a truth she could not admit before. "I know I treated Michael unfairly some of the time. I think I yelled at him when I really should have been yelling at his father. I expected Michael not to hurt me like his father did. I thought he'd be more on my side." A sad, longing smile opened from nowhere, dragging her face down into her shoulder. "Yes, I was angry with Michael," she cried, bolting upward with a shudder. Stunned by her own reckless expression of feeling, she straightened herself, poised herself once again. "But I also loved him dearly," she stated calmly. "And I don't believe he'll ever know just how sorry I am, how much I miss him."

Her eyes glistened only lightly. She could not cry. It seemed important to her to protect herself from that. That seemed to me the saddest part of it all.

It was many sessions later. Their remarks to each other were less cruel, less stabbing. But there was nothing else. No caring, no sensitivity. They were now very much alone together. It was toward the end of our meeting.

"I have some strong mixed feelings," I told them. "On the one hand, it seems important for each of you to continue keeping distant from each other. After all, you've each been badly hurt. But on the other hand, I can't imagine that holding on to hate and bitterness is what you really want to happen. At what point do you think you can begin to forgive yourselves and each other for all that's happened?"

"Aren't some things unforgivable?" Dwight asked.

I looked at him closely. Somehow I knew he wasn't speaking of his wife's actions, but his own. "I believe everything is potentially forgivable. I guess it depends upon what each person is willing to do to make it happen."

Dwight sighed heavily. "Sometimes I want to, but sometimes I don't think it's fair," he said softly.

"I don't think Dwight can be forgiven," Judy jabbed.

The mood in the room immediately changed. Dwight glared at Judy. She looked righteously at me. Dwight was about to say something to her; probably it would be something cruel. I wasn't going to let them get away with it this time.

"I think you should thank your wife, Dwight." They stared at me in amazement. "Every time the two of you start hurting each other with words, you protect yourselves from an even greater pain. The truth is that neither of you has really mourned your son's death. I've watched you protect yourself from that grief, and the way that you do that is by fighting and blaming."

I was irritated. Did they need to be told off? Shaken up? Was I too involved?

I continued while they sat in stunned silence. "I'm sorry. Maybe I'm coming on too strong. It's just sad, that's all. You've been through so much together, you've survived so much pain. But you each push away the only other person who could truly understand and support you. The trouble is that if you admit your own weaknesses, you run the risk that your partner will attack you. So you hold back, take an accusing stance, and you never get beyond blaming and into the truth. And the truth is, I think, that you've both made mistakes, that you've both been hurtful, that you both loved your son, and that neither of you has truly mourned his death, because to do so, you'd have to let down your guard, which you haven't done while you've been so blaming and defensive."

I stopped in midramble. But my words had had an

effect. Dwight and Judy sensed a truth in what I said. For the first time, together, they each had tears in their eyes, and they didn't try to hide it.

Unforgivable? Each could have made a solid case that the other one was just that. But each secretly feared the other was right. Opening up the prospect of forgiving their spouse allowed them to sense themselves as forgivable, too.

That is a powerful reason to forgive. The more you can forgive another, the more you can be forgiving of yourself. The more you can forgive yourself, the easier it is to forgive another. Forgiveness fills the hearts of the forgiver and the one forgiven.

And there are other reasons to forgive.

Forgiveness Reunites When There Is Guilt

When you have betrayed and greatly hurt someone, you are guilty. Judy was guilty of having hurt Dwight. If the other person has hurt you, then that person is guilty. Dwight was guilty of having hurt Judy. There are always reasons why you may have been hurtful, but they narrow down to three: you were hurtful out of anger, fear, or ignorance. Those three reasons exist because you are human but guilty nonetheless (not bad, not unlovable).

Forgiveness is the only final way to end the guilt and condemnation and bring vitality to the relationship and a resolution to your personal pain.

If you think about it, no amount of talking with the other person, no analysis of why the betrayal occurred, will completely do away with the hurt. Since you are dealing with personal feelings and not necessarily involved in a legal matter, no penalty can be handed down that will satisfactorily pay off the debt.

Efforts to make amends may be helpful, but they are also inadequate.

The bottom line is that when there is guilt from having violated a relationship, then you must ultimately be willing to forgive or be forgiven in order to reinvent a meaningful relationship. Without forgiveness, any attempt at reunion will be undermined by lingering resentment and guilt.

Forgiveness Can Stop the Cycle of Hurting

Typically, each person in the relationship has done something to hurt or offend the other. But all that usually comes of seeking vengeance is more hurting, increased bitterness, and deeper estrangement. Soon, the original hurt is but one of many, as each person feels more and more abused, betrayed, misunderstood, and angry.

But when one person decides to forgive, the pain begins to subside. The other person no longer has as much justification to continue to cause harm. Forgiveness at that point won't necessarily prevent future problems, but at least those problems will be addressed without the added burden of unresolved past injuries.

The cycle of hurting will one day end for one reason or another. Why don't you choose to end it now while there may still be a relationship left to salvage?

Forgiveness Frees You to Trust

Without a basic trust, no relationship can survive to be a growing and fulfilling one. And if you now are mistrustful after having been betrayed, then time alone will not remove your doubts sufficiently. If you fail to forgive, then your anger will remain strong enough for you to keep alert for evidence of yet another act of disloyalty. Since no one is perfect, you will eventually find what you are looking for. Is that what you really want to happen?

If you stay in a relationship where you haven't been forgiven for hurtful acts, you will always feel somewhat guilty and beholden to the other person. You will want to make amends. But as your efforts at atonement go unappreciated, your resentment will build. You will also be suspicious that the other person, who still has failed to forgive you, may one day leave you high and dry. You won't trust completely, always feeling uneasy and unable to be yourself.

But with forgiveness, there is a laying aside of resentment and guilt. The crime of betrayal no longer hangs over the relationship. You agree to be vulnerable once again, which is evidence of trust in any relationship. You take the risk of forgiving and being vulnerable because the other person matters to you and you wish to once again experience love.

To be forgiving of your spouse is not to give him or her "just one more chance." In forgiveness, you understand that due to human weaknesses a trust may again be betrayed. You do not pretend that the original hurt never happened, but you still regard your husband or wife as worthy of your trust. You trust that the one who hurt you will endeavor to change those ways of behaving that cause pain, knowing that such changes may take time.

And when you accept the offer of forgiveness, understand that you need not earn the trust of the other person. You already have it.

Forgiveness Leads to Self-Enhancement

You will come to see this process of reconciliation and forgiveness as being a journey of growth, giving, and understanding. You will learn much about yourself and in so doing have a ripe opportunity for self-enhancement.

You will learn what many of your shortcomings are. You rarely receive forgiveness without learning something about yourself that is unflattering. You may even discover that you have hurt others close to you over the years, something that until you were forgiven you either overlooked or deemphasized.

You will also bear witness to your strengths. You will see that you have the capacity to foster healing, even when the wounds penetrate deeply. You have the compassion to be more accepting of yourself and others regardless of faults. You have the freedom to give to others without expecting anything in return. You have the judgment to realize when you may need to end an abusive relationship, despite being forgiving, and when the relationship can indeed blossom.

You will learn that when a hurt against you is particularly painful, it probably stimulated some fear you have not come to terms with. For example, Judy's accusation that Dwight was an unloving father was painful to him. Why? Because it hit a raw nerve: his own fear that indeed he had not been a good enough father. Rather than honestly face his own faults, feel remorse, and find forgiveness, Dwight chose to focus on Judy and blame her for his pain. Judy did the same to him.

Whatever fears you may have, venturing on the road to forgiveness will give you the opportunity to reduce or eliminate those fears so that you can once again be more open and trusting in your relationships.

FORGIVENESS CAN TAKE TIME

Although it is possible to forgive or be forgiven quickly, forgiveness is often a process that takes some time. A thoughtless, insensitive remark by your spouse may be quickly forgiven, especially if he or she shows remorse. But if the hurts are deep and many, then it can be difficult to feel forgiving.

Acts of betrayal seem to be among the most painful to experience. It feels bad enough when someone you hardly know takes advantage of you or makes a fool of you, but it can be shattering when you feel so betrayed by your spouse. By betraying you, someone who knows well your needs and weaknesses makes a mockery of the trust in the relationship.

And yet it is in such a relationship that forgiveness is desperately needed, even if no reunion is possible. For if you fail to resolve for yourself the pain of having been betrayed, you may likely be guarded and wary of openness in other important relationships.

You also need to know that as freeing and joyous as it may be to find forgiveness, it can also hurt a little in the process.

There is the pain you feel when you restrain yourself from getting even, from exacting that pound of flesh, in order that forgiveness can happen. That pain is your frustration and anger at the seeming injustice of it all.

There is the pain that you feel when the person you hurt seeks to forgive you rather than reject you. That pain is your shame and feelings of unworthiness.

There is the pain you feel when, in an effort to understand how the hurts came about, you learn something about yourself or the other person that is hard to accept. That pain is anxiety that comes from realizing you don't know as much as you thought you did, and that others may eventually abandon you.

There is the pain you feel when others try to persuade you that forgiving is a sign of weakness. That pain is your self-doubt and need for approval.

There is the pain you feel when you open yourself up to trust again, knowing how you've been hurt before. That pain could be the fear of looking foolish in others' eyes or in your own. That pain is also necessary if you are to give love.

But once forgiveness happens, there is no more pain, but a healing instead. The relationship is scrubbed clean, invigorating, and vital again.

Why forgiveness? Because forgiveness is more than a moral imperative, more than a theological dictum. Forgiveness is the only means, given our humanness and imperfections, to overcome hate and condemnation and proceed with the business of growing and loving.

WHERE YOU GO FROM HERE

This book is about forgiveness in marriages. It will help you to understand yourself, your spouse, and your family and show you how to find forgiveness when being in relationships (especially a marriage) hurts.

Your marriage is not an island unto itself. The troubles and triumphs you've endured affect other relationships in your life, just as those other relationships can affect your marriage. Particularly, how you feel about your parents and their marriage, and how they feel about you and your marriage are extremely important. In fact, the more difficulty you've had trying to solve your marital problems, the more likely it is that you haven't yet come to terms with your relationship with your parents. That is so because unsettled hurts or issues with one's parents have a tendency to play out in the marriage arena. Consequently, you may have to forgive your parents, or at least let go of your unrealistic expectations of them, before you and your spouse can settle down and fully forgive each other. It doesn't always have to happen that way, but often it does.

This book is divided into two parts. Finding forgiveness in a troubled marriage, especially when other relationships in your life are also troubled, requires some preparation. Part One of this book helps to prepare you.

Part Two describes the phases of forgiveness. These phases are not absolute and invariant. There can be no cookbook formula to forgiveness. But the phases represent the typical transitions that many people experience when they wish to heal a painful relationship. People vary in the amount of time they take to complete each phase. Some people feel genuinely forgiving before completing all phases. Others must repeat certain phases before they finally feel forgiving and forgiven. The more forgiving you learn to become, the easier it gets.

This book provides the nuts and bolts of the forgiveness process, but it does not have all the answers. Life's problems have no easy and absolute solutions, yet I believe that at least some of your pain can be released. But more than that, I want you to know and experience forgiveness so that you can revitalize and reinvent your marriage and other important relationships. I want you to be free to get along productively and lovingly in your life.

This forgiveness process is not a panacea. It is an ideal that we can sometimes reach. Our humanness makes that so. We are simply too imperfect, too caught up in the day-to-day practicalities of living, too human, to conduct our lives routinely with a fully humble and forgiving attitude. As such, the people who we'd like to be forgiving of us, may not. At least not right away. And that isn't always easy to bear.

If you have been hurtful toward your spouse and now feel angry, dissatisfied, isolated, perhaps frightened, or if you have been deeply hurt and feel bitter and sad, you can resolve your pain and reconcile with the one you are estranged from. You don't have to take on the world to overcome all that is burdening you. Begin with that one person you've been thinking about the most, that one person you wish to be closer to but you just can't get past the resentment or guilt you've been feeling.

You can do it. If you've ever forgiven anyone for anything, or if you have ever been forgiven, then you know what is possible. And you deserve every bit of the joy that genuine reconciliation and forgiveness bring.

If you doubt that the last statement is true, please read on anyway. You may discover that there is more good about you than you've realized, that you are worthwhile in spite of your faults (welcome to the human race), and that your capacity to give and receive love really knows no bounds.

Chapter Two

Forgiveness: When It Is Genuine, When It Is False

"I've been over this so many times with you," Lee said to me with exasperation, "but nothing is better. I mean, I don't *feel* loving toward her. Shouldn't I feel that way by now?"

"Should you?" I answered rhetorically. "You're still angry, Lee. Sure, you have reason to be angry, and so does she, but I have the impression you're waiting to feel loving before you can act lovingly."

"I've learned to trust my feelings," he interjected. "I trust them more than I trust Sue."

I was about to focus on his reasons for believing Sue to be untrustworthy when I realized that was what he wanted me to do. That way we could implicitly lay the blame on her for a while and by the end of our session succeed in getting nowhere. Again. As much as Lee complained about uselessly repeating his complaints during our sessions, he was adept at doing just that.

"Sue isn't the easiest person to get along with, you

know," he said, offering me the ball and hoping I'd run with it.

"You're wanting to *feel* better about her, Lee, but you rarely focus on what you can do differently to help improve your feelings. You told me once that you want to forgive her. That's important. But your first step is to *decide* to be forgiving. Make the choice to work toward forgiveness even though you don't feel forgiving now. Do you think you can start that way?"

"I can if she will," he said, shifting the responsibility for his future back into her lap.

"I can't push you into something you don't want, Lee. I know she's hurt you deeply. Actually, from the way you describe it, I'd say you both have treated each other pretty shabbily. But the truth is that one of you is going to have to take the lead on forgiving. Will it be you, or do you intend to wait for her?"

In forgiveness, you decide to give love to someone who has betrayed your love. You call forth your compassion, your wisdom, and your desire to be accepting of that person for who he or she is. You call forth your humanness and seek reunion in love and growth above all else.

Forgiveness is the changing of seasons. It provides a new context within which to nurture the relationship. The changing of the seasons allows you to let go of all that has been difficult to bear and begin again. When you forgive, you do not forget the season of cold completely, but neither do you shiver in its memory. The chill has subsided and has no more effect on the present than to remind you of how far you've come, how much you've grown, how truly you love and are loved.

When forgiveness becomes a part of your life, little resentment is left. Anger may not vanish immediately, but it will wither in time. The hot core of bitterness that was embedded firmly in your being burns no more.

Forgiveness comes first as a decision to act lovingly, even though you may feel justified to withhold your love.

The seed of forgiveness was planted when you were very young and clutching the person who meant everything to you. Remember? Probably that person was your parent. Your existence depended upon your mom and your dad. When you felt hurt or deprived, you could not stay angry for long. That would have been too frightening. So you put aside your anger in the best way you knew how.

The flower of forgiveness bore its first fruit years later when you were old enough to look that parent in the eye and let go, seeing him or her much more clearly. It was at the moment when you saw the limitations, the humanness of that special person and *accepted him or her nonetheless*, that you became forgiving. And you began to believe, right then, that you too were forgivable.

That is how genuine forgiveness unfolds. It begins as a decision and a willingness to accept others as they are. You don't have to like some of the things they do, but you decide not to reject them for their ways. You see others as human and worthy of compassion and fairness. And that is how you begin to view yourself, too. For many people, the ability to be genuinely forgiving of others firmly takes root when they can forgive their parents. That was true for Lisa.

Lisa remembers her mother: "I used to get furious with her when she tried to tell me how to deal with my husband—or my kids. God, she always found something to criticize about my handling of the kids." She pressed her fingers against her temples, rubbing away the ache of a memory. "It was so strange. I woke up one morning; it was the morning after Sally's school play. Mom said she'd go to the play, but she backed out at the last minute. She does that kind of thing a lot. Anyway, I must have had this dream about Mom, and even though I was awake, I could see her face in my mind so clearly. She had such a troubled expression. She had a smile, but it was a pained smile. She was trying so hard to keep me from knowing her sadness, but she couldn't hide it anymore. And that frightened her, I could tell. She turned from me, and I sensed she felt so sad, so ashamed, so sorry. But she couldn't admit it.

"I started sobbing. My husband didn't know what the hell was going on. I just felt so sad, but not for me. For her. Instead of anger and resentment, I felt this incredible sorrow that my mother hurt inside and that she'll probably never let that part of her show. She'll mask it with criticism or with irrelevant statements. Since then, somehow, it's been much easier for me to deal with her. I feel I can forgive her. She's no longer this powerful woman. She's just Mother. Mom. More vulnerable, more human, than I've ever realized before."

Whether her mother changes her ways or not is no longer the issue for Lisa. She has freed herself from pain by finding forgiveness.

Forgiveness is freeing but less satisfying when it is found by only one person in the relationship. That must be the case when your spouse, or parent, either has died or wants no part of your life anymore. At such times, forgiveness cannot bring about a reunion, but it can heal the pain enough for you to move forward in life. Forgiveness can resolve bitterness and guilt even when you have only yourself to help you.

In forgiveness, you do not overlook what it was that

brought about the estrangement. That pain must be worked through. But by forgiving, you admit to loving and wanting the love of the other person more than you want resentment, revenge, and continued separation.

Forgiveness is the place you come to that is like no other place. It is where you are accepted despite your faults and imperfections. It is a welcoming of love where there once was contempt and condemnation. It is the place where you find warmth and where you can sleep easily.

Forgiveness is coming home.

WHAT FORGIVENESS IS NOT

Perhaps while desiring a reconciliation, you shudder at the thought of the words *I forgive you*. You have been deeply hurt or have so hurt another that you can't get beyond the notion that to forgive is to condone the harmful acts. Or you feel that the acts of betrayal or brutality are being glossed over with a casual "let's forget about it" attitude.

"Where is the justice?" one woman asked. "How can it all be forgotten?"

"If I were to forgive her," said a husband, "I'd feel as if I were wrong and she were right. She's going to think that I can be trampled on anytime it suits her and that I'll stick by her."

"All my life I've hated him," another said. "And you sit there talking about forgiveness like he is the poor victim and I'm the persecutor. Well *I* was the victim, and if the only way he can pay for what he's done is to never be forgiven, then he'll keep on paying forever."

Comments like the last one remind me that it can be a mistake to bring up the idea of forgiveness when people are still reeling from a deep hurt. If I raise the issue of forgiveness too soon, people feel misunderstood. More often, they feel I am being insensitive to their pain (they are right), and they resent me for suggesting they turn the other cheek when they have already been badly abused.

If you are feeling misunderstood by me right now, I apologize. Your feelings right now are important and should not be pushed aside. In fact, you will see in Part Two that it is essential to vent and understand your feelings fully if there is ever to be a meaningful reconciliation and easing of your pain.

In forgiveness you never condone or encourage the hurtful acts that led up to the estrangement. Nor can they be dismissed or easily forgotten until you first take a hard look at what happened in order to better understand how the acts occurred and how to reduce the chances of them recurring.

Further, true forgiveness does not take place with strong sentimentality and sympathy at the expense of justice and dignity. There is certainly no justice and dignity if one ignores the seriousness of some human actions in the name of forgiveness.

While your forgiveness of another involves trust on your part, it does not demand that you knowingly lay yourself open to more certain abuse. So, for example, if you are a battered wife who still gets abused even though your husband repeatedly promises to change, get out. You can forgive your spouse later, but get out now. If you remain in the name of forgiveness, it is not a genuine forgiveness. You are operating out of fear and desperation, not love.

Conversely, having been forgiven for something does not give you license to go ahead and hurt others again. Forgiveness is given and accepted with the recognition that while you are human and will make mistakes, you must try to grow and not hurt the people you care about.

FORGIVING TOO EASILY: FALSE FORGIVENESS

True forgiveness can be a struggle to achieve. The more deeply you were hurt and the more you trusted, the more difficult it will be for you to move beyond anger or fear and into acceptance and forgiveness.

Commonly, couples who are estranged from one another realize that each has caused pain at some point and that neither of them is entirely without fault in the estrangement. Reconciliation then involves coming to terms with one's own guilt at having been hurtful, as well as one's anger at having been hurt.

When the process of forgiveness gets difficult and when the need for reconciliation is great, you may forgive too quickly and too easily. You may forgive less out of love than out of fear, less out of a yearning to grow than out of a dread of being alone.

Some people routinely forgive too quickly. That is a forgiveness without freedom, a false forgiveness. Such persons are locked into styles of relating where they are too often hurt because they set themselves up to be hurt and they are too frightened to set limits on the hurtful behavior of others. Often, they do not truly see themselves as worthwhile, so they remain in painful relationships where they forgive in order to feel accepted.

Lucille was like that. She remained for twenty-two years in a marriage that made her miserable. But it was all she felt she had in life. Her husband was a controlling and suspicious man who would use intimidation with Lucille to get what he wanted. Lucille had

no friends. She held a part-time job but felt unful-
filled.

"I don't know why I put up with his ways," she said.
"He blames me for anything that goes wrong, and I
always accept his reasoning. He must really care deep
down, and I know he is a good provider, so I guess
that is why I keep forgiving him."

Lucille's forgiveness of her husband was not genuine, because she was gripped by fear. Most of us
forgive neither genuinely nor falsely as a matter of
routine. We fall somewhere in between, at times forgiving more out of love and at other times forgiving
out of fear. Sometimes we may put forth an honest
effort to forgive but in the process come face to face
with a truth about ourselves or the other person that
is difficult to accept. At such times, frozen a bit by
fear or anger, we may forgive too quickly, and true
reconciliation is stifled for the moment.

Anytime you forgive in a false or distorted manner,
you have an underlying fear that you have not dealt
with properly. Psychological defenses (discussed more
fully in Chapter 5) operate to protect you from the
effects of unresolved fears. This protection, however,
comes at the expense of your ability to clearly assess
all people and situations accurately, since your perceptions of reality are blocked in some fashion by your
defenses.

When you fear something, you anticipate a potential loss. The more common and specific fears, such as
fear of flying or fear of certain animals, often involve
the fear of losing control over one's ability to cope.
Fear of loss of control or loss of mastery over events in
one's life underlies many human actions. Psychologists and psychiatrists also recognize that people fear
loss of love and personal esteem. Unassertive people,
for example, often fear that if they honestly and asser-

tively express themselves, they might lose the love of others and suffer a loss of esteem as well. (For a broader discussion of those three fears, I recommend the writings of David Viscott.)

It is those three basic fears—fear of loss of love, loss of esteem, and loss of control—that may prompt you to falsely forgive someone who has hurt you. We all possess these fears to some extent, but it is essential that we do not let them needlessly complicate, or undermine, our relationships.

Forgiving to Prevent Loss of Love

As long as you believe you are unworthy of true love, you will feel a need to forgive quickly in order to protect whatever relationship exists for you. Unfortunately, you will also be holding back your anger and your inclination to confront the person who hurt you. Essentially, you will be holding back yourself and will end up feeling resentful and depressed.

When you live by pretense to avoid loss of love, you never know if the love that is there for you would remain should you ever come out from behind your facade. You are therefore forced to doubt the sincerity and depth of any love offered to you. The anxiety created by that doubt compels you to maintain the facade in order to ensure that others won't see you as you really are (which is also angry and frightened) and abandon you. As time goes on, your relationships are indeed strained. You don't know how to act. Others around you begin to sense your lack of faith in them, and they feel annoyed, perhaps even mistrustful. And yet, if they were to express those feelings to you, you would become frightened enough to deny everything and back away.

Or you may openly admit your concerns and apologize for your demeanor of pretense but never take the time to change your ways. You'd much rather get the whole matter over with as quickly as possible.

If you engage in that kind of interaction with some frequency, you will eventually brand other people's annoyance with you as evidence of their tenuous love for you. You may even accuse them of being to blame for problems in the relationship, when in fact you never gave the relationship an honest try.

It is an insidious belief that you are unlovable. And it may have developed from the fact that people whom you once depended upon for love never really gave it to you. If so, you started out with a handicap. Regrettably, you then went on to become your worst enemy. You recreated relationships that would leave you hungry for love and acceptance. And your doubt of your own worth made you question the sincerity of any love offered to you.

The power to change is within you. Ultimately, you will have to risk exposing your feelings to the people who matter to you in order to discover whether they can still love and accept you. You will have to be patient and forgiving of them if their initial reactions to your openness are shock, anger, and defensiveness. After all, until now you haven't been straightforward with them. You will be speaking with them in a manner that is not your usual style.

Begin to believe that you are worthy of genuine love, a love that won't be withdrawn because you are human, and you will find it easier to forgive others truly and cleanly. It won't be a forgiveness out of desperation. It will be a giving of yourself in a way that was difficult to do before. It will be a giving that, instead of draining your spirit, replenishes it.

Forgiving to Prevent Loss of Esteem

When your self-esteem is fragile, you may be quickly

forgiving of others as a way to convince yourself that you really must be a good person. This self-sacrificing, forgiving style operates to protect you from your belief that you are an inadequate person.

If your personal esteem is low, you may involve yourself with people who feel worse about themselves than you do. It then becomes easier to feel better about yourself when you are compared with a person you regard as even more inadequate. A complication arises, though, when you need that person to remain inadequate so that you can continue to feel better. And should that person hurt you, you may falsely forgive in order to maintain the relationship you need so much to validate you.

Listen to Marjorie.

"I guess I feel like a dummy, if you want to know the truth of it," she revealed at our eighth meeting. "Everyone thinks I'm stupid. My husband ridicules me even when we have company, and seems to find fault with anything I say. And Gary insults me, too. Sometimes I think he's worse than my husband."

Gary is Marjorie's twenty-year-old son, who was paralyzed after being struck by a car when he was nine. Marjorie had been very dedicated to Gary since his accident, often to the exclusion of her husband. And she could quickly forgive Gary for his insults and insensitivity, in part because she genuinely loved him and in part because she was afraid to challenge him. Emotionally distant from her husband and having felt like a "dummy" most of her life, Marjorie found that helping Gary had been her source of pride and esteem.

"But it's not Gary's fault," she insisted. "He gets upset easily because he can't live like other boys. It's easy to forgive him because he acts out of frustration. But I do wish he'd treat me with just a little more respect."

When I asked Marjorie how long it would be before Gary finally left home, she tensed up before answering.

"Oh, I don't know. Years, I suppose. He wants to leave now, actually. He wants to live away at college. But he's too immature to be on his own. I do practically everything for him."

"I suspect it will be hard on you when he does leave," I said.

"Yes, but I'll . . . get by," she said, unable to hold back tears. "I must be too sentimental. I don't know why I act like this."

As much as she loved Gary and wanted him to be well, she also had an unconscious need for him to be dependent on her so she could feel useful and good about herself.

"You can't keep him, Marjorie," I said.

She had a twisted expression on her face, as if she didn't understand my meaning—and as if she understood it only too well.

"You're his mother, but he's not yours," I continued. "You love him deeply, but you must let him go. It's time."

In six months Gary moved to a dormitory, and Marjorie had to face the issues she had avoided for years.

The moment you believe that you need others to behave in a certain way so that you can feel better about yourself, you give up power over your life. Your task is to admit your shortcomings and then make improvements so that you won't be so desperate when others decide to live their own lives.

Forgiving to Prevent Loss of Control

If you are to experience happiness and fulfillment,

you need to have a sense of mastery and control over aspects of your life. But your need to be in control can get the better of you. Especially if your esteem is low (which you may not consciously admit) and you secretly fear that others would stop loving you if they knew the real you, you may defend against such fears by taking greater and harsher control over your feelings and relationships.

But when you control your feelings too much, you begin to lose perspective. Important data—your feelings—are distorted. You therefore struggle to make realistic assessments and feel increasingly threatened when solutions to problems don't fall into place easily. What you do not realize is that you are more out of control than ever.

Your need to be in control could be subtle. Harriet maintains control by doling out the family finances solely on her terms. Bill is prone to making important decisions that affect his family without first consulting Harriet.

People who are overcontrolling often see others as trying to take control. They justify their controlling stance by claiming that others would always manipulate them if they didn't act the way they do.

If you are a controlling person, you are often trying to control your anger. You may say you are open with your feelings, but your openness is not a welcome relief to those with whom you relate. Probably you are critical and hard to satisfy. You defend your criticisms as being truthful and necessary.

As a controlling person, you manipulate people. You can't let others in your life realize their full potential, because they may go against your way of doing things or even reject you. Instead, you try to coerce or trick them into abiding by your decisions. Whether you behave this way on the job or in more personal relationships, others eventually see through your manipulations despite your efforts to avoid being found out. If they need you to validate their worth, they probably won't confront you and risk your wrath, but they will resent you. And it is only a matter of time before they hurt you or outgrow you.

You don't admit to much fear. The more fearful you are, the more controlling and even arrogant you become. You don't trust easily, and it's hard for you to give freely. Unlike people who are less worried about issues of control, when you give you always have the underlying expectation that you are owed something in return. You feel cheated when you must compromise.

If you are a controlling person, you are actually suffering a great deal of pain. Your esteem is low, although you probably don't consciously admit to that. At your core, you doubt you are worthwhile and lovable. However, your rigidness and poorly contained hostility make it hard for others to see and care about those aspects of yourself. That only stimulates the shame you feel and your sense of unworthiness, which further fuels your anger, arrogance, and need to be in control of your feelings.

The more controlling you are in a relationship, the more inadequate you feel and the less likely you will be able to genuinely forgive others. When you do offer forgiveness, it will be done as evidence of your benevolence rather than to truly reconcile. You will also have difficulty forgiving yourself. That is so because in order to be forgiving, you would have to be open to your faults, which is something your controlling ways have prevented you from seeing clearly.

I know that for you to loosen up your feelings and let others be themselves around you might be tantamount to your world crumbling before you. But if you are estranged from someone and wish to reconcile through forgiveness, it is important that you choose to be more vulnerable. Otherwise, you will lose more relationships than you build, which will only stimulate your worst fear: that down deep you are nothing.

You are someone very special and worthwhile. Believe in that, and set out on a course of change that will ultimately be more satisfying.

TO THE ONE FORGIVEN

If someone has forgiven you but the act of forgiveness was prompted more by fear than by love, then your reaction will probably not be one of feeling reconciled.

If the desperateness of the person who forgave you shines through more than anything else, you may find yourself losing respect for him or her.

If the person forgave you as a means of keeping control over you, then you will have the uneasy feeling of needing to be protected from that person.

If you were forgiven in order to enhance someone's self-esteem, you will sense a great haughtiness and neediness in the person who forgave you.

If the other person can never risk rejection and has a great need for love and affection, you may feel smothered when you are forgiven.

When you ever doubt the sincerity of one's offer of forgiveness, it will be necessary to let the person know of your reaction. That isn't always easy. For one thing, your honesty may not be welcome immediately because it exposes the weaknesses of the forgiver. For another, you run the risk of never being forgiven after that. Some people, particularly those who have difficulty relinquishing control, may not accept your concerns right away. Others may resent what they see as your unwillingness to accept their offer at face value. The correctness of your suspicions does not matter at first. What is important is your willingness to speak up about your apprehensions and cope with what can be an uncomfortable interaction. If you don't do that, if you allow fears and weaknesses to run a relationship, then there can be little hope of joy, growth, and contentment.

Forgiving falsely is common. It need not prevent a reconciliation if it is viewed for what it really is: a human reaction motivated by the belief that one is not truly acceptable and lovable just the way one is.

Chapter Three

"It's Not Fair!": Overcoming Blocks to Forgiveness

Janet gave up her college career because her new husband wanted her to stay home. She quietly obliged. Six months later, she had an abortion because her husband told her they weren't ready to become parents. As her resentment grew over the next year, so did her loneliness. He protested that she was growing distant from him. She struggled to keep the faltering marriage alive by trying to please him. He then complained she had no mind of her own. Infuriated, she threatened a marital separation, hoping he would begin to appreciate her. He presented her with a letter from his lawyer and left with the woman he had been secretly dating on and off since before the marriage. In between bouts of depression and anxiety, Janet cursed his name and declared him unforgivable.

The most common reason given for why forgiveness is impossible is that the acts of brutality or betrayal were just too great. According to the argument, forgiveness simply isn't fair. It is the same as looking the other way and letting the guilty person go unpunished.

It is easy to identify with such a reaction. We have all taken an unforgiving stance after being hurt. But when we are the victims, withholding forgiveness does not heal us. We may feel strong or righteous when we withhold forgiveness, but such feelings pale in comparison to the costs we incur. Keeping our anger burning and unresolved seals in our pain. We then begin to make even greater victims of ourselves.

It is vital to understand that *the blocks that prevent you from forgiving are, ultimately, within you.* No matter how cruelly you've been treated, *the power to forgive does not lie with the person who hurt you.* When you tell yourself you must not forgive because the hurts against you were too great, you are really telling yourself that the person who hurt you has set the guidelines for forgiveness. You are giving that hurtful person more power over you, since *it is in your best interest to forgive!*

But what are those blocks? Those blocks are your attitudes and perceptions. Those blocks are fears you haven't yet come to terms with.

Sometimes you have resented people for hurting you because they exposed your weaknesses. When you hide from yourself, you won't like it when others uncover you.

Jim resents his wife's involvement with her family. He feels neglected. Maybe she is overinvolved with them, but Jim's weakness is that he's been estranged from his own parents for some time. He feels guilty about that but won't do anything about it. Instead, he needs constant reaffirmation by his wife that he's a good person, something that he misses when she is with her family.

Rose resents her husband's overinvolvement with his work. Maybe he is overinvolved, but her weakness is that she has no friends or leisure activities of her own. She's too dependent on her husband.

When you look yourself in the eye and accept your weaknesses, you begin the process of strengthening yourself. And you open the doors to forgiveness, because the hurts against you carry less of a sting.

Some of the more important blocks to forgiveness are visible (that is, you are consciously aware of them), but other blocks are hidden from your awareness. While this chapter provides examples of those hidden, invisible blocks, discovering them for yourself may take more time. The remaining chapters in Part One of this book will help you to do that.

VISIBLE BLOCKS TO FORGIVENESS

Vengeance and Justified Harm

A typical block to forgiveness is vengeance. Vengeance only adds to the pain, with each side then feeling justified to counterattack, thereby making a reconciliation less likely.

When vengeance occurs, a more subtle problem can evolve if you convince yourself that your act of retaliation was *caused by the other person*. After all, you wouldn't have done what you did if you weren't hurt first, or so the reasoning goes. Failing to own up to your responsibility for any action you take is a major block to forgiveness. No matter what the influences on your behavior, once you decide on a course of action, you must own your behavior.

After Janet's husband filed for divorce and left with the other woman, Janet set out on a vindictive course of action. She intended to fight him legally and take away every material possession she could possibly get, even more than she saw as necessary. She downgraded him in front of their mutual friends. She felt he needed to be punished. But Janet's strong retaliatory approach hurt her in the long run. As long as she focused on the damage her husband had done to her, she never evaluated and owned up to her own weaknesses and fears. It was as much her decision to leave college and have an abortion as it was her husband's. By failing to come to terms with her weaknesses, she set herself up to be at a disadvantage later when her fears resurfaced in some other context.

Vengeance not only prevents forgiveness, it also allows you to nurture the false belief that you need not look at and change your own shortcomings as long as there is someone else to blame.

Hating Those You Hurt

If you are not careful, hurting a person you care about—whether your acts were unprovoked or done out of retaliation—can lead you to develop a hateful attitude toward that person. That attitude develops when your acts of harm make you uncomfortable, and you wish to minimize your responsibility for having done them. You can justify having caused pain, and you can reduce your feelings of guilt by nurturing hate. It is much easier to justify hurting somebody you despise than someone you love and wish to be reconciled with.

When You Are Not Forgiven

You may struggle to be forgiving when your partner refuses to forgive you. Why should you show consideration when no consideration is coming your way?

While you may have to one day end a relationship where you can't be forgiven, that does not mean that you must be unforgiving as well. Refusing to forgive someone because he or she is unforgiving of you is to give that person power over an important aspect of your life.

It is good for you to be forgiving. Forgive for that reason even if there can be no reconciliation.

Forgiveness is not a thing that can be traded. Nor is it for sale.

Jodi and Dave have been married for twenty-three years, the last ten of which they have spent licking their wounds, believing the other to be grossly uncaring.

"But what about me?!" Dave argued, his voice deep and grating, betraying a poisonous contempt for his wife. "Look how you've hurt me," he accused. "Don't speak to me about my crimes. If it weren't for you, this marriage could have meant something to me."

Jodi looked at me as if I were a judge. "My husband refuses to consider what a hateful man he is."

Jodi and Dave were too busy attacking and defending to really understand what the other's concerns were. Neither believed that the other could feel remorseful and ask for forgiveness, so neither one tried. In fact, each avoided admitting wrongdoing for fear that the partner, rather than welcome an effort to reconcile, would use the admission as evidence needed to brand the other as guilty and unforgivable. Each one wanted to be viewed as acceptable and forgivable. Each one wanted the other to be really understanding. But neither one was willing to risk going first. At least not anymore.

So they each minimized their hurtful acts by accentuating what was done against them, thereby shrouding their need, their desire, to be forgiven. Then they confronted each other with the added anger that comes from the fear of being judged unforgivable. Often, that anger was just enough to make the other become rigidly defensive and unwilling to listen to all of what needed to be said. Communication broke down, and forgiveness was blocked.

Pride

To offer forgiveness to your spouse, you must desire a relationship built on equality and mutual respect, not one-upmanship. Genuine forgiveness is not offered as evidence of your superiority, but as a reflection of the superior quality of the relationship.

To accept the offer of forgiveness, you must admit that you need it. That requires not only the self-awareness that you are responsible for having been hurtful, but the willingness to be humble. Forgiveness can truly be accepted only with humility.

In humility, you open yourself to witness your strengths and your weaknesses. You do not wallow in guilt or self-pity. You fully accept your complete identity, warts and all. There is no pretense, no facade, just the honest recognition of your personhood.

Do not allow pride to interfere with your opportunity to accept or offer forgiveness. Pride, by the way, does not refer to self-respect or the satisfaction of having achieved some important goal. Pride is insistence on seeing things in only a certain way, usually in a way that bolsters sagging esteem. When you are prideful, then you feel that you are always right (better) and that others who disagree with you are wrong. When pride gets in the way, you won't be able to evaluate your guilt realistically, and you may balk at an offer of forgiveness.

INVISIBLE BLOCKS TO FORGIVENESS

Inability to Forgive Oneself

Probably the greatest block to being able to forgive another is the inability to forgive yourself. Such a failure is due either to a denial that you are culpable for any act that might require forgiveness (that is, your guilt is invisible) or to an insistence on self-punishment (which means your fear of how others would treat you, if you didn't punish yourself, is invisible). If you repeatedly denounce yourself for mistakes you've made and end up feeling more needy and depleted as a result, you are blocking your path to forgiveness. You are confusing punishment and self-condemnation with forgiveness. Eddy is like that.

Eddy is thirty-six years old and a Vietnam veteran. He came for counseling to help stop his explosive behavior and his suspiciousness of others. He had been through two marriages, and now his third was threatened. His wife had separated from him after continued verbal abuse by Eddy. She also could not trust him to change and found it hard to forgive him for his chronically angry and hurtful ways.

When Eddy came to see me, he was desperate and pathetic. Desperate because he was losing another marriage, and pathetic because he held only minimal regard for himself. He saw himself as an unacceptable person and unworthy of a loving relationship. To placate his wife, he would make sacrifices for her that she saw as hollow. He would then hold back his anger and disappointment and belittle himself further. When she was not around, he would impulsively punch walls and yell obscenities, condemning her as uncaring. In effect, he had an invisible fear that if he should stop torturing himself for his past ways, his wife might finally just abandon him.

Eddy also could not quite forgive himself for having killed in Vietnam and having been witness to atrocities there.

"Eddy," I asked one day, "what is the price you must pay for having hurt others?"

He had no ready answer. But he began to realize that his persistent self-punishment was getting him nowhere. His punitive ways were holding him hostage to a past he wanted to be rid of. And they were keeping his wife at bay, too.

His wife, Linda, seemed unnerved by my question to Eddy. "I guess I still feel that he owes me for how he treated me. Maybe it isn't fair but still . . . it annoys me when he constantly berates himself, because I feel I have no right to be angry at him then."

"But you do get angry," Eddy protested. "You make me feel that unless I publicly condemn myself for how I've abused you, you'll never accept me back into the relationship."

I tried to clarify matters. "Eddy, it seems that whenever you sense her anger, you begin to berate yourself, putting yourself down before she has a chance to. And Linda, when you see that happening, you eventually get even angrier because you feel he's shutting you out. Then you sense her anger again, Eddy, and this whole thing goes full circle."

They agreed.

By working through the phases of forgiveness, Eddy was able to forgive himself. He refused to let his past run his life. He accepted himself as imperfect but worthwhile nonetheless, and persevered in his efforts to change his hurtful ways of relating to others.

He told his wife that he had forgiven himself and hoped she would one day find it possible to forgive him, too. He expressed sincere remorse for having hurt her, and was willing to work on the relationship without being his own worst enemy.

Displacement

When we refuse to forgive and choose instead to keep our anger alive "for justice's sake," we may unfairly redirect that anger at others through what is known in psychology as *displacement*. Yelling at your children or spouse when you are really upset with your boss is a common example of displacement. A more subtle but equally common example occurs when unresolved emotional issues with one's parents are displaced onto one's spouse or children. You may have a difficult time then forgiving your spouse or child because their actions are colored and intensified by the unsettled issues with your parents.

The woman who vows never to become the critical, strict parent her mother was may place an unfair burden on her husband and children. If the children misbehave and she is unwilling to set limits on their behavior (for fear of behaving too much like her mother), her husband may have to. Predictably, his limit setting will spark her fear that the children are being handled too strictly. Soon she'll criticize him much as her mother has criticized her. The husband and wife will fight a battle over "being critical," and she may find it hard to forgive him, when the issue that really needs to be addressed is between the woman and her mother.

In our day-to-day lives, we often notice when we are unfairly displacing our anger onto the innocent. But if there has been a deep, painful betrayal that we cannot forgive, it becomes more difficult to stop taking out our anger at those who don't deserve it. For example, if your former spouse betrayed you by constant lies and infidelities, you may have a hard time trusting a new partner. Now your new relationship is suffering because you have not satisfactorily resolved your past hurt and anger. To insist that it would be a gross injustice to forgive your ex-spouse is missing the point. Failing to forgive that spouse can be more unjust for you, since your anger and your new marriage remain trapped.

The solution to overcoming displacement isn't easy. You must learn to identify and express your feelings to the people who prompted them as soon as possible after you experience them. The longer you wait, the more you keep your feelings to yourself, the more you risk displacing those feelings onto others unfairly.

Loyalty to One's Family of Origin

Sometimes forgiving your spouse (or other family member) would result in being disloyal to another family member, often a parent. So, to avoid being disloyal, forgiveness is withheld. Blocking forgiveness out of loyalty to one's family of origin is usually the most invisible block to forgiveness. Therefore, it is among the most powerful.

Lynn and Scott were married for eighteen months. It was her first marriage at age twenty-two. Scott, thirty-one, was divorced and had one child, whom he visited regularly. Lynn was the youngest of four sisters, all married.

"When she called me from her parents' house and told me she wasn't coming back, I was devastated," Scott said. "She told me I had forced her to make a choice between me and her family and that she'd made her choice. I didn't force anything. I just didn't want us to be as involved with her family as she wanted.

"They are nice people, believe me. But they're always around. Lynn calls them constantly. Between scheduling time for my son and having to visit her parents each weekend, Lynn and I never have had time for ourselves. I felt she was asking me to make a choice between spending free time on weekends with either her or my son. But she wasn't about to give up visiting her parents. This may be hard to believe, but in each of the last five years, Lynn, her sisters, their husbands, and Lynn's parents have vacationed together in the summer. This summer I said no because the vacation interfered with plans I had with my son. That was the straw that broke the camel's back."

Lynn agreed to attend one meeting. She was not interested in reconciling.

"How did Scott hurt you, Lynn?" I asked. She told me a story that paralleled Scott's. She felt an obligation to her parents that he didn't understand, or want to understand.

"What worried you about the fact that you didn't vacation with your family this year?" I asked.

"It hurt my family's feelings, especially my dad's. He's always wanted us to be a close family. That's very important to him. When he was growing up, he was shipped off to different foster homes. He hated it. But he's made a wonderful life for us despite his childhood. He's been a good, loving father. We owe him."

"Do you owe him your marriage?" I asked, perhaps too bluntly.

"I thought this would be a waste of time," she said, believing I was siding with her husband.

Since this was the one and only scheduled meeting with Lynn, I decided to be completely candid, even though I wasn't sure she was ready to hear what I had to say.

"If you have to lose your family in order to save

your marriage, Lynn," I said, "the marriage won't last." She nodded in agreement. "But if you have to lose your marriage to protect your dad from his fears, then your family isn't working well, either. Something is terribly wrong in any relationship if you are forced to make choices like the ones you've made."

"I want Scott to care about my family," she blurted.

"And he wants you to care about him and his son," I said. "I think you can each get what you want. But by your becoming closer to Scott, your dad may have to face some fears of his that he really hasn't faced yet. He's so afraid of losing his family he is strangling it to keep it close. Part of your marriage problem may really be his problem."

Despite the rough going in this meeting, Lynn eventually reconciled with Scott. There was turmoil in her family for some time afterward as the family questioned her loyalty to them. But eventually the family adjusted to a new, more productive way of relating.

If you have trouble forgiving, consider the family rules you grew up with. All families have rules. And all families have rules about what to do when other rules are broken. The way your family handled matters when rules were broken can give you a clue as to why you may be reacting the way you are. For example, was your family rule "Don't rock the boat"? If so, you may deal with troubled relationships today by being tentative. If the rule was "Don't upset your father," then you may act like Lynn, settling problems in any manner that will protect your father. Any rules that once stifled meaningful efforts to repair relationships can cause problems for you later on, if you continue to abide by them out of loyalty.

You aren't really being loyal to a parent or spouse if

you must deplete yourself in the process. Yes, there
are times when you must make sacrifices. But if you
must continually weaken yourself to prove your
loyalty, then you won't be at your best when a legitimate sacrifice is called for. You will deprive the very
people you are trying to protect at the time they need
you the most. Is that loyalty?

Labels

Labeling is a common yet often unrecognized block to
forgiveness. It is more difficult to forgive someone
when you've labeled him or her as bad, hurtful, evil,
or unchangeable. Labels may be accurate to a point,
but they never provide a full picture of the person you
are describing. And if you want to find forgiveness,
you will almost always need to broaden your perspective about the person who hurt you.

Think of the many labels often used by warring
couples to negatively describe a spouse: selfish, controlling, hysterical, manipulative, frigid, castrating,
misogynist, unaffectionate, martyr, crazy, bitch, bas-
tard, lazy, perverted, stupid, inadequate, and so on.

The problem with labels is not that they aren't true.
Often, they do accurately describe aspects of another's style of behavior. The problem with them is that
they limit your understanding of the real nature of
your marital problems. Once you unfavorably label
someone, that *description* is regarded as the *cause* for
your problems. It no longer becomes necessary to look
for alternative reasons for your difficulties.

Whenever you label someone else, there is probably
something about yourself you are avoiding. As long as
your husband is "perverted," you never have to examine how your attitudes about sex and sexuality have
affected your sex life. As long as your wife is "a

bitch," you never have to examine how you may have failed to be considerate of her when she needed it the most. As long as your spouse is "controlling," you always have a justification for your manipulations.

Yes, people do have personalities and attitudes that are uniquely their own. But it is also true that people act not just in accordance with what they think of themselves, but according to what they think others think about them.

You may have wrinkles, thin hair, and a pot belly, but when your spouse holds you and tells you how attractive you are, you feel attractive. If you treat your spouse *as if* he or she has a particular quality, that quality will show itself. If that quality was there to begin with, it will be displayed more often—or at least you'll think it's being displayed more often—just because of your expectations.

That doesn't mean you are responsible for traits of your spouse that are hurtful or undesirable. Each person is ultimately responsible for his or her own feelings, thoughts, and behaviors. But if you are stuck in your effort to forgive your spouse, you'd do well to consider whether you are unwittingly reinforcing certain attitudes or behaviors by virtue of your labels and expectations.

Tina is furious that her husband Rob is so loud and strict with their three-year-old son. To her, Rob is demanding, critical, insensitive, and a bully.

Rob sees it differently. To him, Tina is lazy and too lenient with their son. "I want him to learn that there are rules to follow, but she always makes me the heavy. I do all of her dirty work."

There is merit to each of their views. And the more lenient Tina is, the stricter Rob becomes. But until they each stop negatively labeling each other and consider how they are reinforcing each other's behavior, nothing will change for the better. They also need to broaden their view of one another. A good place to start is to realize that each of them seems to have the boy's best interests at heart.

If you think that labeling has prevented you from finding forgiveness, your first step is to become aware just how often you speak or think in terms of labels. The best way to begin is to keep a small notebook handy to record which labels you use and how often you use them. Couples who are locked in conflict are often surprised at just how frequently during the course of the day they negatively label their spouse. Such hardened views can be a major obstacle to forgiveness.

Next, you need to challenge the validity of those labels. Start by checking to see if you describe others with words such as *always* or *never*: "Mitch is *always* trying to control me. He *never* lets me do what I want to do."

Such a statement is probably inaccurate and unfair. You need to rephrase those statements accurately and include evidence to the contrary. That is, recall examples when your spouse behaved in more desirable ways: "Right now I feel that Mitch is trying to control me. He gets this way a lot when it comes to my wanting to visit my parents. But when it comes to the children, he seems to respect my ways of doing things."

Challenging your unfair labels takes practice. A quick and easy way to reduce your unfair use of labels is to do the following:

1. Imagine yourself labeling your spouse. Get as clear an image of the situation as you can. Is it happening while you are driving to work and thinking about your spouse? Is it happening during an argument?

2. Now immediately imagine yourself correcting

that view. Imagine yourself remembering evidence that would contradict that negative label.

3. Repeat this exercise ten times. As a result, you'll be able to catch yourself when you actually are labeling your spouse, and you may even prevent it from happening as often.

If you've used the labels as weapons against your spouse during an argument or discussion, and you catch yourself doing it again, apologize to your spouse. Let him or her know that the label is unfair and that there have been times when he or she has acted much more considerately. It is only fair.

The blocks to forgiveness can seem formidable. That is particularly true when your focus for change remains away from yourself. When you emphasize how others have hurt you, you fail to face and come to terms with your own needs, strengths, and weaknesses. The more you know about yourself and understand your feelings, the better equipped you'll be to overcome the blocks to forgiveness.

Forgiveness is our saving grace. It is the only means to contend with the fact that in life we will cause pain to others and ourselves. It awakens us to our goodness and allows us to be all that we are, unbridled by anger, guilt, or fear.

Chapter Four

The Real You: Knowing Yourself and Taking Responsibility for Your Life

"There is a beauty to all your sadness."

My words gently nudged open the eyes that had closed to memories long forgotten until this hour. Grace's arms were folded loosely across her chest. She had cradled herself while sobbing, and for the past few minutes she had been quiet, nearly sleeping, in her memory of someone she could finally accept had never cradled her before.

The meaning was clear to us both. Her anger and grief over never really having been loved by a mother, who was seemingly closed to everyone, was spent. She had finally given up the belief that her mother was a loving woman. She also gave up the belief that she must have been an unworthy daughter to have been so unloved. And the recognition, painful as it was, that her own ten-year-old daughter had to some extent been left wanting because Grace had not faced her past squarely, gave her new direction.

"What is next for you?" I asked later.

Home. My little girl is waiting. I'm going home to her now." Grace had found the courage to know herself better, and she saw that there was purpose in her life after all.

To see yourself as clearly as possible, to be able to understand the truths about yourself so there is no more denial or pretense, is an ongoing task that is both burdensome and freeing. And it is a task that prepares you for the times when you will want to find forgiveness. The less you know about yourself, the more you are forced to operate out of ignorance and fear. The less you know yourself, the less you can love yourself. The prospect of forgiveness then becomes compromised.

It is hard to find forgiveness and revitalize a special relationship when you are essentially estranged from yourself.

RECOGNIZING YOUR STRENGTHS AND WEAKNESSES

At your most human level, you wish to love and be loved, to avoid and overcome all that creates fear within you, and to grow and discover meaning in your life. From such basic yearnings develop every other emotion and thought. If you take the courage to know yourself and search for the meaning of any current problem you have, you will come to rest at one or more of those places of truth.

The more you can love and be loved, the less will fears hinder your life. Conversely, the more you are threatened by your fears, the more you will need to protect yourself, and in so doing will place barriers on your willingness to give and receive love. The more you put up barriers and cloak your ability to share love, then growth and meaning in your life will wither.

What is ironic and gratifying, however, is that when you feel that your life possesses little meaning, there begins the preparation for productive change. The place you are at right now in life, however painful and meaningless it may seem, points the way for your growth. Your own growth and knowledge of yourself are guided by where you are coming *from*.

Thus, if your life is tainted by the belief that nothing you do matters, then the direction you must choose is one whereby you accept full responsibility for your actions and their consequences.

If your life has been shadowed by loneliness, then you give. Give freely of yourself with no expectations of return. You need to be needed.

If your life has been calloused by mistrust, then you start trusting by first looking for what is good in other people.

If you are plagued by self-doubts, look around you. You are not alone. Your real problem is that you believe you are unique, so no one else could feel the way you feel.

If you are so competitive in your relationships that the only way you can feel good about yourself comes at another's expense, then openly give full credit to others for their efforts and accomplishments. Praise them no matter how well or poorly you performed.

The changes you need to make in your life are probably not major. Typically, your weaknesses, or potential weaknesses, are more extreme forms of your strengths. The assertive person's weakness is hostile aggressiveness and insensitivity toward others. The perceptive person's weakness is suspiciousness and impulsiveness.

The organized and responsible person's weakness is

rigidness, compulsiveness, and often a need to hold the reins of control. The analytical person's weakness is indecisiveness and emotional restraint.

Cautious people seldom take appropriate risks. Confidence can lead to arrogance; optimism to a Pollyannaish view of life. Kindness can sometimes mask timidity. Perseverance is admirable, but not headstrong pursuit of a goal when the situation is clearly a losing battle. Intimacy and vulnerability may lead to greater attachment, but overattachment leads to dependency and desperateness as you give up too much control of your life.

If you want to identify your weaknesses, or potential weaknesses, look at your strengths and nudge them to an extreme. The more you know of yourself, then the more these words will make sense to you, and the more you will be open to change.

But the principal reason for knowing yourself better has to do with the notion of self-acceptance. Self-acceptance becomes difficult when aspects of yourself are hidden from your view. And self-acceptance is the cornerstone of a healthy self-love and any attempt to grow.

Vicki's husband would sometimes beat her up. More often his abuse was verbal. He'd blame her when anything went wrong. He'd humiliate her in front of his family. And when she'd get so angry and so hurt, he'd complain that she was immature for holding a grudge.

I asked Vicki to give me reasons why she stayed in the marriage. She listed the following:

- I can't afford to take care of the kids myself.
- I'm too dependent on him.
- The children need a father.
- What would my family think of me if I left?

The list was revealing in what it didn't include. Vicki was out of touch with her feelings, her needs. Her concerns had more to do with what other people thought than what she needed to have happen. The fact that there was little happiness in the marriage, and no respect, was not an issue for her—at least not anymore. Vicki had no idea who she was. She had no sense of herself as a unique, worthwhile person with needs, wishes, and strengths. She regarded herself as a nonentity. Forgiveness was a meaningless concept. Forgive who? For what? Somehow, she believed that life was supposed to be the way it was for her.

But over many weeks of therapy, she began to look more closely at herself, which was the first step toward self-acceptance. Long-held fears gave way to anger—anger at her husband for sure, but also an anger for never having treated herself the way she deserved. She realized it was time to make constructive changes in her life. Her first major change was to confide in her closest friend all that had been happening over the years. Until then, she had feared her friend would think less of her if the truth were known, a fear that more accurately reflected how she felt about herself. Two weeks later, her lip bloodied and her makeup smeared, Vicki called on her friend to accompany her to a women's shelter. Vicki was finally taking a stand. She was owning up to the truth of her life. No more denial. No more pretense. It was time for a real change.

Ned was still living in a world of pretense. He had had an affair for two years before his wife, Toni, found out about it, and he had little sympathy for her when she spoke of her hurt and anger. But when she then had an affair, he was outraged. He couldn't understand how she could be so cruel. He berated her for taking the easy way out instead of trying to work on improving the marriage. Was Ned really in touch with who he was? Did he know himself? Hardly. And his unwillingness to look at himself, along with his insistence on focusing on his wife's actions, cost him his marriage.

Earlier in this chapter, I spoke of Grace and how she had tried to pretend about her past. But the most important part of her past that she tried to run from was not just the fact that her mother was an unloving woman. It was a truth about herself. She recognized that while her early years had indeed been painful and lonely, *she had used her past as the sole justification for why her life was so miserable.* She had failed to admit that she could have done things differently as an adult that would have changed her life for the better.

She could have stopped blaming her ex-husband for all the problems in her life. She could have stopped expecting her daughter to prove to her that she is a lovable mother and person and start believing in it herself. But she was fearful of taking responsibility for changing her life. To change at any time implied that perhaps she could have changed sooner, a discomforting thought for her, given the pain she and her family had endured.

"Grace, what about your daughter?" I asked during an earlier session. "It has never been easy for you to deal with Shana and her tantrums. I know she opposes you on anything you say. And I know you feel she hates you, and that scares the hell out of you because you understand what hating a mother can feel like."

"You don't think she hates me?" she asked.

"I'm sure that some of the time she does hate you, Grace. Most kids feel that way about their parents now and again but. . . ."

"She should know better," Grace insisted. "She should care more about my feelings. I'm always doing things for her, and she doesn't appreciate me."

I must have had a pained look on my face, because Grace stared at me with a knowing gaze. I had heard her words before, numerous times, and she knew my response.

"Same old thing again, ain't it?" she said with a scanty grin.

I nodded.

"I always look for things to blame Shana for when I don't want to look at myself. But at least now I can recognize when I'm doing it."

In truth, Shana didn't act the way she did because she was selfish, unruly, and insensitive to her mother's feelings. She was reacting to a mother who had given up control over her life. Grace couldn't provide herself or her daughter with security, and the girl was rebelling.

Grace was able to own up to her guilt and then do away with it by forgiving herself. There was no penalty to pay, only the willingness to build a relationship with a daughter who needed her. And by forgiving herself, she discovered it was possible to forgive her mother. She no longer had a reason to keep alive her anger at her mother. Grace still had a slight longing within her for a childhood unmarred by pain, but it wasn't a yearning that depleted her. Grace let go of the blaming and the guilt and was able to live more fully in the present, unburdened by the past. And all of that came about after her willingness to take a closer look at herself, to know herself (and therefore to love herself) better.

ACCEPTING RESPONSIBILITY

To accept responsibility for your life does not mean that you are entirely to blame for your problems. You are not responsible for the way your parents acted, for example. But it is your responsibility to do something about your current problems regardless of how they arose. If you refuse, you have only yourself to blame if matters don't work out in your favor. That may frustrate you and seem unfair, but life is unfair. Give up the belief that it is supposed to be fair.

When you accept responsibility, you are willing to own up to all you've done. Even if you hurt others unwittingly, you need to come to terms with the fact that you sometimes act blindly. And you then need to improve your self-awareness so that you won't be unintentionally hurtful in the future.

Taking responsibility for your life involves a measure of self-acceptance. If you can't accept yourself, then you will deny responsibility and appear blameless so others will accept you, or at least not reject you. You'll want to protect a fragile self-esteem. Or without self-acceptance you will hold yourself accountable for more than your due. You will take on an exaggerated sense of responsibility and blame as an unconscious maneuver to appease others into not rejecting you at a time when you are about to reject yourself.

That was Vicki's problem. She believed her husband when he blamed her for every marital problem, every child problem, every missing sock, and every burned-out light bulb. Nothing she did was good enough and everything that went wrong was her responsibility. She was even grateful when he let her off easy some days. She had a distorted sense of responsibility that, instead of enhancing her self-acceptance, diminished it.

RESPONSIBILITY AND FORGIVENESS

Accepting responsibility for your life prepares you for

forgiveness. You can forgive yourself for mistakes you've made, whether you intended to make them or not, only when you are willing to own up to what you've done.

But when you blame others for your problems, you deny yourself the opportunity to be forgiven. At an unconscious level, you tell yourself that to admit to being human and fallible will cause others to leave you. So you deny your failures and seek to place the blame elsewhere. And you never learn that by finding forgiveness you can discover just how much you are accepted and loved by the people in your life.

When you accept responsibility for yourself, you will be able to point out your partner's shortcomings without much blame or criticism. Your purpose will be to get a clearer understanding of all the obstacles in the relationship so that the two of you can decide how to proceed.

Know yourself better, and accept responsibility for your life. It is when you fear admitting the truths about yourself that you end up hurting others. That is also the time when you need forgiveness the most and when you are most likely to resist it.

The Story of Adrianna

Adrianna was twenty-nine when she came for marital therapy with Ted, her husband of six years. They came at her husband's insistence because he felt his wife had become "lazy and neglectful of her duties." Adrianna's duties were to care for their two children and the household. Adrianna saw her husband as insensitive and demanding. She also believed that her "laziness" was really a general melancholia she'd been experiencing on and off for ten years.

It didn't take long to see that each partner had a style of relating that interfered with getting along well

with each other. Ted often acted in an overly controlling and demanding manner. Adrianna would rebel
against that by being less effective at home, thereby
prompting more criticism from Ted. They both
realized that. So why continue to lock horns?

"I get the impression that you two are dissatisfied
with more than just each other," I said. "Adrianna,
you say you've been melancholy for ten years. What
have you been holding back?"

"I don't know," she answered quickly, looking at Ted
to answer for her. Ted was about to speak for her, but
I interrupted.

"You say that Ted is too controlling, Adrianna, yet
you let him speak for you often, even when you know
the answers yourself. Are you deferring to him because you know he likes to take charge? Or is it that
you would prefer that others run things for you?"

"I'm not sure," she answered, true to form. She
struck me as a very intelligent woman, yet she had
little insight into her behavior. The more I spoke with
her, the more apparent it became that she tried to be
whatever anyone around her wanted her to be. In the
process, she lost sight of who she really was.

The couple also argued about finances. Over time it
became clearer that Adrianna's resentment over a
tight budget reflected her anger with herself for never
having obtained the education or the job she really
wanted.

"I was afraid to fail, so I didn't go to college," she
admitted one day. Until that moment, she had used
the fact that she had to raise her children as the
understandable but convenient excuse for why she
couldn't go to school. She found reasons outside herself to explain away her behavior, avoiding taking a
closer look at her own fears and weaknesses. Her
reluctance over the years to know herself better and

to accept responsibility for doing something about her concerns allowed her to blame others for her unhappiness. But that came with a cost. She was periodically depressed, often feeling helpless, and had no real sense of who she was.

When Adrianna accepted responsibility for her situation, she was empowered with the opportunity to change for the better. The shift in her attitude about responsibility did not reduce the tension in the marriage, however. Although she was less inclined to blame her husband for difficulties, she was also making decisions on her own and not looking to her husband for support she could give herself. That made him uneasy.

"I sometimes think it was better the old way," Ted remarked. Ted felt uncomfortable giving up some control in the marriage. But despite the rough going at first, they adjusted to the changes by virtue of their commitment to each other. And the adjustment was made easier the moment they stopped blaming one another and started taking responsibility for their own thoughts and feelings.

Chapter Five

Shedding Your Defenses: Being Open to Forgiveness

Henry glared at me. Arms folded, straight in his chair, he nonverbally challenged me to try my best shot at getting him to be involved in psychotherapy with his wife.

"I still don't see why I need to be here," he exhorted. "And if you can't convince me to stay," [there was that glare again] "I'll leave now."

Henry wasn't an uncommon type. He refused to believe that he had any part in his "wife's" problems and was gearing up to attack my profession before I might think that his daughter's school problems had something to do with him, too. In other words, he was being defensive. He was frightened of being blamed, so he acted as if the problems with his family didn't involve him in the least.

When defensiveness gets in the way of seeing the truth, the process of reconciliation and forgiveness can grind to a halt.

SEEING YOURSELF AS YOU ARE

When you are estranged from someone who matters to you and you wish the relationship to be healed, a task is required of you. Your task is to shed some of your psychological defenses, your cloaks of protection, and be more open to your feelings, the pain and the joy, that are within you and generated by the relationship.

Even if no reunion is possible and you are left alone to resolve either your guilt for having betrayed your spouse or some other person, or your bitterness for having been betrayed, you must lower the defenses that have kept you from getting a clearer look at who you are.

For you and everybody else, the fear of future hurt and the memories of past pains keeps you from being completely open and trusting. And that is a good thing at times, because some people may really wish to hurt you. Some people really would use your honesty about yourself as a weapon against you. It is then good judgment to keep some of your thoughts and feelings to yourself.

But the problem lies not so much when you consciously decide to withhold those thoughts and feelings, but when it happens unconsciously. Then you can't distinguish between safe and unsafe situations as well as you should.

When you can't be sure whether a situation is safe, you probably won't risk exposing your truest feelings. But you can't become close to someone unless you risk closeness. You can't resolve a deep hurt when you keep quiet about it, when you pretend that the hurt wasn't that bad, or when you exaggerate the hurt until you decide the relationship is too painful to endure.

You must get a handle on what is hurting you and what your truest feelings are. Otherwise, your ignorance will cause you to set yourself up for more hurt later on.

THE NATURE OF DEFENSES

Psychological defenses come about after you have been hurt. They are internal reactions that enable you to protect yourself from past, present, and future pain. They typically do that by moderating your impulses to act (giving you an opportunity to think about what you want to do) or by denying and distorting your thoughts and feelings about a situation. The shock and dreamlike state people experience when a loved one dies unexpectedly are a common example of how defenses can operate to protect one from overwhelming stress and pain.

You can never rid yourself completely of your defenses, nor would you want to try. When they are working to your advantage, they shut out some degree of stress and anxiety you are facing so that you can cope better. Many overworked professionals and business people in high-stress positions never realize just how pressured they are until they have an opportunity to take a vacation. Then they become sick or exhausted, finally feeling the effects of stress that their defenses protected them from while they had work to do.

When they work well for you, defenses operate like a short-term loan. They buy you some time, to give you an edge, to help you catch your psychological breath so that you can decide where to go from there. Unfortunately, they are often used as long-term answers for problems that require different solutions. In the long run, you can't solve problems by avoiding them or pretending they are no big deal when in fact they are. If you do that, other areas of your life begin to unravel. You find yourself becoming increasingly unhappy, irritable, less effective, bored, anxious, sickly, or depressed. And your personal relationships suffer from the fallout.

To properly shed your defenses, you need to better understand how they operate. You can't really work on any major problems effectively if your defenses are blinding you from some truths. Defenses may help you to pretend at a time when a little escapism can ease the pain, but it's time now to face reality.

The less you know about yourself and the more fearful you are about taking appropriate risks, the more your psychological defenses will run your life, leaving you to react in a knee-jerk fashion to situations. As defenses become more rigid, they are often applied when they really aren't needed. Consequently, you begin to regard many of your feelings as bad and many situations as unsafe, jumbling up your ability to make sound judgments.

An analogy I like to make is of a man who spent a night in the woods, camping for the first time. Frightened by unfamiliar forest noises, he stayed awake all night should a wild animal discover him and try to devour him. Indeed, if a wild animal did attack, the man was prepared to defend himself. But as it turned out, he remained awake all night afraid of the wind in the trees.

Of course, there is danger in this world, and nothing is ever completely safe. But if you live your life like the man in the forest, overreacting to events and always imagining the worst, you will lose more than sleep.

It is the nature of defenses to build upon themselves. For example, suppose you regard yourself as being honest and frank with others. Suppose further that if the truth were known, your honesty is your excuse to be critical. You have lied to yourself (put up a defense) that your frankness is for other people's benefit when in fact it is a way for you to express anger. Anger is something you feel you cannot admit to openly, so you disguise it somewhat. You convince yourself you are being honest and helpful with your comments, not hostile.

Your defenses are now many. First, there is the defensive distortion that you have made comments purely in the name of honesty. Second, there is the defensive denial of the anger and hostility behind your comments. Third, by denying your anger, you have to deny or distort memories of past hurts that made you angry in the first place. And fourth, you deny your basic fear that you will one day be deemed unlovable by those you care about. After all, if you believed you were worthwhile, you would have been more open to the hurts and feelings all along, never having to hide or disguise them for your protection.

As you can see, defenses can pile up and complicate matters. An immediate complication is that your defensiveness has irritated others. If other people get defensive (or offensive) in return, is it due more to their degree of maturity or are they *reacting* to you? It isn't easy to tell. The only legitimate way to find out is to lower your defensiveness and watch what happens over time.

Of course, you do not need to uncover all layers of defense in order to reinvent your relationships through forgiveness. Aspects of yourself will always remain out of your consciousness. But the more you know of yourself and the less you distort your perceptions, the greater are the chances that your reconciliation will be lasting and fulfilling.

BECOMING LESS DEFENSIVE

How do you know when you are too defensive? How can you recognize your styles of defense? There is no one, easy answer to those questions, since defenses, by their nature, operate out of your awareness. Becoming aware of them is a major step in changing them. You must strongly desire to know more about yourself if you wish to get a better handle on your defenses.

Still, there are clues you can look for that will tell you what you need to begin to know. Are you anxious these days? Depressed? Frightened? Are you often sickly, and your physician seems to be unable to ease your suffering? For some people, those symptoms are the defense.

Josie, for example, came to me because she was constantly preoccupied with health concerns. Despite assurances from physicians that she was a fit twenty-seven-year-old, she would check her blood pressure many times during the day and be frightened that any ache or pain was the beginning of a cancerous tumor. Her preoccupations were ruining her new marriage. Her husband was growing impatient with her, and their sexual relationship suffered due to her health concerns.

Josie had lived with an extremely close family where everybody knew about each other's business and relatives lived only blocks away. Her mother was very protective of Josie through the years, keeping her home from school for the slightest health reason and cautioning her about the perils of dating and the dangers of sex. When Josie left home to get married, she and her husband rented an apartment only minutes from her parents' home. The real trouble began

when her husband, a computer engineer, was trans-
ferred to another state.

Then her physical concerns worsened. Her parents
became alarmed and suggested that the couple move
back home. Feeling too tugged at by her parents, Josie
stopped calling them. When they called her, she said
she was not feeling well enough to phone them regularly or to move back home. (She was trying to be
loyal to her husband.) But her symptoms made her
marriage miserable, too. (She was also trying to be
loyal to her parents.) Thus, her hypochondriasis was a
defense, unconsciously designed to keep her in everyone's good graces until she could figure out what to
do. Her parents, hurt that she moved away, were not
about to disown her, since she was suffering so. Her
husband, hurt that she was being so "irrational," was
not about to leave her, since she "obviously had a
psychological problem."

For others, physical setbacks, depression, and anxiety are indications that the defenses have weakened.
If you respond that way, those symptoms might give
you access to thoughts and feelings that otherwise
would be unavailable to you if your defenses were
running full power.

Choose one of those feelings and nudge it further.
Take anxiety, for example. There may have been moments already while reading this book when you felt
the uneasiness that comes from sensing a truth about
yourself that is hard to accept. Begin there.

- What is that uneasiness about?
- What is being threatened? Is it love? Security? Esteem? Integrity? Control? Success?
- Are you absorbing the anxiety for someone else in
  your family (that is, taking on some of their respon-
  sibilities as your own)?

- When did you feel threatened or anxious like that before?
- How did you handle it then? By blaming? By pretending to minimize the threat?
- What is there about yourself that you dislike?
- What about you could cause someone to reject you?
- Do you hide these shortcomings? How so?
- Are they really shortcomings, or are you someone who rarely gives yourself the benefit of the doubt?
- Do you feel that you must perform in some way to earn and keep the love of others?

Take the time to answer those questions. Come back to them again. In your efforts to reconcile, forgive, and reinvent your relationships, you will face those questions and others like them. Without some answers, your efforts at reconciliation will be more cumbersome.

When you have a better sense of what the things are that hurt you, of what makes you angry or frightened, happy or dissatisfied, optimistic or despairing, you are one step closer to understanding what you do with those feelings when they stir within you. And what you do with those feelings is what defenses are all about.

Anxiety as an Opportunity

Anytime your anxiety increases, it signals not only a threat but an opportunity to know yourself better should you risk lowering your defenses and exploring the meaning of the anxiety. As soon as you begin to feel anxious, ask yourself what the threat is. Pay attention to your immediate reaction. Is it one of denial? ("There is no threat. I don't know why I'm

anxious.") Is it one of blame? ("It's not my fault.")
Does your stomach or your head hurt? Just what is it
that you do with the anxiety once you experience it?

In the final analysis, this process of learning more
about yourself and lowering your defenses is not just
an intellectual exercise. It necessarily becomes an
experiential process where you must face the things
that frighten you. You do that in order to test your
expectations of harm and try out your coping skills.

So, for example, if you find yourself forgiving too
quickly the husband who betrayed you because you
fear you'll be abandoned if you talk too much about
your anger, you could face that fear head on. You
might tell your husband, "You know, part of the
reason I'm forgiving you now is that I'm afraid that if I
take too much time or say all that's really on my mind,
you won't care about our relationship anymore." If
that is still too threatening to say, you might tell him
weeks later when things seem a bit more settled that
sometimes you fear losing the people who matter to
you.

Instead of dealing with your fears and uncertainties
in your head, and instead of drawing conclusions
about others without first checking out your assumptions, speak aloud your concerns at a workable pace
for you. In all likelihood, if you give the fearful situation a fair shot, you will discover that your worst
expectations do not come true. The person you love
won't abandon you, the plane won't crash, and the
world will go on just as it always did.

And if the people you care about do reject you
because you want to be honest and be yourself, you
are fortunate to no longer have them in your life. Yes,
it will hurt you if they leave, but it is not fatal, and it
will mostly be their loss.

COMMON DEFENSES

All psychological defenses force you to deny or distort some aspect of reality. Some defenses are healthy and evidence of maturity. The effective use of humor in a tense situation is one. Another positive defense is the ability to temporarily suppress thoughts and feelings that would be too intrusive if you gave them their due, say, when you have important work to do. Many other defenses, though, are negative. Unlike the healthy defenses, which are called into action only when necessary, negative defenses are more permanent and applied under too many conditions when they aren't helpful.

The more common problematic defenses in marriages are discussed here. Everybody has used them at one time or another. Your task now, especially since you want to be reconciled and know forgiveness, is to try to recognize which of these defenses you may be using so you can begin to render them obsolete.

Projection

The method of defense called projection involves denying a feeling or attitude as your own (when in fact it is your own) and attributing that attitude to others. For example, if you are frightened by your hostile impulses, you may deny them while accusing others of being hostile toward you.

You read about Grace in the beginning of Chapter 4. She was fed up with her daughter and her husband and accused them of taking her for granted. They both wanted to take from her but were unwilling to give, she thought.

Grace grew up feeling unloved, especially by her

mother. She believed she had to work twice as hard as her siblings to get half the appreciation from her parents. Unfortunately, but understandably, she married young and had a child in order to feel loved. But her concern for her own need to feel loved was so great that her ability to provide for her family's needs was compromised. When her daughter became anxious or upset or wanted more of Grace's time, Grace resented her and saw her as selfish. She would often deny her husband sex because she regarded his advances as evidence of his concern only for himself.

What mostly was happening with Grace was that she could not be sensitive and giving to her family because she was too preoccupied with feeling needy herself. She then projected that insensitivity onto them and branded them as being selfish and inconsiderate. It then became even more complicated because after a while, Grace's daughter was desperate for love and attention and became even more demanding of Grace. Grace saw that as evidence of her daughter's inconsiderateness and for a long time was unable to see how she had contributed to the problem by her use of projection.

Of course, Grace's husband was not innocent. His ways of dealing with problems at home also contributed to the marital difficulties. But the point is that it was helpful when Grace could better understand her role in their estrangement.

Projection is a real problem when you are trying to reconcile and forgive. It is a defense that lends itself to an accusatory style of relating rather than one of humbleness and mutual understanding. If you are locked in a harsh conflict with another where each of you accuses the other of being hurtful while refusing to admit your own mistakes, this defense is probably operating.

Unlocking this kind of defensive hold on one another can be a struggle, but it is possible. Begin by owning up to anything at all you did that might have hurt the person now accusing you. Reduced defensiveness on your part will ease the tension. From then on, whenever the other person hurts you (even if it is denied), you need to stop the action and inform that person of the hurt you just experienced. That person may believe that no harm was intended, but you must state clearly that you felt hurt, regardless of the intent. If you do that often enough and in a manner that conveys your desire to reconcile rather than attack, you may be able to unblock this defense.

Projecting our responsibility for matters onto others is the most common use of this defense. Be aware of that. You alone are responsible for doing something about your problems. Others may have hurt you, but if all you do is blame, then you are denying your responsibility to change the situation for the better.

"What are you going to do about it?" is the most aggravating question I can ask some people.

"What am *I* going to do about it?" they argue. "I've been trying to tell you *I'm* not the problem. It's my husband (or wife, or mother, or father, or boss . . .). It's not my fault that things are the way they are."

"Uh-huh. So what are you going to do about it?"

Projective Identification

"My husband is a cold fish. I need affection. I crave it. But he's too aloof and distant to even care."

"I can give affection," he says. "But she gets so damn emotional . . . I feel smothered."

"My wife relies on me for everything. She's too afraid even to go shopping. I'm glad to help, but it can be exhausting."

"Without him, I don't know what I'd do. I depend on him so much. I have no confidence in myself."

"It is his anger that troubles me. He gets so furious, so enraged. I can talk things over calmly, but he can't." She was composed, sure of herself, at ease.

The husband sat there quietly, gritting his teeth, struggling not to explode.

When a couple seem to be polarized over certain issues or traits (emotional/logical, angry/calm, helpless/competent, neat/sloppy, strict/lenient), projective identification may be operating.

Projective identification occurs when couples unwittingly bargain with each other to take on their partner's unacceptable qualities while giving up their own. Thus, a rational, unemotional husband who fears the part of him that is emotionally needy and yearning for intimacy gives that part of himself to his wife. She, on the other hand, likes the emotional side of herself but fears the part that prefers to be distant, or perhaps even emotionally cold and withholding, so she gives that part to her husband. As a result, each carries certain traits to an extreme, and they fight with each other about those qualities instead of battling with themselves over their mixed feelings.

"You're too damn unfeeling and uncaring," she accuses, never realizing she is talking about aspects of herself.

"You're too emotional. You never think!" he jabs, not realizing that he doesn't have to face those aspects about himself as long as his wife plays out those qualities for him.

Like projection, when projective identification is in force, the partners project unacceptable aspects of themselves onto their partners. But unlike projection, each spouse then unwittingly tries to cajole, persuade, or manipulate the partner into expressing those unacceptable parts. The never-angry wife subtly provokes her husband to be angry. The emotionally restrained husband behaves in ways that provoke his wife into being hysterical. Or the partner who has been fighting off depression or alcoholism chooses a mate who is more able to act in such ways. And as much as partners outwardly dislike the expression of such feelings by the other, they need those feelings to be expressed to reduce their own internal anxiety.

Projective identification may also be working when one spouse does modify his or her behavior in the "desirable" direction, but then the other spouse reverses roles. Kim and Ken are a good example. Kim is the emotional pursuer in the relationship, often wanting more closeness and affection. Ken is the emotional distancer, often backing off and trying to make space for himself that doesn't include Kim.

"I'm wondering if you can each try something," I said to them. "Kim, I'd like you to stop trying to get Ken to change. Stop asking him about his feelings, and stop trying to get him to be more affectionate. Just for a week. Will you do that?"

"I could, but then he'll never be intimate. Look what I have to go through just to get him to be a little more emotional with me."

"Ken," I said, "if Kim agrees to stop trying to get you to be affectionate and intimate with her for one week, will you agree to make more of an effort on your own to express your feelings? To be more affectionate?"

They both agreed to change their own style of relating. One week later, all was fine. Ken was expressing his feelings more, and Kim was giving him the space he needed by not trying to pressure him to be more forthcoming with his emotions. But one week after that, matters were not fine.

"She doesn't seem to want me around," Ken complained. "I ask her 'What's wrong?' and she tells me she doesn't want to talk about it. She's not letting me in on her feelings."

Kim defended herself. "I just decided that if I have to hold back from expressing my needs just to give him the space he needs, then I want no part of him."

All of a sudden, Ken was the emotional pursuer and Kim was the emotional distancer. What was happening? Projective identification was still in force. They simply reversed roles so that the battle could remain *between* them instead of *within* them.

To unlock the grip of projective identification ultimately requires that each person face his or her own *ambivalent* feelings. Kim and Ken each had mixed feelings about wanting both intimacy and autonomy. As long as Kim viewed Ken as the detached one, she never had to come to terms with her own need for (and fear of) autonomy. As long as Ken viewed Kim as the overemotional one, he never had to deal with his own need for (and fear of) closeness and intimacy.

Rationalization

This defense is easy to spot and occurs with great frequency. It amounts to coming up with an excuse or list of excuses in order to justify a feeling, thought, or action that is otherwise unacceptable. No one likes to admit his or her faults and vulnerabilities, so it is easier to make excuses for why things go badly:

- "I know he beats me, but he's promised me he'll change for good this time. He has so much on his mind."

- "It's your fault I hit you (lied to you, mistreated you, etc.)."
- "My marriage would have survived if we had had more time to work on it."
- "I'm not being critical, I'm being honest."

If the fact that you were betrayed is hard for you to accept, you may rationalize what happened as being a misunderstanding rather than face the truth of a betrayal. Rationalizing can numb the feelings you would otherwise experience if you were being more honest with yourself. If you make excuses to explain away the behavior of those who hurt you, you will delay in confronting the person about what happened and may therefore open the gate for more hurting later on.

Having to put up with people who often make excuses and who don't make much progress in their life is frustrating. They often complain that you are making mountains out of molehills by questioning them when in fact it is they who are dodging the real truths about themselves.

Rationalizations can also make it hard for you to admit it when you've been hurtful. Since owning up to your behavior and accepting responsibility for your actions is a necessary prerequisite for any genuine and lasting forgiveness, making excuses can be a real problem.

If you are making too many excuses, you'll eventually know it, because your problems won't be getting better. They'll linger.

If your spouse is making too many excuses, don't invest your energy trying to change him or her. Your spouse may just resent it after a while and fight you on it. Couples too often try to "psychoanalyze" each other anyway. That typically results in the couple arguing about *that* and allows the more important issues to get lost in the cross fire.

If you conduct your life by looking out for yourself and don't take responsibility for trying to change your spouse, you'll allow for the possibility of improvement. Certainly, your spouse will need to come to terms with his or her own fears and defenses, but that can be accomplished only if your spouse takes responsibility for it, not you.

In the final analysis, if you hurt someone you care about, you need to own up to your actions and change your ways if the relationship is to be a caring and growing one. No excuses.

Repression

When you use the defense of repression, you shut out from your awareness a thought or memory of an event because remembering it would be too painful. Often, the feeling associated with the event is still somewhat conscious, leaving you depressed or frightened but unsure why. Complications in your relationships can result.

This defense can be especially problematic when you are trying to reconcile through forgiveness. You may deny that you were hurtful and therefore feel no remorse for the actions you did that caused another pain. Your lack of remorse makes it hard for the person you hurt to be forgiving. Or, more commonly, you may repress the fact that you were hurt, thereby sidestepping the need to offer forgiveness at all. People who have had traumatic or abusive childhoods often repress much of what they experienced. Whenever you deny or minimize problems, you lose the opportunity to change hurtful ways of relating.

Another form of this defense is called isolation. It is

the opposite of repression in that memories of painful events are remembered, but the feelings associated with the memories are lost, isolated from the thoughts. Many women, for example, can recall that it was painful when they gave birth to a child, but their memory of the actual pain has faded.

Donald came for psychotherapy with his teenage son, Mike. Mike was a discipline problem. Primarily, he was staying out too late at night and was inclined to talk back to his parents when he didn't like what they had to say. The problem had been going on for months, and Donald was beyond feeling angry and frustrated.

"I guess you could say I feel contempt for Mike," he confided one evening when Mike refused to attend. "I can't wait until next year when he turns eighteen. Then he'll be out on his ass."

"I certainly would be angry if I were you," I said later on. "But contempt is such a strong feeling. I'm not clear how Mike's behavior warrants such a reaction by you. It seems a bit extreme. Is there something else I'm missing?"

Donald sat stone faced. His wife, Michelle, who usually remained quiet and seemingly uninvolved, spoke up.

"Don, you've always had it in for Mike. Always. And anytime I try to talk to you about him, you shut me out."

Indeed, there were deeper problems, including a strained marital relationship. But the use of repression and isolation surfaced in this way.

"Don," I asked a few sessions later, "how would your father have handled this situation with Mike?"

"There would be no problem if he handled it," Don answered. "My father ruled with an iron fist." Don went on to describe his father as a critically harsh, hard man, cold in his feelings toward people.

"How did you react to your father's ways toward you?" I asked.

"I just did what he wanted."

"What were your feelings at the time?"

"I don't remember much feeling," Don said. "I just did what he told me. There was no other way with my father."

"Other kids in your shoes might have felt angry or frightened," I prodded.

"I don't remember feeling anything about him then. And I don't feel anything toward him now. In fact, I see him as little as possible. I suppose you could say I'm indifferent."

Don's blocking of his feelings was stunning. He had repressed many memories of his father, and for those memories he could recall, he repressed (or isolated) his feelings about the man. He denied, of course, that hurt and anger lay behind his indifference. And the idea of forgiving his father was a meaningless concept. "There's nothing to forgive. He was the way he was."

If Don were more aware of his feelings, he would have sensed that his son Mike was, among other things, fearful and angry that his father might not really love him. But Don couldn't empathize with his son in that way because he had repressed so much. All Don could do was to try to control his feelings and other people in his life. But Mike's disobedience put a dent in Don's armor of control. To feel contempt for his son, a clear overreaction, was in fact the stirring of feelings of contempt he held for his father (and himself). But he had repressed such feelings until Mike did something that Don always wanted to do: rebel against the father in the family.

Mike eventually left home at age seventeen to live

with a college friend. Therapy sessions ended shortly thereafter. "Since Mike is away, there is no more problem," Don concluded. Michelle was still silent, quietly angry at the man she felt pushed their son away, but afraid to do anything constructive. She had her own fears, her own defenses, her own pain.

Even though the strain in Don and Mike's relationship continued, Don made some encouraging attempts to break through some of his defenses. Notably, he spoke with his father and let him know why he felt so indifferent toward him. To Don's surprise, his father owned up to some mistakes, arousing both anger and grief in Don.

My hope is that Don will acknowledge enough personal pain (hurt, anger, guilt) to be able to understand Mike better. I hope that eventually he can admit to Mike that he was hurtful so that the seeds of a new relationship can be sown. And I hope that together, Don and Michelle can heal their wounded marriage.

If Don can forgive himself for his faults and overcome some of his defensive ways of dealing with pain, he might one day believe that his father, too, is forgivable. Without that resolution, Mike may be left to carry on and grapple with a belief handed down to the men of each generation in that family: that they are not good and worthwhile sons.

There are numerous other defenses not mentioned here. With them, too, the protection offered usually comes at a cost. Your perception of reality becomes distorted, possibly enough to interfere with the complex business of honestly relating with your spouse in a manner conducive to reconciliation and forgiveness.

When you hold back or disguise your feelings, they begin to take on a life of their own. They tell you there is danger in places where there is none, and they blind you to some real dangers, since your focus is so narrow. Distorted perceptions make it hard for you to understand others, accept them, fight with them, and forgive them.

And you can't hold back your feelings selectively. If you block your anger, then you necessarily block your ability to feel joy as much as you otherwise might.

When you experience what it is to lower your defenses, you may begin to wonder whether the risk of being open to your feelings is too great. You may decide it is better to leave well enough alone, that while the relationship in question is far from perfect, it is at least tolerable. You fear rocking the boat.

Understand that while such types of compromised relationships exist everywhere, there is little growth. Much is stifled. And by trying to not disrupt matters by keeping your feelings at bay, you wind up feeling tenuously safe at best. You find yourself fluctuating between periods of boredom, loneliness, and then high stress, all in an effort to preserve the status quo.

You worry that all will be lost should you be yourself, and you feel an aching inside. The aching comes not from the fear of losing what you have so painstakingly preserved, it is the aching recognition that you may never be able to let go of it. It is the recognition that all along you have been estranged from your true self as well as from others, that you have denied growth in favor of predictability, been dishonest in the name of safety, quelled your yearnings in the hope that you would then be saved from fear. And you may also wonder if you will ever know how it is to love fully and deeply, and be fully and deeply loved.

But there is much hope. You really are worthwhile and do have the capacity to experience love. And despite your faults, you deserve acceptance, surely from yourself. The more you recognize your worthwhileness, the easier it will be to lower your defenses.

Then you are on your way to resolving all that lies unsettled within you.

If you have unsettled fears, you see the world as a hurtful, frightening place that threatens your control and self-worth.

If you have unsettled sadness, you see the world as a lonely, uncaring place that leaves you grieving and feeling misunderstood.

If you have unsettled guilt, you see the world as a condemning place.

If you have unsettled resentment, you see the world as an insensitive place that leaves you feeling cheated.

If you have unsettled anger, guilt, or sadness, you have unsettled fears.

Settle your old debts. You have the power to contend with your relationships honestly, straightforwardly, and with the compassion that comes from being fully human and in God's image.

The gift that comes to you when you can own up to your weaknesses, when you can find the courage to remove your heavy cloaks of protection, is the gift of self-forgiveness.

Chapter Six

Anxiety and Forgiveness: "I'm Afraid—What Do I Do?"

When you make the effort to know yourself better, when you accept responsibility for having to do something about your problems, and when you begin to shed some of your defenses, you will expose emotions. As you proceed on the road to reconciliation and forgiveness, those emotions will be pushed and prodded until you at least accept them, and understand them as well.

The uncovering of your emotions is impossible to avoid. Some feelings will be of joy, love, and enthusiasm for life. But you may also experience anxiety, anger, guilt, or depression. Perhaps you feel them already.

It is time to face the truths about yourself, your feelings, and your relationships so that you can live a more satisfying, authentic life. The next four chapters will deal with emotions that will unsettle you on your journey to forgiveness. Most people experience them before they try to find forgiveness. Others experience them as the forgiveness process unfolds.

The first of these emotions is anxiety.

ANXIETY

Anxiety is a vague, unpleasant feeling that something bad will happen. It is characterized not just by worry and apprehension, but can also include obsessive preoccupations and uncomfortable body sensations such as trembling, heart palpitations, profuse sweating, dizziness, shortness of breath, nausea, headaches, and other body aches. Some people suffer from sudden panic attacks where breathing becomes so difficult and their hearts race so fast that they fear they are about to die.

Anxiety is a sign that you feel threatened. It is a warning by your body that you are feeling endangered in a way you can't completely control. The anxiety you feel may also be a strong indication that you are frightened by both the estrangement in your relationships and the prospect of reconciling. True reconciliation can be a scary process for some.

You may not automatically connect your anxiety or panic attacks with a troubled relationship. You may say that your anxiety is limited to planes, or to leaving home, or to speaking in public. And that may be true. But if in your relationships, particularly with your spouse and parents, there is a strong element of risk in being open about your feelings, then anxiety stems from there as well.

SOURCES OF ANXIETY

Anxiety over Not Being Forgiven

In your efforts to reconcile and reunite with your

spouse, there are many potential sources of anxiety. You may, for example, become anxious at the possibility of not being forgiven for hurts you've caused. If so, you probably believe that now you've gone too far and that it would be impossible to be forgiven and accepted back into the relationship. Although your hurtful acts may have been horrendous, this anxiety over not being forgiven stems ultimately from your doubts of being a worthwhile person.

While the issue of acceptance will be discussed more fully in Chapter 13, there is one thing about it you need to know now: Your fear that another person will find you unacceptable and unforgivable is evidence of your unwillingness to accept and forgive yourself. People who can be accepting of themselves do not live their lives in fear that others will reject them.

When you do not accept yourself, you fear genuine closeness in relationships because you believe that greater intimacy will one day lead to your being found out. You are on guard that the unacceptable side of you will be discovered and lead to your rejection. It is even possible that your anxiety over being found out became so unbearable that you did something hurtful just to get the "truth" about you exposed and the entire matter done with. You provided the justification for why you should be rejected because you couldn't tolerate the waiting.

The flip side to your anxiety over not being forgivable is, ironically, *a fear that you might be forgiven*. It can be scary to be accepted and forgiven by someone you've hurt when you hold a basic belief that you are unworthy of such acceptance. You may then continue to be hurtful until you do get rejected. But if that happens, understand that it isn't because you really are unforgivable and unworthwhile. It will be because time after time you rejected the offer of love to you. Those people who are productively involved with life and who want to grow have better things to do than to continuously put up with your abuse and testing of them.

Give up the belief that you are unworthy of forgiveness. It is only *your* belief. If others believe that about you, then you shouldn't be involved with them.

When you perpetuate the false belief that you are unworthy of forgiveness, you are really playing it safe. As long as you can use your unworthiness as the justification for why your life is an unhappy one, you never have to look further and admit your *real* weaknesses (and strengths). You never have to take any of the risks that come with being honest about yourself and improving your ways. It is that, not your supposed unworthiness, that is preventing you from being happy.

You may also fear being forgiven because you feel you are therefore beholden to the one who forgave you. You believe you are in debt to the forgiver and now must make sacrifices to pay off the debt. Such a line of reasoning only diverts you from what you really need to be doing. You don't need to make sacrifices. Instead, you need to make a concerted effort to change your style of relating that led you to causing harm and feeling guilty in the first place.

The person who truly forgives you does not want you to feel beholden or to somehow "make up" for what you've done. That person simply wants you to stop violating the relationship. The best way to do that is to admit your faults, accept forgiveness, and endeavor to change your hurtful ways.

Anxiety That You Won't Be Able to Forgive

If you don't believe that you can forgive the person

who hurt you, then you are not alone. Some hurts cut deeply. Your doubt and anxiety are a strong indication that your feelings of hurt and anger are still unspent. Let your feelings be known.

Your anxiety may also be due to the expectation that you will be hurt again, even if you offer forgiveness. That is a realistic concern. But the nature of trust is to accept the uncertainties in order to restore a loving relationship. There is no such thing as a sure thing. If there were, then the issue of trust would be moot. Go to the person in question and say that you are still unfinished about what happened that hurt you and that you'd like to settle matters; perhaps even agree on steps that could be taken to reduce the likelihood of future problems.

Your anxiety about offering forgiveness may really be a fear of disrupting the status quo. Often, relationships level off at a point where there is no real fighting but no real loving either—just periodic skirmishes that are well rehearsed and well worn. You may fear that by raising old issues and stirring up emotions that have been dormant (perhaps dormant for years), you may lose the relationship. That is a risk you must decide whether to take. But do not fool yourself. Don't believe that by playing it safe or pretending to forgive, your relationship will blossom into a loving, growing, and sharing one. It cannot as long as your truest feelings are held at bay.

You may also be uneasy about forgiving the person who hurt you because you have underlying feelings of guilt. You feel guilty over the fact that while you were hurt, you were also hurtful in return and have yet to fairly own up to that fact. Instead, you focused your anger at the person who hurt you, feeling entitled to experience the victim role without considering how you victimized the other person.

If that is true for you, then it is important to admit

your wrongdoings with no excuses. Arguing, "I didn't mean it," or, "This wouldn't have happened if you had only been more considerate," is keeping you anxious. Part of you knows the real truth and won't let you get away completely without owning up to your guilt and accepting responsibility for your actions.

Admit your mistakes, and apologize. It doesn't matter who started it. Be sincere. Show remorse. In so doing, you may make it easier for the other person to admit his or her faults, which in turn will make it easier for you to offer forgiveness.

If you overlook your guilt and only accuse the other person of being hurtful, that person will become too preoccupied defending against your accusations and not listen to the truth of what you are saying.

The Story of Arlene

Arlene suffered from severe panic attacks. Without warning, she'd become so engulfed with anxiety that breathing was an ordeal. Her heart would assault the inside of her chest like a jackhammer against clay. She got to the point of avoiding public places and not driving her car for fear that a sudden anxiety attack would render her helpless.

After several months of medication and behavior therapy (whereby a client learns to relax in the face of fearful events and unlearn the phobia), her symptoms were markedly reduced. But a nagging anxiety lingered. While the anxiety was less intrusive than it once was, she lived through each day with the quiet apprehension that bad things would happen to her. And she also felt guilty for "the ordeal I've put my family through," referring to the time when her symptoms were at their worst. Her family, especially her husband, told her she need not feel guilty, but reassurances didn't help.

A closer look at her relationships, however, revealed that her anxiety and guilt had a realistic basis. She was guilty of something she had not owned up to, and her unconscious anxiety over being found out was what haunted her.

Before the onset of her panic attacks, Arlene and her husband did not have a satisfying relationship. One divisive issue involved her father. On the one hand, Arlene spoke highly of her father, almost revering him. But, on the other hand, she kept an emotional distance from him. She would be happy in his presence but never felt free to be herself. There was a superficial quality to their relationship, yet Arlene would chide her husband for not being more like her father.

In truth, Arlene was angry with her father, but it was much later on in therapy before she recognized and accepted her anger. Then she revealed, "He made me so angry and confused. First he'd comfort me whenever my mother got mean and critical, and she was like that all the time, but he never protected me from her. I thought he was my savior, but he wasn't. In fact, of his three daughters, I was the one he paid the least attention to. If anyone was to be scolded, it would be me, even if my sisters were to blame. But where have they been since my mother's death and father has needed them? Far away, leaving me to take care of him. And all he seems to want to talk about is how he wishes they could visit more often. I wonder if he ever appreciated me."

For the time being, though, those feelings remained hidden in Arlene. She was frightened by her resentment of her father, fearing that exposure of those feelings would cause him to reject her. So she defended aginst such feelings by pretending he was a wonderful man, a man better than her husband.

As Arlene's husband felt more distanced from her, he began to work longer hours. She felt neglected. When her father became ill and had to be hospitalized, some of her mixed feelings toward him began to surface. Arlene rarely visited her father when he was in the hospital. Since she and her husband had only one car and he was working more hours, she blamed his unwillingness to modify his work schedule as the reason she couldn't visit. When her father died unexpectedly, Arlene lashed out at her husband. She accused him of never caring enough about her or her father. "All you ever think about is yourself," she'd accuse. It was shortly thereafter that her panic attacks began.

Arlene could have found a way to visit her father if she had really wanted to. Her decision not to visit him often (and her unwillingness to take responsibility for that decision) was her way of passively showing anger at him without having to feel guilt. But acknowledging that anger was so uncomfortable and risky that she projected her guilt onto her husband and branded him as the culprit. Her dishonesty with her feelings, combined with the loss of her father and strain in her marriage created an anxiety that became overwhelming, resulting in panic attacks.

To prevent future attacks, Arlene chose to avoid dealing with any stressful or emotionally laden topic. That only succeeded in keeping important feelings unsettled. Her family didn't want to upset her, and they then found that they couldn't be themselves around her. Everyone walked on tiptoes. Arlene noticed their cautiousness, which increased her guilt and anxiety. She had plunged into a morass of fear, anxiety, and self-doubt.

When, after several months of therapy, her symptoms were at a manageable level, she began to look a bit more honestly at her situation. First, she was able to admit that she had always been hard on her husband and that she had unfairly blamed him for her unwillingness to visit her father when he was in the hospital. Unfortunately, with that admission, she began to put herself down, wondering aloud how her husband could put up with her. She restricted her activities, believing that she didn't deserve much enjoyment in life anymore.

The unconscious motive behind that was to punish herself enough so that others wouldn't. She feared that she might not be accepted with her admitted faults and acted as if punishment was necessary to alleviate her guilt. But her anxiety was kept alive under such conditions because she was doing nothing constructive about her guilt.

Fortunately, after being confronted numerous times in therapy about her self-punishment stance, she set on a course whereby she sought forgiveness from her husband for the ways in which she hurt him. She also forgave her father, her mother, and herself. Her husband showed remorse as well, admitting how out of anger he had distanced himself from Arlene.

Forgiveness did not allow Arlene to get away with anything. On the contrary, the process of forgiveness required her to take a hard and honest look at herself. She exposed her faults as well as her strengths. And with the people who mattered most to her, she risked being honest about her feelings.

In time, she began to believe that she was acceptable in spite of her weaknesses and no longer needed to deny or distort them. Free to clearly own up to her shortcomings, she made a solid effort to change them and improve her style of relating. Arlene's anxiety attacks stopped, and her general apprehensiveness lifted.

Anxiety over Changing Your Behavior

After you have admitted your part of the responsibility for the estrangement, and *even after you have been forgiven*, you may get anxious at the prospect of changing your style of relating that caused problems in the relationship.

Forgiveness is not an experience where one says, "Forget about it. It's over now," and the two of you go on to relate in exactly the same manner as always. If there is to be a satisfying reunion, hurtful ways must be changed.

When you are forgiven, there is no condition placed on you to change. You simply are forgiven. The forgiver can't demand that you change as a condition of forgiveness. However, your failure to try to change any of your hurtful ways is to rebuke the love offered to you. Over time, you may lose the relationship, since the forgiver is under no obligation to continually put up with your abuse.

When you recognize your faults and have been forgiven, it is up to you to change your ways. That prospect can create anxiety. Generally, the anxiety you may feel comes from three basic areas: anxiety that you lack the skill or know-how to change; anxiety that changes you do make will be inadequate or "too little, too late"; and anxiety that by changing, even for the better, you will give up something important.

Anxiety That You Lack the Know-How
"Where do I begin? What do I do? I've been this way

all of my life; how can I change now?"

Those are common questions, and of course no simple answer can be applied to each and every person. And there is disagreement in the fields of psychology and psychiatry about whether or not people already possess the necessary skills to change, or if they must learn some skills before changes can occur. I believe that most of the time people benefit from learning (or improving) some skills. Certainly, if you have created problems in your relationships because you need to be more assertive, a more effective parent, a better lover, and so on, you may do well to read any of the available books on such topics and become better educated.

As far as general skills that can be applied to most efforts to resolving problems, three often need polishing. The first vital skill, especially when you are trying to reconcile and forgive, is to *listen* well. Being able to listen actively can be difficult, particularly when the other person is complaining about you or falsely accusing you of something. Then you are preoccupied with your anger or fear and thoughts on how to defend yourself and can't really hear what the other person is saying. Feeling defensive is normal and understandable, but if it causes the other person to believe you aren't really listening, then that person's frustrations could lead to more battles you could do without.

You can learn to listen more effectively. Start by waiting for the other person to finish a thought, and then tell that person your understanding of what was just told to you. Do that *before* you agree or disagree with the person's comments. That way, if you misunderstood what was said, it can be immediately corrected. And if your understanding is accurate, the other person will feel better knowing that you are taking the time and effort to hear him or her out.

Often, others get more obnoxious or adamant while speaking if they doubt that the listener is really trying to understand what's being said.

If you practice giving that type of immediate feedback to one another, your listening skills will improve, and you will also find that you are discussing matters at a slower, more workable pace. It seems awkward and artificial at first, as the dialogue seems to progress in a herky-jerky manner, but you'll soon get comfortable with it.

If your efforts at active listening fail because you end up interjecting critical or defensive remarks, then the second skill you need is to stop reflexive responding. Reflexive responding is any thought, feeling, or action that has the effect of cutting short a dialogue or escalating it to dangerous levels.

Giselle and Steve respond so reflexively to one another that listening, and productive communication, rarely occur.

"I want you to show consideration for my feelings," Giselle said calmly.

"That's just a fancy way of saying you want me to give up what I want and always go along with you," Steve shot back. "You always want to keep me under your thumb."

"I hate it when you say 'always'! I don't *always* do the terrible things you say I do," Giselle volleyed.

Each of them was responding to the other in a reflexive, unproductive manner.

One useful technique for overcoming reflexive responding is to agree to let the other person speak uninterrupted for at least fifteen minutes. Initially, the spouse who is listening will get irritated at what's being said, but there is time later to respond. It is also important to take the full fifteen minutes, if not more time. Typically, spouses can't talk for that long if all they do is complain. Eventually they must use the time to focus more on their feelings, faults, and wishes, which will help reduce reflexive responding as well.

A third useful skill is being able to prioritize problems and potential areas of change. You may have so many things to modify that you don't know where to begin. For example, you may have a list of complaints about the other person, and you aren't sure which to raise first. You do know that you want to discuss your concerns, but you also know that some issues are harder to bring up than others.

One way to approach it is to make a list of those aspects of the other person you dislike (and that person could do the same about you). Then, rate from one to ten the level of anxiety you feel as you imagine yourself talking with the person about each issue. The items rated high on anxiety are important but perhaps too much to deal with right now. Those rated low to moderate are likely to be more workable.

While addressing each point is a goal, a more immediate and important goal is to learn to tolerate levels of anxiety while trying to resolve problems. You will never get rid of your anxiety. The process of reconciliation creates anxiety. But you need to be able to cope with a moderate amount of anxiety as you contend with your problems. By prioritizing the areas of concern based on your anxiety level, you increase the chances that you'll be able to stick with your efforts to change.

Anxiety That Changes Made Will Be Inadequate

When you fear that the changes you make in your life won't be good enough or come fast enough, the fear may be due to your low self-worth. You are worried that the person who forgave you will come to regard you as unacceptable if you fail to mend your ways soon.

Of course, it is possible that you were forgiven too quickly, and the other person is still angry with you. If so, discuss your concerns and clarify your expectations of each other. However, it may also be that you simply doubt your worth no matter how much love and forgiveness someone offers you.

If you persist in holding dear the belief that you are not a worthwhile person, you will never work honestly and productively at changing your ways. You will always hold back, even just a little. To go all out would be too honest a test of both your abilities and the strength of the relationship you want preserved. It is easier to hold back on your efforts and then blame any subsequent failure on your unworthiness. That way, you can keep alive the fantasy that had you really put forth a solid effort, everything would have worked out. You never have to address the possibility that had you done your best, you still might not improve your ways. You never have to address the possibility that had you done your best, you might have been rejected anyway.

It is painful to work hard at mending a relationship and improving your shortcomings only to discover that the relationship just won't work out. But believe that you are worthwhile, and make strong, concerted efforts to improve yourself. If the relationship doesn't survive, then at least you did your best and are not kidding yourself about the future of the relationship. That pain is cleaner and able to be healed better than the pain that comes from deceiving yourself about your worthiness, being left to wonder that things might have been different "if only I. . . ."

A sad irony here is that any amount you hold back from putting forth your best efforts to change is probably just enough to keep you from succeeding. You then markedly increase your risk of losing the relationship, the very thing you wanted to avoid.

Finally, some people blame the other person for their failure to make improvements. They argue that the other person is basically unaccepting of them, no matter how much effort is put into changing for the better.

Don't do that. You must accept full responsibility for your efforts to make productive changes in your life. If the other person is finding you to be unacceptable, why were you offered forgiveness? If you believe that the forgiveness offered was not genuine, why did you accept it? If you truly believe that your relationship can't work out no matter how much you change, why haven't you left?

If there is to be hope for the relationship, you owe it to yourself not to use the other person's weaknesses as the excuse to not be your best in trying to improve your ways.

Anxiety That Changes Made Will Bring Loss

Finally, you may be anxious because you sense that even if you change for the better, you will give up or lose something of value to you. A common fear is, "If I change too much, maybe the people I care about won't like the new me."

Sometimes changes can make the relationship feel awkward. Even desired changes can be a bit disruptive at first. Let's face it, anytime you start being more open about your feelings, no matter how sensitive you are to the feelings of others, some people get a bit rankled.

Give yourself, and others, more time. Let go of any inclination to revert to your former style of relating, even if the old way seems more predictable and comfortable.

Other possible losses come from change. When

Fred tried to be less critical of the way his wife disciplined the children, he became aware of his strong
need to be in control of family situations. To Fred, not
criticizing his wife about discipline issues meant he
was not in charge. And he wasn't sure if he wanted to
give up any control.

Fred grew up in a household where nothing he did
was ever "good enough," so now he tried to prove his
parents wrong by being the perfect father to his children. But to succeed now meant that his wife couldn't
be "good enough." By toning down his criticisms of
her, he had to admit he was wrong for having been so
faultfinding. That only opened up old wounds, where
now he had to wonder if perhaps his parents' criticisms of him were justified, since he was no longer the
"perfect father."

He needed to accept the fact that he was human and
therefore imperfect. And he needed to address his
anger at his parents and begin the process of forgiving
them. If he could not forgive them, he would be
showing himself that not being "good enough," as his
parents weren't "good enough," can be an unforgivable offense. That would only impede his ability to
forgive himself, since he too was far from perfect.

You have been hurtful in part to get some need met.
Fred was harshly critical of his wife because it met his
need to feel that he was a good enough father. It also
met his need to prove his parents wrong.

Everyone has needs for attention, affection, control,
approval, sympathy, achievement, and the like. Relationships suffer, however, if the needs are satisfied by
engaging in problematic, inflexible patterns of behavior.

As you begin to modify your ways of relating, you
will become aware of what some of your needs are.
There are ways to meet those needs without damag-

ing your relationships. But that requires an openness on your part as to what needs you want met, and a willingness to discuss with others how to best go about getting them met.

This chapter was designed to inform you of the ways in which anxiety will creep in (or pounce in) on your efforts to reconcile, forgive, and heal your marriage.

Your anxiety is a signpost. It tells you that you are uneasy and frightened about something. And it tells you the direction you need to travel in order to better cope with the anxiety, if you take the time to read the sign carefully.

Anxiety is a constant, pulsing tension. It is all hope. And it is despair. It is the gulf between the past and the present, the longing for that which once was and is no longer. It is the space between what is and what can be, the yearning we call desire. It nestles in all of us.

You cannot overcome all anxiety. In its absence you would be dead. But you can come to accept it, and ultimately transcend it, by basing your security on something that is not fleeting.

You want security. Your security is understanding that there is a greater purpose for your life, if you would but take the time to extend yourself beyond your fears and into the faith that comes from loving within a relationship that matters.

Chapter Seven

Anger and Forgiveness: "I'm Mad—What Do I Do?"

"I hate her now. No, I loathe her. Every time I think about her, I'm consumed with hate." Charlie's words shot out like venom as he spoke of his ex-wife. "She took my money, my kids, and my integrity, and I'll never forget that."

Charlie has a relationship with his former wife that is most potent. He is connected to her by an iron bond of anger and hate. He is passionately involved with the woman he says he wants no part of. And he cannot be free of her until he is free of his anger.

ANGER FELT

Anger is the emotion that follows shortly after you have been hurt. It is a normal response to pain. Any pain. When you stub your toe, you feel hurt and then angry. Even when a dear friend who is always reliable is late for a dinner appointment with you, you feel a little annoyed. The pain there may come from the fact that you worried about the friend's safety. Or you felt that the friend was a trifle insensitive in causing you to wait.

It is not a sin to feel angry, nor are you a bad person because you feel it. Anger is an all-too-human emotion. Anger is not a problem. But how you contend with it can be.

Anger unchecked and allowed to burn can lead to bitterness. Anger held back out of fear of expressing it leads to guilt and depression.

When you are angry, you may notice that your body is more tense, your pulse is rapid, and you are increasingly preoccupied with what is making you angry. You find it difficult to concentrate on other matters. You are mobilized for action.

Feeling angry does not by itself help or hinder a relationship. What matters is what you do with the feeling.

If you typically express your anger in a hostile, demeaning, controlling manner, then the relationship will be scarred at best. People will resent you if they put up with you at all.

If you hold back your anger and fear expressing it, then the relationship will die a slow death. There is opportunity for growth and deeper trust when you can express anger honestly, directly, as soon as possible after the hurt, with a sensitivity to the other person's feelings, and with an attitude of respect. Impossible to do? Of course not. But it isn't always easy.

If you want to be reconciled with the other person, if you want to forgive and get on with a healthy relationship, then you must let go of your anger.

If a reconciliation is impossible or undesired but you still wish to end your suffering from having hurt or been hurt, then you must let go of your anger.

To achieve that, you will have to do two basic and related things. First, you must express your anger at the source of your hurt. Don't fool yourself about this. If you want to renew a relationship or at least settle your feelings, you need to go to that person and say, "I'm angry, and let me tell you why." As discussed more fully in Chapter 17, express that anger even if the other person is unavailable. Writing a letter to an unavailable person is one excellent way of stating, and clarifying, your feelings.

The second thing you need to do in order to let go of your anger is to decide to nurture a forgiving attitude. That involves your being open to knowing yourself better, too. It requires your willingness to take responsibility for the way your life is running. As soon as you can admit that it is your responsibility to do something about your pain (anger, guilt, grief, depression, anxiety, estrangement from others), you can take an honest look at what your strengths and weaknesses are. When you do that, you will be more open to forgiving yourself. That in turn makes it easier for you to understand and accept the weaknesses of others. Knowing that another person is weak (and not just malicious) helps you to not take things so personally, and your anger is then eased.

While anger is an important factor in your estrangement, it is not anger per se that is keeping you estranged. It is what you are doing with the anger that is of most concern.

Consider Jack and Cynthia, who were in their late fifties. They came in for family therapy with their son, Robert. Robert was thirty-two years old, divorced, and for the past four years had been living with his parents. He had no secure job. Every time he tried to live independently, an emotional or financial crisis erupted. His parents would bail him out and accept him back home.

Both parents were angry with Robert. Jack was especially furious. He said he was angry because Robert was lazy, refusing to pay even a modest rent at home. Robert also argued with his mother, using foul language when she complained to him about his laziness.

"Then throw me out if you don't want me anymore," he would taunt. "Go on, I dare you."

Jack's anger at his son was easy to understand. But there was more to it than what was on the surface. By being open to the idea of knowing himself better, Jack admitted that a second layer of his anger was toward Cynthia. He was angry because he saw her as domineering and too protective of Robert. Jack wanted him out of the house. Cynthia refused. Jack admitted to his wife, "Sometimes I think that you care more about his feelings than mine." Caught up in his anger, Jack went on to claim, "Ever since we've been married, my feelings haven't been that important to you. Mostly, you've wanted things done your way, and I always went along with it. With no appreciation from you, I might add."

Things heated up when Jack insinuated that it was Cynthia's overprotectiveness of Robert that led to his being so irresponsible. Cynthia argued that Jack's laid-back, passive style was the reason for Robert's problems.

When Robert interrupted their arguing to announce he was leaving for good, Cynthia became upset. She stopped fighting with her husband, almost as if she were telling Robert that there would be no more fighting if only he would stay. Jack sat back and said nothing. Robert agreed to stay home. Frightened, miserable, and seething with anger, the family stayed stuck.

But Jack's anger was starting to overflow.

"Did your mother appreciate you, Jack?" I asked one day.

"Hardly," he answered. "I even took care of her after my father died. I postponed getting out on my own so I could stay home with her, but all she did was criticize."

"That's true," Cynthia said, supportively. "You really did make a lot of sacrifices for her, and she never gave you the credit you deserved. She just criticized you all the more. That wasn't fair."

"Much of my life I've felt spineless," Jack said later. "I hate to say it, but it's true. And it's hard not to view Robert in the same light when he acts so irresponsibly, when he seems afraid to get a real job and work hard at it."

"Are you saying that your anger at your son is unfair, Jack?" I asked.

"Partly," he said. "He is acting irresponsibly, but I've been irresponsible all these years every time I sat back and let my wife make all our decisions. That wasn't fair to either of us."

Jack never would have been free of his anger if all he ever did in therapy was focus on his anger at Robert. That is so because his anger at Robert was laced with an unresolved anger toward his wife, his mother, and himself. Thus, anytime Robert acted irresponsibly or unappreciatively, Jack was likely to overreact because he was carrying excess emotional baggage.

Once Jack saw what his anger was all about, he had a clear direction for change. Not only did he need to be more assertive with Robert, he had to resolve his anger with his wife and mother, and come to terms with his need to please.

When you are feeling angry, consider these questions:

- How were you hurt, and who hurt you?
- Was it your sense of esteem that suffered? Your sense of being loved? Your sense of control? Of competence? Of pride?
- Did you ever experience that kind of hurt before?
- How did you deal with it then?
- Did your method of handling it lead to a resolution of the problem or a greater estrangement?
- Could you have prevented the hurt?
- If not, why not? If so, why didn't you?
- Do you use your hurt to control others?
- Is that why you hold grudges? Or does holding a grudge give you a reason to stay angry?
- Could you ever feel so angry that you would vow never to forgive?
- What would you do with your anger then?

Use the energy that comes from being angry to help you confront the person who hurt you rather than withdraw or seek retaliation. And then face yourself. If your anger is deep and long-standing, then there is something about yourself that makes you angry, too. Determine what that is, do your best to resolve it, and your anger at others will be diminished.

ANGER RESTRAINED

People who frequently withhold their feelings of anger are one of two general types. The first type is chronically angry and well aware of it. A strong (but always unsuccessful) effort is made to keep the anger in check because once it leaks out, the person fears losing control. Many such people have periods of sudden, explosive behavior marked by physical aggressiveness or verbal abuse. Sometimes they appear to feel terribly guilty afterward, but they never seem to change.

The second type of person is much less in touch with the full extent of the anger and is mostly afraid. Such a person is afraid of being rejected or disliked if that person says what he or she feels. This person may not admit to being angry, but only to being "annoyed" or "disappointed" or confused about his or her feelings. The more confused this person is, the more fearful and angry he or she is. Such a person may say he or she is "slow to burn." There are usually no uncontrolled angry outbursts. Anxiety and depression are common.

If you hold back your anger, then you doubt your self-worth. It is hard for you to experience a full joy about anything because you can't be too spontaneous. Any spontaneity necessarily involves a loosening of control over your feelings. You don't want to risk doing that, so every experience becomes somewhat tainted.

When you hold back your anger you are probably afraid of something. When you restrain your anger, it becomes more difficult to be forgiving. You may want to lash out instead. Or you may offer forgiveness quickly, saying "It's all right, forget about it," when in fact you are really pleading, "Don't hurt me. I'm frightened enough as it is."

To forgive, you must acknowledge your anger fully so that you can let go of it. But if you are afraid and admit to only some of your anger, it lingers and begins to take on a life of its own. It forces you to pay attention to every hurt or inconsiderate act against you, and it blinds you to the more positive things in your life. And with every new hurt, you feel weakened as old hurts reemerge to accost you. It was that way with Jack when his unresolved anger at his mother and himself hurt his relationship with his wife and son. His unspent anger left him weak and exasperated, unable to cope well with new problems that arose.

Not only is it difficult to forgive when you restrain your anger, it is difficult to feel forgiven. That is because matters are still unresolved for you.

You can give many reasons for not expressing your anger. But if you believe that your life will become too complicated should you be open about such feelings, just hold back on their expression and see how much more complicated your life will become.

ANGER EXPRESSED

There is still much public misinformation about the nature of anger and whether it is helpful to express it. Confusion probably persists not because there is no clear consensus in the field of psychology about the usefulness of expressing anger, but because the topic of anger still creates anxiety. And anxiety leads to misunderstanding.

The bottom line is that anger, like any other feeling, needs to be expressed if you are involved in a caring relationship. When you feel angry, that is simply how you feel. It is as much a part of your being at that moment as anything else about you.

But in your effort to reconcile and forgive, the expression of anger can be problematic when it is done out of fear and defensiveness. That is the case when anger is expressed in an openly hostile and attacking manner or when it is expressed subtly and passively.

Hostile Expression of Anger

Expressing your anger hotly may sometimes be the

only way to get heard. Some people refuse to listen unless you scream. It isn't ideal, but it happens that way. But most of the time, expressing your anger in a hostile way serves less to inform than it does to attack. It is an assault made at the expense of the other person's vulnerabilities rather than a means to heal and reunite.

"You don't give a damn about my feelings!" Cheryl shouted to her new husband. "Just because your ex-wife ran around on you, you think I'm going to screw any guy I meet. Well, I'm sick of your accusations. Why don't you grow up for a change?"

No matter how justified her anger was, Cheryl's verbal attack did nothing to help resolve matters. Her husband reacted angrily and defensively to her remarks, and then they argued about *that* rather than deal with the issue of his mistrust.

Indignant that her husband reacted angrily, Cheryl accused, "I can't even express my feelings to you without you being upset and critical. This marriage is nowhere."

Their lines of communication were destructive. And their anger, however legitimate, was kept alive not because they expressed it but because they expressed it in a manner designed to hurt, not heal.

The process of reconciliation and forgiveness gets sidetracked, sometimes permanently, when hostile, verbal attacking is done in the name of honest expression of anger. The person being attacked often sees no choice but to attack or withdraw, both options only postponing the necessary work required to reconcile.

Passive Expression of Anger

As difficult as it is to contend with someone who is venting anger at you in an openly combative way, at least the anger is overt and you know what you are dealing with. But when blatant expression of anger is somehow unacceptable to the person who feels angry, then it may be expressed in subtle, indirect, and passive forms.

What psychologists and psychiatrists refer to as *passive-aggressive* behavior takes the form of such actions as stubbornness, procrastination, dawdling, gossiping, forgetfulness, and "humorous" remarks that are hurtful. The person on the receiving end of these kinds of attacks feels hurt and angry but is not always sure if the other person meant to be hurtful. And if confronted, the passive-aggressive person denies any harmful intent, so there is no resolution.

The exquisite nature of this form of attack is revealed when the aggressor (who may honestly be unaware of his or her hostile feelings) not only denies harmful intent but goes on to suggest that you are being too petty, too sensitive, too critical. "You can't take a joke," the aggressor might say. That leaves you frustrated and angry, knowing that any further attempt you make to discuss the concern will be thrown back as "your problem." Meanwhile, the passive-aggressive acts continue.

When anger is expressed passively, an insidious process develops that can eat away at the foundation of your relationship. Any effort to reconcile, even about matters not related directly to the passive aggression, is at an impasse. How can you reconcile about a past problem if the other person is hurting you now? How can you reconcile if the other person denies that a problem exists? Resentment builds, and the relationship deteriorates.

One way to try to handle the matter is to tell the person the specific things being done that bother you the moment they occur.

"Look, Marge, it may not seem like a big deal to

you, but it really bothers me that you end up working late on days you're supposed to drive me home. When I'm the one driving, I make it a point to leave on time so you won't have to wait for me. Would it be possible for you to let me know a day in advance when you think you may be needing to work overtime?"

The point is not to accuse the other person of being inconsiderate or hostile (they'll deny it anyway), but to inform him or her that you simply don't like what is happening. Your feelings and reactions are the issue, not the other person's motivations. If that doesn't get you any results, then you will eventually have to set limits so you don't suffer too much.

"It's not working out, Marge. I'm getting resentful that I still get home late on the days that you drive. Rather than continue feeling resentful, I think it's best that we drive our own cars to work from now on."

If a person who is passively aggressive really does care about the relationship, then you will notice a sincere effort to change. But don't expect perfection overnight. If the person doesn't change, then you are setting yourself up for more hurt if you continue to remain as involved with that individual.

Appropriate Expression of Anger

For reconciliation and forgiveness to have a fair shot, you must express your feelings truthfully but tempered with love. If you express anger passively and then deny that you did it, then you are not truthful. If you are hostile and abusive, then you aren't loving.

It is possible to convey that you are angry without making a big deal out of it. There is no need to be dramatic or caustic. Simply be direct and clear about what you feel. Be respectful of the other person's feelings, but don't soft-soap what you really mean.

Know that it is probably as uncomfortable for the other person to have to listen to you as it is for you to speak.

When you finish what you have to say, check to see if you feel better. If you do, tell the other person that. It will make him or her feel better, too. And it is an indication that any future offer of forgiveness by you will be viewed as sincere.

And when the other person is angry with you, let him or her talk. Hear the person out. Don't defend. Your task is to demonstrate that you understand what is being said and that you care about what the person has to say. There is plenty of time later for you to give your side of the story.

If you find it hard to listen, say so. Ask the person to repeat what you didn't get.

It is true that when you come to terms with your anger by acknowledging it, experiencing it, and honestly, straightforwardly, and compassionately expressing it, you take a risk. You may be attacked, abandoned, or you may become closer to that person, more able to forgive and accept forgiveness.

But when you hold back your anger or use it as a weapon, the risks reduce dramatically. Resentment, rejection, and deeper estrangement then become a sure thing.

Move forward. Take the risk of honestly and compassionately expressing yourself. For in a forgiving marriage, anger is neither a weakness nor a sign of loss of love. It is the first mark of a relationship on the mend.

Chapter Eight

Guilt and Forgiveness: "I'm Bad—What Do I Do?"

"I'm a good-for-nothing father," Stu said. "How can she still love me? All her life I ignored her. I never found time for her, especially after the divorce when she went to live with her mother. But she thinks I'm wonderful! I don't deserve her. But I hate feeling this way. It's my guilt that is doing this to me. Why am I feeling so damn guilty for something that happened years ago?"

"How often do you see your daughter now, Stu?" I asked.

"Not often," he answered, his head bowed low. "I can't face her."

"You're still hurting her then, Stu. You're not spending time with her now, just like you didn't years ago. You're feeling guilty because *you are guilty*. When do you want to stop feeling sorry for yourself and repair the damage?"

When I asked you in the previous chapters to look

117

honestly at yourself, to see the truth of your feelings without defensive distortion, it was with the knowledge that you would struggle the most with your guilt.

Guilt is both an inner, subjective feeling state as well as an outward, objective condition. Subjectively, guilt is a painful state of anxiety whereby you feel badly about having been hurtful and you worry about being found out and punished.

Guilt is an internal fire that burns to frighten and condemn you. But it can also be a light that guides you. It lets you know that you are doing something wrong, something undignified, and makes it hard for you to try to pretend otherwise.

Behind your feelings of guilt there is always some anger that you haven't dealt with adequately. Maybe you vented it in a harsh, hostile manner, or maybe you held it in and feared expressing it. Regardless, it has contributed to your now feeling guilty.

Objectively, guilt is a condition of estrangement between yourself and someone who matters to you. It is brought about when one of you deeply hurts the other. If you have been hurtful, then you are guilty, *whether or not you feel guilt inside*. In compelling and thoughtful articles on the topic, E. M. Pattison wrote of the condition of guilt occurring when one violates a relationship one has been committed to by treating the other as a thing instead of as a person.

If you want to reconcile, find forgiveness, and heal your relationships, you must come to terms with your guilt. You must recognize when you are feeling too guilty or not guilty enough. And regardless of how you feel about it, you need to do something about your hurtful actions that are keeping you estranged, if there is to be any meaning to the reconciliation.

SUBJECTIVE GUILT—FEELING GUILTY

The condition of *feeling* guilty is always a bit compli-cated. Sometimes you feel guilty about something you've done because you really were hurtful and should feel guilty. But other times you feel guiltier than is appropriate, and instead of being guided by your guilt, you are overburdened by it. It gnaws at your self-esteem, and you feel frightened that others will abandon you if they ever know the "real" you.

Sometimes you feel guilty about something, but your feeling masks a deeper guilt that you haven't come to terms with yet. For example, Carl felt guilty when he forgot his eleventh wedding anniversary. But a more meaningful guilt lay elsewhere. He had been bored with his marriage for some time, overin-volved at work, and had been toying with the idea of having an affair. His real guilt was that he had failed to do something constructive about his marriage con-cerns, a guilt that was stimulated when he forgot his wedding anniversary.

Sometimes you feel guilty unnecessarily due to overly rigid belief systems that cause you to condemn yourself for thoughts, feelings, and actions that aren't bad at all. The most common example of that is feel-ing guilty about anger. Anger is normal and reason-able after you have been hurt. It is not wrong to feel angry, but it is wrong to express it in a hostile, attack-ing manner. And even if you do act in a mean or vicious way, you are not a person unworthy of love. Unfortunately, people with exaggerated guilt feelings do believe they are unworthy of true love.

People with religious beliefs that tell them they are first and foremost *sinners* often condemn themselves. While I am not a theologian (but someone who believes that sin is real), I nonetheless believe that God loves us and does not condemn us. Our real sin is perhaps not becoming all that we are. We do that by focusing primarily on our guilt, convincing ourselves we are not capable (worthy) of doing more for ourselves, and thereby hold back on the God-given talents and ideas we have.

Sometimes you may feel guilty but then become consumed with guilt. You are racked by waves of unyielding anxiety and self-condemnation. At times, you may not even allow the other person in the relationship who is also responsible for the estrangement to accept any blame. You place the burden of guilt squarely on your shoulders, intensify the feelings, and stagger under the weight of it.

Danielle was like that. The slim, thirty-four-year-old who has been married for eight years doesn't know what it means to be free from feelings of guilt.

"I know it's my fault that Russ is having an affair," she said, trying uncomfortably hard to appear at ease with herself. "I haven't been able to give him what he needs."

She listed all of the "terrible" things she's done to Russ over the years. First, there were the four miscarriages, which pained Russ because he so much wanted to be a father. Since the birth of their daughter ("I should have given him a son"), she is worried that she's neglected Russ. "Let's face it," she told me, "since Maria's been born I've had no time. I feel exhausted. Sex is a fading memory. But I should be making more of an effort for Russ. He knows that."

"What was your job in your family growing up?" I asked her one day.

"That's easy. I was the responsible one. I took care of my younger sisters, I cleaned the house, and I guess you could say I tried to keep everybody calm. I didn't want there to be any tension."

"Where was the source of the tension?" I asked. "Between your folks?"

"I don't know if there was more between my parents or between my mother and me. Everything had to be spotless at home, and it was my job to keep it that way. I wanted to please her. Partly because I knew she was unhappy about something. I think there was some secret between my parents. Something they didn't talk about, but when it was on their minds you could cut the tension with a knife. That was when I made real sure my sisters stayed out of trouble because when my parents were in that mood, the least little thing would set them off." She paused, looking guilty again. "Don't get the wrong idea about my parents. They were wonderful."

It is common for very responsible children to grow up and become very responsible adults. But Danielle was taking on too much responsibility and then feeling guilty when things didn't run smoothly.

You may have the opposite problem. You may feel less guilt than you should. If so, you are probably a caring person to some extent but you think mostly about yourself and not about how you hurt and offend others. You defend yourself against any effort to accept more responsibility for your actions by branding the person who feels hurt as too sensitive or a troublemaker. Or you argue, "I've got to look out for number one," as your justification for being hurtful and inconsiderate.

If that sounds like you, then there is an underlying anger you haven't admitted, much less resolved. If you want your current relationships to remain intact, you need to do something about the ways you are acting, even if you don't agree that you are being hurtful.

As much as Danielle was overresponsible, her husband Russ was underresponsible. Maybe that was always his style, or maybe he was simply adjusting to Danielle. After all, she was responsible enough for the two of them.

"Danielle tells me that she's responsible for your having an affair, Russ. Is that right?"

Russ nodded.

"She held a gun to your head?" I said, smiling, not sure if he'd appreciate my remark.

"She might as well have. She spends more time cleaning the house than she spends with me. When I want her time, she tells me she's too tired from all the cleaning. But will she cut back on her cleaning? No."

"He's right, he's right," Danielle cut in, practically pleading for leniency.

"It sounds as if you've made some mistakes, Danielle," I said. "But I can't get it out of my mind that you're taking on too much guilt. Doesn't Russ have a mind of his own? Isn't he responsible for his actions?"

Russ burned a hole through me with his eyes. "Of course I'm responsible," he said coolly. Danielle shifted uneasily.

"If there is any good to your having an affair, Russ, it's that it has brought you two together to straighten some things out," I said, hoping to find a common ground where everyone could take a stand. "Danielle, maybe you're still being loyal to your mother; I don't know, but obviously you're taking on too much responsibility. Funny, but that's pretty irresponsible, don't you think? I mean, it only leads to more problems, and you treat Russ as if he isn't old enough to make his own decisions."

"Sometimes I feel that she's treating me like a kid," Russ blurted. "Everything has to be on her terms."

"If that's how you feel, Russ, then the time to make your own decisions is now. Your first decision is whether to work on the marriage and stop the affair, or keep the affair going. Marriage therapy won't work as long as there is another woman in your life."

"This is all my fault," Danielle concluded.

"This is your husband's choice and responsibility," I said. "No matter what you say or do, there is no way you can make the choice for him."

Therapy was just beginning. The first step was regaining some balance in the relationship over the issue of guilt and responsibility.

The common thread that connects people who feel too much guilt with those who don't feel enough is their focus on their inner, subjective feelings of guilt without doing anything about their outward, objective behaviors that are hurting others. As guilty as Danielle felt, she'd continue to feel that way as long as she never modified her behavior. And since Russ was in the "less guilty" (which means "less painful") position, she would have to do most of the changing first. Until she gave up some of her guilt and gave it back to Russ where it belonged, their situation would probably stay the same. So she did give up some guilt.

"Russ, I've made mistakes in this marriage, and I want a real opportunity to change our marriage around. For that to happen, your affair has to stop. I'm not saying this as a threat, I'm just letting you know that as long as your affair continues, my heart won't be in this marriage. I won't work on this relationship myself. That's my choice. What's yours?"

Russ said he wanted time to "think about it." Over a two-week period, without having stopped his affair, he watched his formerly guilt-ridden wife stop feeling guilty. She didn't argue with him or berate herself.

She spent more hours at work and signed up for a computer course she'd always put off taking. As her anxiety from her guilt began to disappear, Russ's guilty feelings emerged. A week later he stopped his affair, and the two were ready to work on their marriage.

OBJECTIVE GUILT—BEING GUILTY

No matter how much or how little guilt you feel, when you hurt others (or yourself), you are guilty. Maybe you don't intend to be hurtful or maybe you do, but when you violate a personal relationship by causing harm, then you are guilty. Not bad. Not unlovable. Guilty.

If you honestly believe you haven't been hurtful, then talk about that with the person who feels hurt. You may be right. The other person might have misperceived your actions or may be making mountains out of molehills. But more than likely, if another person is complaining that you are being hurtful, then you probably aren't fully in touch with all you are doing.

Another type of guilt is relevant here. In psychology and philosophy, it is called *existential guilt*. Existential guilt occurs when you fail to realize your potential or when you conduct yourself in a manner that is unauthentic to your nature. So if out of anger, pride, or fear, you don't do something about a problem relationship of yours, then you are guilty. You are guilty of holding on to anger and fear when you have the potential to let go of those feelings and resolve the pain. It may not be easy to resolve such feelings, but to hold onto them only results in more hurt later on. You and your relationships suffer when parts of your past haunt you and you do nothing to try and stop the process.

Hank was a fire fighter. He suffered overwhelming bouts of anxiety that interfered with his job performance. At home he was irritable and argumentative. Kathleen, his wife, went from being patient and understanding to angry and aloof. When I asked Hank if any major losses or stressful events had been occurring around the time his anxiety attacks began, he could think of nothing important. Then he remembered that his uncle, a man who raised Hank and who he'd been estranged from for ten years, had suffered a near-fatal heart attack.

"I guess it bothered me, but I don't know why. I haven't talked to him much since I left home."

He went on to detail how he and his uncle had become estranged. It became clear that Hank wanted a better relationship with the man but was reluctant to make the first move. Somehow, appearing to be "in the right" was more important than reconciling.

In time, Hank went to his uncle for the purpose of reconciling. One of the things Hank did while talking to him was to apologize. He apologized for not coming to the man sooner to try to settle their problems. The fact that his anger at his uncle had a legitimate basis wasn't the point. That was a separate issue, which Hank did confront his uncle about. But Hank recognized that out of anger and fear, he had stayed away from his uncle for years. It was an all-too-human reaction that Hank owned up to.

"I didn't like admitting it at first," Hank said to me. "I was angry at him, and to apologize for waiting so long to confront him made me feel a little like a kid again. But the truth is I did wait too many years. He did, too, for that matter, and he was sorry as well. I guess we were equal on that score. But I know it was the right thing to say. I know that deep down it has bothered me that I can stay distant for so long while we all just get older and older."

Hank also owed his wife Kathleen an apology. He had treated her poorly during the time his anxiety was at its worst (which actually added to his stress), and had done little to repair the damage there, either.

Often, the anxiety you feel is the anxiety of guilt. It is your awareness (perhaps subconscious) that you are doing something that keeps you distant from those you care about. Look at what you are doing that is keeping you separated, and begin to change those ways of behaving.

OWNING YOUR GUILT

Owning guilt is seeing yourself for all that you are, for all you have done. It is accepting the fact that you did something to violate a close relationship. You violated it out of anger, fear, or ignorance. When you own your guilt, you put the responsibility for changing on your shoulders.

Owning your guilt can be difficult. You may expose yourself to the onslaught of others who seek a scapegoat in order to avoid accepting responsibility for their actions. They may be unwilling to own their guilt, so you become a convenient target as one willing to accept blame.

That is a frustrating situation but one that must be risked in an important relationship. For if you fail to own up to your guilt, then no genuine or lasting reconciliation can occur. You will only see how the other person is guilty, not recognizing how you contributed to the problem.

Another difficulty with owning your guilt is that you don't have any excuses. It isn't quite the same with other emotions that make you feel uneasy. If being frightened or angry is unacceptable to you, for example, then you can justify such feelings with statements like, "Who wouldn't be angry?" or "What happened was enough to make anyone afraid." Such remarks are said to convey the idea that somehow the feelings weren't your own. You try to sidestep the issue of responsibility. But when you admit guilt, you admit responsibility and a willingness to stand alone. Otherwise you would plead innocence.

A third burden in admitting your guilt is that it removes the sting when you condemn others. It is much easier to attack and blame when you are guiltless. But by owning your guilt, you begin to view the other person's guilt in a more compassionate light. You see that everyone is imperfect, blameworthy from time to time, and human. It is in such a light that the seeds of forgiveness take root.

To own your guilt is to accept the truth of who you are. If you fall short of the truth by denying or exaggerating your guilt, then your relationships will suffer. At best they will stagnate.

Access to the truth of who you are isn't easy and is perhaps a lifelong pursuit. It is easier when you establish relationships where defenses are minimized and where trust, openness, and love are allowed to flourish. It is easier when it is acceptable to make mistakes.

Remember, when you are guilty, you are not worthless. Guilt is part of being human. But do not use your humanness as the excuse to do nothing about your faults; otherwise you will begin to feel ashamed. Your humanness requires that you do what you can to overcome those weaknesses so that you can experience all that is indeed human.

THE HINDRANCES OF GUILT FEELINGS

Your guilt feelings are important because they tell you something is wrong. You feel threatened. And, most likely, you have done something that caused someone else to suffer.

Guilt feelings become a hindrance to reconciliation and forgiveness when you try to alleviate them without doing anything to change your hurtful ways. There are three common ways (other than forgiveness) in which you may act in order to try to feel less guilty. Note that these methods do nothing to make you no longer *be* guilty. These methods are:

1. To be kind and extra caring to the person you've hurt so as to somehow atone or "make up" for what you've done
2. To punish yourself
3. To place the blame on somebody else

If you routinely engage in any of these methods without owning your guilt and making a sincere effort to change your ways, you will set yourself up for more pain. "Making up" for what you've done may placate the person you hurt. But if you do nothing to modify the things you do that hurt others, your atonement will eventually be seen for what it is: not genuine. If you try to buy back the person's favor, then there will be little security in the relationship.

If you punish yourself as a way to alleviate your guilt, then you do little that is constructive. Instead, you are adding negativity to an already negative situation.

Some people overly punish themselves and then feel that they've earned credits against a future hurtful act. Then when they eventually hurt another, they try to alleviate their guilt by convincing themselves they already paid the price.

When Brian felt guilty over an argument with Maureen, he'd spend his Saturdays sprucing up the yard or putting up Sheetrock in their fix-up home.

When Maureen felt guilty over hurting Brian's feelings, she'd reduce her food intake and eat bland, soupy food instead of anything substantial (all in the name of saving money, something she knew Brian appreciated). Of course, neither of them really knew what the other was up to, so the sacrificing wasn't acknowledged as it might have been. Brian was *supposed* to clean up the yard and put up Sheetrock. That was his job, according to Maureen. Maureen was *supposed* to be budget-conscious, since the money was her responsibility. But more importantly, neither of them invested any energy in changing the ways about themselves that were hurtful to begin with. Nothing substantial changed.

So the next time they had a fight, each was puffed up with a "look at all I've done for you" attitude, an attitude that made each feel entitled to be hurtful or insensitive, since the other was so unappreciative.

By being self-punishing, you also overlook one essential factor in healing a relationship: empathy. Feeling guilt without feeling empathy is to be concerned only with *your* feelings when you need to be focused on the other person's feelings. When you are stuck in a rut of guilt, you can climb out only by caring about how the other person must be feeling. It was nice that Brian and Maureen were trying to be helpful to one another, but it would have been more empathetic, and therefore more helpful, if they'd been up-front with each other.

"I'm sorry, Maureen. And I cleaned the yard up especially nice today, since I know you enjoy it when the place looks clean. I'll try not to be so insensitive next time."

Blaming others as a way to rid yourself of guilt causes severe difficulties. The other person is forced to defend against your unjust claims while each of you feels resentful. By refusing to acknowledge your responsibility for your actions, you give up power. You close off avenues that could lead to a resolution of problems, because you don't regard yourself as accountable.

Feeling Guilty Holds Others Hostage

Another hindrance to feeling guilty comes when you become so highly focused on that feeling that you are blind to almost anything else. You see others as accusing or poised to accuse. Or you anticipate punishment or abandonment. Simply stated, you overreact to what others say and do and are not free to act realistically.

You then hold others hostage. They cannot be free to be themselves without you overreacting and taking things personally. Your intense guilt has distorted all of your perceptions, giving the relationship little room to breathe, let alone grow.

Feeling Guilty Can Keep You from Being Curious

When your guilt feelings are strong and your fear of punishment overpowering, you won't be able to be curious enough to seek a reasonable solution to your problems. Your guilt can be such a force that you do not wish to discover any more about yourself or the relationship because of what might be revealed.

Without the curiosity necessary to be able to evaluate your situation carefully, the solutions you eventually come up with will be ineffective and narrow-minded. "I hurt him because he hurt me," may be all the reasoning you need to justify your behavior and feel less guilty. "This marriage is a dud, so why shouldn't I have an affair?" may become a reasonable solution when you don't want to see your guilt for all that it is. If you want to overlook or deemphasize your contribution to problems, it is easy to come up with simple solutions that solve nothing.

When you feel very guilty and are frightened by your guilt, you do not want to be open to all of the truths about what happened. But it is precisely an honest look at what happened that is needed, if worthwhile changes are ever to take place. When your guilt makes you fear the truth, then the solutions you come up with eventually become part of the problem.

Feeling Guilty Impedes Your Ability to Accept Love and Forgiveness

When you don't come to proper terms with your guilt, you will have to defend against the anxiety it raises. The defenses you put up to block anxiety also impede your ability to accept love.

If you defend against your guilt by making sacrifices for the person you've hurt, any offer of love to you from that person may only add to your guilt feelings. Having made sacrifices to atone for your guilt, you now feel the need to make even more sacrifices to pay for the love being offered to you. "I don't deserve it," you claim as you become exhausted from all the self-sacrifices you must make.

If you defend against the anxiety of guilt by punishing yourself, you will hold the basic belief that you aren't worthy of any love offered. So you won't accept any.

If you defend against your guilt by blaming others for hurtful acts you've committed, the person you blame probably won't feel loving toward you. He or she will be too busy defending against your false or distorted accusations. And should that person act loving toward you anyway, even though you are blaming unfairly, you won't trust the love. You may regard it as an attempt to manipulate you.

In the same manner, you will be less open to receiving forgiveness if you don't contend with your guilt properly. You may believe yourself to be unworthy of forgiveness. Or you will doubt you've made enough sacrifices to earn forgiveness, adhering to the false belief that forgiveness and love are always given conditionally.

THE ONLY SOLUTION

When you feel guilty about anything, look to see who you are keeping estranged from. Begin to close the gap, and your guilt will take care of itself.

Chapter Nine

Depression and Forgiveness: "I'm Sad—What Do I Do?"

Melissa doesn't seem to know how to think or act anymore. Most of her feelings are blunted. When she does feel something, it is an overwhelming sense of hurt, grief, and helplessness. She is depressed. The feelings are thickened with fear and choke off her ability to know what to do next. "What's wrong with me?" she achingly repeats to herself.

She wants intimacy, she desperately needs her husband, but she can't accept it when he tries to please her, to help her, or to cheer her up. She senses that about herself and feels guilty about that, too. That adds to her depression. She's so afraid that she's lost herself, her abilities, her sense of purpose, that she's frightened of being dependent. It would be a surrender. But she can't function well by herself. She knows that. Her husband is frustrated by his inability to help her. Sometimes he tells her to pull herself together, to stop being so self-centered. Then he feels guilty and tries to make it up to her. She questions his sincerity.

Try as they might, they can't stop hurting each other.

The weakening or snapping of the bond between you and the spouse you are estranged from can result in feelings of depression. Studies indicate that marital difficulties tend to precede depression in women and that recovery from depression is more likely if marital problems are dealt with properly.

If you betrayed your spouse and now believe you will never be forgiven, you may condemn yourself and perhaps even hate yourself. Self-hate brings depression.

Maybe you were betrayed but are afraid of your anger. If allowed to burn, the anger can turn against you and result in depression.

Any loss you experience leads to sadness. If you believe you are helpless to overcome your pain, you can become depressed.

Common features of depression include sleep disturbances, appetite loss or increase, concentration difficulties, chronic fatigue, and loss of enjoyment for most pleasurable activities. Enthusiasm disappears. You withdraw socially. You may have crying spells. You have a pessimistic attitude about yourself and the world. Feelings of inadequacy stir. It is as if a great weight has pressed down on you, squeezing you dry of energy, strength, and hope; constricting your range of emotions; and leaving you with the belief that nothing you do matters anymore.

In severe cases of depression, the biochemistry of the brain is also altered. Certain medications can then help restore a proper chemical balance. While a person on such medications may then feel less depressed, reports of diminished self-esteem and anxieties about being open with one's feelings are still common.

In almost every instance of depression, except perhaps in a normal grief reaction (the loss of a loved one), there is a truth you need to know. The truth is that you are depressed partly because of your belief that you must forever earn other people's love and that somehow you've failed to measure up. You didn't meet the standard. You view your worthwhileness as a spouse, parent, child, sibling, or friend as conditional. You hold to the basic belief that no one could fully accept you for all you are, faults included. You truly believe that others will love you and put up with you only under certain conditions. And those conditions always involve your limiting, hiding, or denying some real part of yourself.

Certainly you may open up some sad feelings during the process of forgiveness. Often that sadness is the letting go of the past. It is a recognition of loss, of having to say good-bye to a part of your life that you've relived every day, even if that past was painful. (Chapter 15 says more about that sense of loss.) But if you are depressed, it is likely that the depression began before you started out on the road to forgiveness.

You are depressed, lonely, and estranged from others—some of whom you want to be closer to, but it is just too risky. And you have lived your life, and handled the relationship now in question, by at times walking on eggshells. You've been an actor putting on a facade. Your style has been one of pretense. And you are afraid.

That is why you did what you did with your anger. Whether you hid it, denied it, or intensified it in a hostile attack on another, you believed that if anyone discovered your truest feelings, that person wouldn't remain long in your life.

That is why you did what you did with your guilt feelings. Rather than accepting yourself as worthwhile in spite of your faults, you punished yourself repeatedly for having them. You saw your guilt as evidence that you are not a worthwhile person and thus became depressed.

Now you feel ashamed and helpless, too. That is because you weakened your power by denying aspects of yourself (such as your anger at people you've felt hurt by), and now you cannot move with strength. You can't be yourself, but you are exhausted from living a masquerade. And the thought of making changes scares you. You fear that if you begin to act with strength and openness, then others will regard you as having been a phony and abandon you. So you remain where you are, focusing inward on your perceived inadequacies, and your depression seems all-encumbering.

All you wanted was to love and be loved by others who are distant now. But the road you took that led to your depression led you further away from all that.

To be forgiving, you need to be honest with yourself and others. You are depressed in part because you have been dishonest. You held back some feelings and convinced yourself that they didn't matter or that they were too dangerous. You distorted your anger and its meaning by holding it back or never fully expressing it. Then you continued being dishonest by telling yourself you had no right to your anger anyway. You also tried to sell yourself the idea that your happiness would be secure if only . . . you could find a better job . . . the children would behave more responsibly . . . your spouse would be more considerate . . . your parents could have been more loving . . . all the while being afraid to believe in the power of yourself to move you out of depression.

To be forgiving, you must be more accepting of yourself and others. You are suffering now because you have not accepted your feelings as legitimate or yourself as worthwhile. And by holding back your truest feelings from others, you are, in effect, questioning their loyalty. You stop short of accepting them fully when you don't give them an honest chance to know you.

Anytime you can't be accepting of the people closest to you, you remove opportunities to give them your love. Any such act of withholding makes you feel worse about yourself. We all need to give ourselves credit for giving our love to others. We all need to recognize that we are capable of showing love. By failing to be accepting of others, you have removed many opportunities to show your love. As a result, you've failed to accept yourself.

To accept forgiveness, you must own any guilt and begin to make productive changes in your ways of relating. You are depressed because, after owning your guilt, you let it consume you. Instead of using your guilt as a springboard for change, you sank deeper into it. You did admit to some guilt but never followed up with a constructive plan for change.

To feel forgiven, you must first feel remorseful for the ways you hurt yourself and others, enough to want to try to change. You are depressed because any remorse you once felt gave way to fear and confusion. The desire to admit your anger and guilt to others was undermined by your fear of being yourself. And now you feel trapped. To reveal yourself is to risk rejection. But to fail to be open about your feelings keeps you depressed and smothered with guilt, emotionally aloof from the people who matter most to you.

THE STIRRING OF CHANGE

Even though you are hurting and feeling helpless and hopeless, you do have choices and there is a way out.

But you must at least recognize the truth of three facts. You may disagree with them or say they are true for some people but not for you, but that is because you have worked hard over the years to convince yourself otherwise. Give up that fight and consider these three truths:

1. In spite of your faults and whatever pain you have brought to yourself and others, you are worthwhile and able to be loved.
2. You can't always try to earn love. In its fullest state, it is given freely to you. Accordingly, you must give love to others who do not always give love to you.
3. You aren't as helpless as you think you are.

Regarding the first point, your faults are evidence of your worthwhileness. It is through them that you know you are indeed loved. If you never expose your weaknesses, then you'll always doubt the genuineness and durability of any love offered to you. It is the love that is there for you, in spite of your faults, that you can trust as being sincere.

But that doesn't mean you should hold on to your weaknesses as a test of another's love for you. Nor does it mean that you must tolerate the abuse of another as a sign of your love for that person. In genuine love, one works to change one's hurtful ways so as not to harm the beloved.

Because you fear that your faults will cause others to reject you, you may try to hide your faults. But don't fool yourself. You can't ever hide completely from others. To be sure, they may not be able to see through to all of your weaknesses, but pretense is eventually recognized. In fact, you are probably still estranged and depressed now, not because of whatever faults you possess but because you have been insincere about them. It is your deceit, defensiveness, and perpetual fears that have hurt others enough for them to want to move away from you.

When you doubt you are worthy of love, you arrange to make it difficult for others to show their love of you. Your holding-back style is irritating to them. They wonder whether you are testing their love for you. Nobody likes to be tested and not accepted at face value.

When you doubt you are worthy of love, you begin to view your anger as either bad or your only weapon. You then can't deal cleanly with others when they hurt you. You are left to act out of fear, shame, or guilt, which can hardly begin to improve matters.

Believe that you are unlovable and unworthwhile, and you will thrive on self-punishment. Your guilt and fears will be unrelenting, and periodic depression will become a way of life.

You are the only person stopping you from recognizing your worth. If people in your life try to convince you that you aren't worthwhile, they do not belong in your life.

The second important truth is that you can't go through life always trying to earn love. Nor can you offer love to others only if they repay you in kind. You have the opportunity to feel genuinely good about yourself when you can give love to someone who may not "deserve" it. Love is at its fullest when it is given freely.

It is common in our society to believe that love must always be earned. Our society is built on the premise that not much is provided for you that you don't earn. But as far as love is concerned, the matter isn't that simple.

You may wonder, "Isn't love earned at least to some extent? Isn't it necessary to treat people in a kind and respectful manner if they are to offer us love?"

Well, yes, especially in the early phases of a relationship love may be kindled when there is kindness
and consideration. But to say that love is *earned* sug-
gests that love can be bought or sold, which is not true
of genuine love. You might be generous, even to the
point of being self-sacrificing in a relationship. You
could be sensitive and understanding. *But that doesn't
necessarily earn you the love of another.* You may be well
liked because of such actions, and you may increase
your opportunities to spend more time with people,
but others' love for you won't always follow.

Through a variety of complicated and incompletely
understood processes, love will be offered to you or
not. And in its most genuine and lasting form, it will
be offered with recognition of your faults. And it is by
your degree of love for the other person that you will
try to improve yourself.

A main difference between you and someone more
loving and enthusiastic about life is this: You act
kindly much of the time in order to earn another's love
or to rid yourself of unwanted guilt. The happy person acts kindly much of the time to demonstrate love.

It is normal to want to show people your love. And
you can't expect to be loved forever if you don't act
lovingly (although you may be loved anyway). But if
you are always trying to prove your love, then you
never feel reassured. The moment a problem arises,
your doubts will surface, and you'll have to double
your efforts to feel loved once again.

Where are the roots of the idea that love must be
earned? In the mind of a young child, love is something that is earned. And it is also something that can
be withdrawn suddenly and permanently.

When a child is naughty and parents react with
disapproval, the child internally experiences a loss of

their love and a corresponding drop in self-esteem. Of course, in most cases, the youngster's misbehavior does not dry up a parent's love. However, the parents may temporarily (and understandably) lose some affection for the child. But the youngster doesn't understand that disapproval is different from loss of love. Believing love to be lost, the child feels a need to somehow earn back the parent's love by undergoing some kind of punishment or by trying to modify his or her behavior according to the parents' wishes. Such is the normal process of development that helps create the child's conscience.

But some adults can get stuck at that emotional level of understanding they first experienced as children. Or they may retreat to it (through a defensive process known as regression) when under great stress or fear. As a result, they view their faults too harshly and question whether they can be loved as long as they possess such shortcomings. They hold back their feelings out of fear of being revealed for who they are.

When they do hurt others, they deal with the situation defensively, instead of constructively. They may deny their anger and guilt. Or they may admit it but then punish themselves harshly, or arrange to be punished by others. Or they make sacrifices in a pathetic attempt to buy back the love that was supposedly lost, never feeling certain they have done enough to earn it back in full. Through it all, their basic feeling of being unlovable is stuck inside them, distorting their perspective and their relationships.

If you believe that love must always be earned, then you turn it into something it is not: a payment, a price paid for some service. Consequently, you limit the amount of love you can give and receive, because you're always conscious of the payback.

Give yourself permission to not always feel loving

toward the people you do love. When the person you love hurts you, then your anger will temporarily overpower any feelings of love. But that doesn't mean you are unloving.

Abandon the belief that love must always be earned, and you will be able to give freely to others. You will especially be able to give the gift of forgiveness. And you won't be giving so the other will regard you as a worthy person, you won't be giving to make the other beholden to you in some unspoken way. You will give because you trust and love and are no longer depleted as you were when you gave love with conditions attached.

Finally, you aren't as helpless as you think you are. You may not be able to control the *outcome* of an effort to improve your marriage, but you can control your ways of trying to improve it. You have control over you. The game isn't over just yet.

STEPPING OUT FROM DEPRESSION

Once you are open to the truths that you are worthwhile and able to be loved; once you conduct your life with the understanding that love is ultimately given to you, not forever earned by you; and once you realize you are not totally helpless, you can do something constructive about your depression.

First, you need to own up to your faults and weaknesses. Don't wallow in guilt or self-pity. Forgive yourself for possessing them. Then forgive yourself for doing little to change them until now.

Second, identify some basic assumptions about yourself, others, and life in general, that are probably unrealistic and that keep you feeling depressed. Then tell yourself repeatedly that they are false and not something to live in accordance with. Most depressed people conduct their lives as if the following assumptions are true and indelible:

- To be happy, I must be accepted by others virtually all the time.
- If people disagree with me, it means I am stupid and they won't like me.
- Since I'm willing to make sacrifices for others but they don't make them for me, I'm not worthwhile.
- If I make a mistake or look foolish, I'll never be successful, and people will not want me around.
- I have no real needs. It is my job to put other people's needs ahead of what I might want.

Third, go to the people you are estranged from and have a heart-to-heart talk with them. Let them know how you've felt hurt by them, and admit to how you have been hurtful. Hear them out if they have anything to say to you. Then forgive them and ask for their forgiveness.

Fourth, set out on a new path in life whereby you reduce the amount of time that passes from when you first feel hurt (or joyful or grateful) and when you express those feelings to the others involved.

Being open about your feelings is crucial if you are to alleviate a serious depression. But such openness without a willingness to nurture a forgiving attitude is cumbersome at best. And it could very well be destructive.

Finally, give of yourself. This is the most difficult but important thing you need to do when you are depressed. I know you are already exhausted and depleted. I know you've been hurt and treated unfairly. You didn't deserve that treatment. I know you may have felt that others "owe you," but you've also sensed that sometimes that belief has caused you to justify hurting others. You must give of yourself and demonstrate that you are a good person (since you really doubt that you are). You feel depleted mostly because you haven't been as giving toward others and gained the self-acceptance that comes from giving. Don't give by making tremendous sacrifices. You're too tired. Besides, you don't want your giving to be an act of punishment but an act of love and caring. How do you give? By extending caring.

Anytime you respect and consider another person's feelings, you are caring. Anytime you give comfort (not necessarily solutions) to someone who is troubled, you are caring. Anytime you can express your feelings honestly and respectfully, you are caring. You are also being intimate, perhaps as intimate as one could really ever be. Anytime you give the kids their breakfast and let your spouse sleep in late, you are caring. Anytime you wipe your child's nose, you are caring. Anytime you smile at yourself and pat yourself on the back for doing any of these things, you are caring for yourself. Anytime you *attempt* to find forgiveness, *whether or not you succeed just yet*, you are caring.

Get the idea? These are not insignificant tasks. If you do them out of love for the other (with minimal or no resentment), and if you give yourself credit for doing them (you won't give yourself the credit you deserve if you do them with resentment), the effects will be powerful.

The more forgiving you can be of others, the less you will need to hold on to your anger. Therefore, depression will rarely come about.

The more forgiving you can be of yourself, the less you will need to hold on to your guilt, thereby blocking depression.

It can be arduous to lift yourself out of depression, but you must begin. It is a lonely task. Even with support, you know only too well that no one else feels exactly the way you do.

Often the people who care about you don't know how to act around you if your depression lingers. They feel helpless, perhaps angry at your fragility, and then guilty about their anger. They treat you with kid gloves sometimes, and other times with heavy hands. They can't be themselves.

Foster a forgiving attitude toward the people you want to be closer with but who don't always know how to act around you. When that attitude surfaces, your depression will ease. People can start being themselves because forgiveness doesn't overlook or sidestep their faults but faces them squarely. And it reveals everyone's strengths and integrity.

GIFTS OF THE MAGI

A woman dreams of her son. He is seven, smiling, handsome, and smart like his . . .

She stops. The father doesn't deserve the credit for her son's intelligence. He didn't care about him as much as she did anyway. She tries to dream again but . . . it fades, she . . . can't.

For a few seconds, her dream had been real. Until she remembered it was a dream. That made the act of trying to dream again too painful, for it only pointed out the cruelest reality she ever survived. Her son Timmy was dead. He had always tried to please his father. The man's approval and affection meant everything to the boy. Allison never understood why, given her husband's tendency to be harsh and unapprecia- tive. So one day when his father was busy cleaning a paintbrush, Timmy climbed the extension ladder to touch up a spot on the house his dad had missed.

When he fell, he landed on the cement stairs and never regained consciousness.

Allison looked blankly over at her husband, Gary. His jaw was tight, his eyes . . . were they moist? He couldn't return her gaze.

"You each hurt so much. It's hard to believe that Timmy died almost twelve years ago," I said tenderly.

Allison nodded. But they had come to talk about her most recent depression. Her father had died six months ago, and it seemed to reopen old wounds. They had also come to talk about their marriage; they just hadn't told me that yet. Gary didn't say much as Allison spoke about her father. At one point, she became insistent.

"He was a saint," she said, as if I had challenged her to think otherwise.

I knew she was grieving. And I knew she was idealizing her father. When that happens, as it so often does in the process of mourning, it usually means that the surviving person is feeling some guilt. When we love someone, our humanness does not allow for perfect love. We have ambivalence. That means that sometimes we can hate, or be unloving, toward the persons we love. Allison was not yet accepting of her ambivalence. Raising her father to sainthood was one way of making reparation for the guilt she felt over her anger.

It was later when they spoke of each other.

"It's hard for me to love Gary," Allison said. "And he knows why."

Gary looked both angry and ashamed. "She's always believed that I wasn't a good enough father to Timmy," he said quietly, his lips quivering. "And in a way I know she's right. For some reason, I always was impatient with him, intolerant of his mistakes. I wasn't all bad, I want you to know. I did love him."

His eyes were pleading, but hesitating. He wanted forgiveness but didn't believe he deserved it. Neither did she.

Their pain was excruciating. He had suffered guilt for twelve years, believing himself to be inadequate, even loathsome, and deserving of whatever punishment he got. She was enraged, lonely, and grieving, but unable to ask for comfort and support from the husband she needed.

Their stories went on and on. Like his son, Gary sometimes had been unfairly treated by his own father. Estranged from the man, he had learned of his father's death the morning of his funeral. Only by then it had been too late for him to attend.

Allison's mother had had a drinking problem early on. Her father had been protective, in a passive kind of way. He always seemed to idealize his wife, while at the same time he tried to give the children some of the pleasures he knew they were missing. Allison's anger at her mother, and at her father's occasional passivity, had been what gave her the strength to care for her younger brother, keep the house clean, and get straight A's in school.

It was many sessions later. They'd been trying so hard to unravel the hidden threads that had kept them together, and in pain, for so long. I wanted them to finally hear something about themselves I prayed they could now understand. I began with Allison.

"You and Gary have stayed together for twenty-one years. The one thing you've needed to survive, Allison, to get through the pains of your youth, of Timmy's death, of your marriage, and your dad's death, has been anger. Without your anger you'd have . . .

"Crumbled. Fallen apart," she interrupted.

"Yes," I continued. "But couples don't stay together without some good reasons. Needs have to get met.

Even though your marriage hasn't gone the way you say you've wanted it to go, Gary has given you the very thing you believe you've needed the most. He's helped you to stay angry. He's protected you from the more painful feelings of loss."

I let my words sink in before continuing.

"If he'd been more loving toward Timmy, if he hadn't been guilty of treating Timmy and you unfairly, you might have ultimately lost touch with your anger and 'fallen apart.' I can't help but think, Allison, that on some level of awareness, Gary knew what it was you desperately needed from this marriage, and he gave it to you."

They each stirred, their faces puzzled (possibly hopeful?), certainly troubled.

"And, Gary," I said, turning to him, "I believe that, at that same level of awareness, Allison has given you what you believed you've needed the most. Punishment. As a child, you doubted you were a good enough son. Missing your father's funeral, being estranged from the man so many years, only made those doubts more certain. By punishing yourself, you're hoping to atone for that. You're also hoping to atone for how you treated Timmy before he died. If you weren't being punished, if you weren't almost an outcast in your own marriage, your guilt would be unrelenting. Allison has spared you that pain."

She trembled at the truth of it. He nodded, disturbed, looking toward his wife for some sign.

Tears formed in her eyes that had been too angry to hold them, until now.

For them, years of pain were beginning to life. Each could see how the other had been both very needy and yet very giving. They felt a deeper sense of caring. And of sadness. For the very things they felt they needed (anger for Allison, punishment for Gary) came at a cost. Those things kept them from fully mourning their past losses and from finding forgiveness.

By finally forgiving himself, Gary had no need for punishment. His guilt, ravenous until now, was sated. By forgiving Gary (and her parents), Allison had no need for her anger and could get on with grieving the losses in her life. This time, they could grieve together.

You are undertaking a journey that you hope will lead to a reconciliation with the person who matters to you. At least you want to resolve your own personal pain and revitalize your life. You are on a road where you will know the meaning of forgiveness. It is a journey that will expose your fears, your anger, your guilt, your depression, and your love and all of your strengths.

Accept your feelings and yourself. Believe in your worthwhileness. Demonstrate your love, and you will never be lost.

Chapter Ten

Before You Forgive: What You Need to Know About Your Marriage

You need a relationship in order to exist. You need someone you can give to, provide for; someone whom you can rely on, take from. Without relationships, our purpose and meaning in life loses its shape, color, and fragrance. Without relationships, we have no place to go that is of any importance.

Homes can be lonely places without relationships.

But relationships can hurt. Not only do we hurt when those we care about treat us unkindly or inconsiderately, but we hurt when we lose them to death.

And there are deeper hurts. Wounds suffered by estrangement can be the most enduring and the most damaging. For an estrangement in one relationship, even if you tell yourself that the relationship doesn't matter to you anymore, almost always spreads to other relationships that do matter. Estrangement can be insidious.

Forgiveness heals the wounds suffered when you

are estranged. And healing in one relationship almost always spreads to others.

EIGHT ESSENTIAL INSIGHTS INTO YOURSELF AND YOUR MARRIAGE

The goal of the first part of this book has been to prepare you for the five phases of forgiveness. As a final preparation, consider well the eight points discussed in this chapter. Come back to these eight points anytime you are feeling stuck in your efforts to find forgiveness in your marriage.

1. Husbands and wives each have needs for closeness *and* separateness. Problems erupt when one person's need for closeness threatens the other person's need for separateness.

For many couples, resolving this problem seems impossible. For her to have the distance she desires, he must give up the intimacy he wants. Someone always is a loser, or so it feels. The pattern is predictable. The emotional pursuer (the one who is mostly aware of a strong need for intimacy) chases after the emotional distancer (the one who is mostly aware of a strong need for separateness). Each can comfortably tolerate only so much distance from the other—with the pursuer able to tolerate less.

Eventually, the pursuer gives up in anger and exhaustion. The distancer holds steady a bit, maybe comes in for a closer look to see what's happening, and there is a stand-off. Temporarily. Then the pursuer will chase once more, this time giving up much sooner. If the pursuer is too angry now, he or she will back away, maybe far away. If the gap between the two becomes too great for the distancer to tolerate

(remember, even the distancer wants some closeness),
he or she will close the gap by pursuing. A role rever-
sal.

This pattern could repeat itself often, or the couple
could reach a point of distance from each other that
neither one is comfortable with. They'll stay there,
occasionally warring with verbal gunfire, but resolving nothing. Each one believes the other's need for so
much intimacy or so much isolation indicates a serious
psychological problem.

What the couple doesn't admit is that the conflict
should really be taking place within each of them, not
between them. They each fear the same thing—complete loss of self—but they don't know that. The
pursuer feels a strong need to connect with someone
so as to complete him- or herself. The distancer feels a
need to avoid intimacy to protect him or herself from
being swallowed up, annihilated in another's quest for
emotional fusion.

The solution scares them because they say they
really don't trust each other enough to try. But if the
pursuer would agree to slow down, and *out of love for
the other* provide that person with some needed space;
and if the distancer would agree to reverse direction,
and *out of love for the other* provide that person with
some needed intimacy, the conflict between them
would subside. If they give to the partner what the
partner needs, they won't feel so controlled as they do
when the partner tries to *take* what they want. Over
time, they develop faith in each other. Then they
aren't threatened by the other's occasional needs for
intimacy or isolation.

Once partners act this way, though, the conflict
moves from *between* them to *within* each of them. Each
must struggle with the conflicting human needs to be
both intimate *and* separate. If that gets too uncomfort-

able, they may resume the pursuer-distancer relationship.

2. Partners are at the same level of emotional/psychological maturity when they marry. It is possible to outgrow a partner, but when that happens, the marriage won't survive unless the other partner grows, too.

It may not appear to be true at first glance. We all know many couples who've been together for a long time and yet seem so unhappy or mismatched. So why do they stay together? It is tempting to think that economics provides the answer: "I would have left him long ago but I couldn't afford it." To be fair, economics is a factor in many people's decisions to remain in an unhappy marriage. But it isn't always the primary reason. People select, and keep, their mates for many reasons, conscious and unconscious. And the mate that one chooses tends to be remarkably similar to oneself in terms of emotional development and maturity.

One of the first couples I worked with brought that point home to me in a forceful way. He was domineering, in charge of practically everything at home. She took care of the children, and that was all. She couldn't even drive because she had never learned how. He told her she didn't have the intelligence to drive. She believed him.

They came to me because he was exasperated.

"I can't keep doing everything for her anymore. I work full time plus I'm in charge at home. It's unfair! What the hell am I, Superman?!"

She slumped in her chair, despondent that he was suffering, telling me that he was so right.

At first, in my naïveté, I believed them. Then there were little things, subtle things, that didn't fit. As much as he claimed he wanted her to do more, he undermined her every effort with criticism and discouragement. As much as she claimed she was helpless and incompetent, she was a dedicated mother who helped her two learning disabled daughters every day with their writing skills. She did volunteer work at a nearby nursing home. And she had an uncanny ability to gauge just how competent her husband needed to feel on any given day.

Was he so domineering because she was so submissive? Was he so competent because she was incompetent? Sometimes it really seemed that the reverse was true: that without her, he'd be nothing.

In truth, as fearful as she was of being too competent or too responsible, he was just as fearful of being regarded as less competent and responsible. They needed each other. So they traded off to each other the aspects of themselves they were most uncomfortable with. She traded some of her competent parts for some of his helpless parts. Then they both could avoid viewing themselves as they really were.

That such an unconscious exchange took place was revealed months later. He had left her for another woman. She went back to school. She learned to drive. She found a part-time job. He came back to her after his mistress kicked him out. But she was changed. Within six weeks he took a leave of absence from his job due to "pressure." He became severely depressed. He couldn't care for himself and eventually had to be hospitalized.

People marry people who are at the same level of emotional development. If partners exchange aspects of themselves to keep from facing who they are, they may struggle when it comes to being genuinely forgiving. To forgive is to *let go* of what is hurting. But if you are hiding from yourself, you may wish to hold on to some hurts to protect you from the truth of who you are.

3. All symptoms postpone development.

Sometimes it is frightening to grow, to move on. It can be scary to see yourself more clearly, in the light that comes from greater maturity. When those fears become too intense, symptoms may develop. The symptoms can be physical, emotional, or both. You may show them, your spouse may show them, or your children or parents may show them.

All symptoms postpone development.

In some families, if the children weren't so symptomatic, then Mom and Dad would have had time to grapple with their marital problems sooner. They would have solved the problems and become happier, or not solved them and become divorced.

In some families, if a parent weren't so sick and helpless, then the youngest child would finally get to leave home and start a life of his own.

In some marriages, if the wife weren't alcoholic and irresponsible, then the husband would have no way of proving to his estranged father that some men really can care for their children, even under adversity.

In some marriages, if each partner weren't so insensitive and critical toward the other, they wouldn't have the excuse to avoid dealing with different, more relevant issues, such as how they feel about themselves, how uncaring they've been toward one another, and how they feel about their parents.

The longer that symptoms persist, the more likely that one person in a family won't proceed well with new phases of life (going to high school, dating, going to college, leaving home, getting married, staying married). The longer that symptoms persist, the more likely that at least one person in the family isn't coming to terms with some truths about him- or herself.

4. The more issues and relationships that remain unsettled for you before you are married, the more likely your marriage will suffer.
This is especially true if there are emotional cutoffs in the family you grew up with. When some people in a family are so estranged that they want nothing to do with one other, members begin to view others in black-and-white terms. People are either for you or against you, friends or enemies. That attitude wreaks havoc in a marriage.

People who've cut themselves off emotionally from a family member often expect much more closeness and loyalty from their spouse. The more intense the cutoff, the less flexibility they'll have when their partner eventually is hurtful, inconsiderate, or, worst of all, disloyal.

Of course, there is an opposite problem. Some people come from families that are too close. In such families, people assume that they always know what's best for others and that they can always tell what others are thinking before words are spoken. People think more in terms of "we" than "I." There is much giving, but it is with a cost. The price paid for others' loyalty to you is your agreement never to be disloyal to the family. In families that are too close, being an independent thinker can be an act of disloyalty. Living out of town, or out of state, can be a disloyal act. So can putting your spouse's needs ahead of the needs of your family of origin.

Some people decide that their families of origin come first, and that their spouses must always come second. Probably that will lead to difficulties.

Some people in overly close families marry people from emotionally cutoff families. At first, the spouse with the cutoff family is attracted to a partner with a loving family. But, depending upon how much the partners have come to terms with their families of origin, the cutoff spouse may resent what he sees as his wife's overinvolvement with her family. He may tell her to make a choice: "Them or me."

If you cannot forgive the people you are emotionally cut off from, you will (unfairly) expect too much from your spouse and eventually feel hurt by that spouse. And you will struggle at forgiving all over again.

5. When you try to change chronic problems, they will get worse (initially).

Expect it. Chronic problems initially get worse because the longer a problem remains unsolved, the more likely it is serving an adaptive function for someone. Or others have adjusted to your problem, and to have to readjust is too cumbersome. Even when husbands, wives, and family members "can't wait" for the problems to go away, they often undermine efforts at improving matters because they are afraid of disturbing the status quo. So you must hang in there and expect problems to worsen (and not take it personally when they do) before lasting improvements come about.

A woman was afraid to drive for twenty years. Her dedicated husband took her everywhere. Finally, in psychotherapy, her symptoms improved. She started to drive more every day.

Then her husband said, "*Are you sure* you want to drive today? It is raining out, you know." She hesitated, grew more anxious, and decided he was right. The next day she was afraid even to sit in the car, let alone drive it. The phobia has roared back.

Eventually, the husband was able to face some fears

of his own. "I guess I'm afraid you won't need me anymore," he told her when her fear of driving was practically gone. Who was protecting whom in that marriage?

When symptoms serve a purpose, they won't go away quickly. And when you try to get rid of them, they usually worsen at first.

6. All behaviors are attempts at solutions.

When you think about it, everything one does is really an attempt to solve, or settle, some issue or problem. Eating dinner may solve the problem of feeling hungry or the problem of boredom.

Watching television may solve tension by helping you to relax. Rolling over to the far side of the bed solves the problem of a leg cramp, or is a way of telling your wife you're angry at her. Being depressed may solve your problem of feeling depleted by lowering your energy level. It may also "solve" your problem of how to tell people they've hurt you without actually telling them.

The value of thinking along these lines is that it can help you put a positive light on some negative behaviors. If you have trouble forgiving someone, asking yourself what that person was trying to solve by hurting you may help you understand that person better. Ninety-nine percent of the time, the person who hurt you wasn't doing it simply to be malicious. Yes, he or she might have been angry or wanting revenge, but there was probably a lot more to it. That person was trying to address and solve some problem. You might do well to ask that person what the problem was.

7. If the qualities that first attracted you to your spouse are now the very same qualities you object to,

you have some ambivalence within yourself that you haven't yet resolved.

You first saw, and loved, her sentimentality, her willingness to care about so many things. Now you are disgusted with her lack of logic, her heightened emotionality.

You first saw, and loved, his strong sense of purpose and his ambition. Now you are angry that he is distant, seemingly more involved in his own interests than with you.

You feel that your spouse has let you down. He isn't the man you married five years ago. Something has shifted. But what? If you look closely, you'll discover that the qualities you married your spouse for were qualities you needed in order to complete or validate yourself. But in such an arrangement, you left yourself vulnerable. You believed that you no longer needed to complete yourself since you had him. (But no one else can do it for you.) You remained less in charge of your life while your spouse took responsibility for some of your happiness and satisfaction. Now you need him more than is healthy for a relationship. You recognize that, and you resent him for it. You always run the risk of resenting those people who expose your weaknesses.

Probably, he feels you let him down, too. As much as you needed him to complete yourself, he needed you to complete himself. You each used the other. It is common to do that, and it isn't fatal. But now each of you has grown dissatisfied as you discovered that your spouse hasn't lived up to the image you married.

If you really require someone else to make you feel complete, what will you do when that person hurts you or leaves you?

Maybe you loved her sentimentality because you could never allow yourself to be that way. But how can you continue to love in her (especially over many years of married life) those qualities you can't accept in yourself?

Face yourself. Accept that you have fears and desires that make you very uncomfortable. Everyone has them. When you can accept yourself as a whole, complete person, you won't have to deny your faults and fears. It is when you deny aspects of yourself for the purpose of avoiding rejection that you feel incomplete and seek others to complete you. But the very qualities of yourself that you denied you will eventually discover in your mate. Then what will you do?

8. Don't try to change your spouse. Change only yourself.

This is crucial. Spouses who try to change one another almost always meet resistance. Typically, the "problems" become more imbedded. And if you should "succeed" in changing your spouse, you'll really never give that person credit for his or her part in it. So you won't completely trust your spouse because you'll think he or she changed only because of your manipulations instead of his or her own desire. Your spouse will start to feel controlled and resentful. You'll feel hurt and frustrated.

When you say that your spouse has to change in order for you to feel happy, you've given up power over your life. You must change yourself. You must focus on your areas of emotional inflexibility. Specifically, you must change the ways you react to your spouse's objectionable behaviors.

That doesn't mean you must "give in" or tolerate behaviors that you know are hurtful. A good way to begin is to determine whether you and your spouse are polar opposites when it comes to the behaviors in question. Is he lazy about housework while you are scrupulously clean? Is she boring while you are the life of the party? Is he too strict with the children while you are too lenient? If so, then each of you is probably reinforcing in your partner the very behaviors you object to. If your husband is irresponsible about finances, he'll never have to change his ways as long as you protect him from natural consequences by being obsessively frugal.

The more lenient you are, the more strict he'll become. The more emotional you are, the more logical she'll become. If you are overcompensating for your spouse's "faults," chances are your spouse is doing the same thing with regard to you.

So you must constructively modify your behavior. Don't make up for what your spouse isn't doing. Do what you believe to be necessary and right for you, regardless of how your spouse feels. Chances are good your spouse will change in a direction you desire. But not necessarily. And if you change your behavior *for the sole purpose of trying to change your spouse*, it won't work. You'll get too frustrated. You'll think it's unfair because you're doing all the labor of changing. You'll give up too soon. That is why you must change yourself in a positive, constructive way, a way that eventually feels good for you (you won't be happy about making changes at first), or else the changes will be too difficult to maintain.

A next step is to analyze other areas of your life, such as family relationships, job satisfaction, leisure, friendships, finances, and your physical and spiritual health. Which of those areas could use improving? You may be so reactive to your spouse partly because other areas of your life are not a source of esteem and satisfaction for you. As such, you may be expecting too much from your mate, wanting him or her to fill in the gaps that those other areas have left open.

When you neglect other areas of your life, you set yourself up to be hurt more deeply by your spouse. Forgiveness will be more of a struggle then because your spouse is having to pay for more than just the hurts against you.

It's time now, you know. The estrangements, the pain, the resentment and the guilt—all of them have remained too long. It's time to find forgiveness and begin again.

After you have read this far in the book, your perspective should already have changed. Now you may no longer see the problems as unresolvable or the hurts as unforgivable.

But you can still have doubts; you can still be mistrustful. The problems haven't been settled yet. You can still be bitter at the unfairness of it all. Probably it was unfair, no matter what your role in the estrangement was.

But you can also let go. Let go of the injustice, of the anger, of the guilt. Let go of the estrangement. You've been looking for forgiveness, and you can find it. It is in a place you've overlooked until now. It is within that part of you that knows how to care and love, and that knows you deserve more love in your life than you've allowed so far.

PART TWO
THE PHASES OF FORGIVENESS

Chapter Eleven

Phase One: Identifying the Hurt and Feeling Remorse

Tom's wife warned me about him. Since her lawyer sent him the papers that proved her divorce threats were real, he'd been angry and agitated. "He doesn't trust psychologists either," she alerted me.

I was prepared. But not for who I saw. The bright executive with the fast-rising career mustered most of his strength just to shake my hand. He looked ragged. I imagined his dark eyes had once been penetrating, even hypnotic. Now they were shallow, pleading eyes, made sickly by the heavy circles under them. All of his movements seemed in slow motion. He couldn't even blink his eyes without appearing to wince in pain.

"I want to save my marriage," he blurted with a desperation that broke through his coat of depression. "I'll do anything I have to. Just tell me what to do."

I had just met him, and he was begging me. I wanted him to get more comfortable. (Or was I the uncomfortable one?) "You look so tired, Tom," I said, my words hardly able to express all of my feelings.

"It's been a long forty-eight hours. Too little sleep and a little too much Scotch. I know I look like hell."

He went on to tell a story his wife had told me many times. I was surprised that their versions matched so well. For two years, he'd refused to believe the signs that his marriage was in serious trouble. When his wife went from exasperation to indifference with him, he chose to be "patient and considerate." When he suspected her of having an affair, he quietly "forgave" her and hoped that in time she'd regain her senses. Now she'd left him, and her lawyer had sent him legal forms that made it impossible for him to pretend. His fears mounted; he'd do *anything* now if he thought it would save his marriage.

If you don't acknowledge when you are in a painful marriage, the relationship may not survive. If it does, it won't be rewarding. If your relationships are to last, you must risk losing them by at first being open to your feelings and then (as discussed in the next chapter), sharing them.

You are estranged from someone, and now you want to be reconciled. You want the relationship restored but with greater trust, openness, and love. At least you want to be able to forgive and let go of your resentment, or to be forgiven so you can let go of your guilt.

Your task at this first phase of healing your relationship is to admit *to yourself* all that was hurtful. While it is possible to forgive or feel forgiven without proceeding through all five forgiveness phases, this first phase is a must. If you cannot admit and identify your feelings, forgiveness may be regarded as a meaningless exercise.

If someone betrayed you, you must acknowledge

the full extent of your sadness and anger. You need to assess what you lost. Was it love? Power? Esteem? Pride? Control? Is what you lost going to be important to you a year or five years from now? Or, when you think about it, does your loss make little difference? Did the person who hurt you do so callously? Or, if you understood that person better, might you look at matters differently?

If you were hurtful, then you must acknowledge your guilt. And you must look at your anger that led to your guilt, and whatever hurt or loss is behind your anger.

Most importantly, you must nurture any feelings of remorse for having been hurtful. Your remorse is evidence that you care about the other person's feelings.

If you never acknowledge your anger at having been hurt, you can't forgive fully. You won't be able to confront the person who hurt you about your anger if you don't even admit it to yourself. The relationship may survive, but you will never feel content. You will always harbor some anxiety, an apprehension that you could be hurt in the same way again, and an aching dissatisfaction with everyday events.

If you never acknowledge your guilt, then you run the risk that the person you hurt will want little more to do with you. And who could blame him or her? That person may be able to forgive you, but if you don't admit your guilt, the relationship will never be more than it is already.

Once you acknowledge your guilt, you must nurture your remorse if there is to be firm ground for the relationship to build upon.

Acknowledging your feelings of anger and guilt may seem to be fairly easy. But this phase can be a trouble spot.

DISTORTING THE TRUTH

Trouble occurs at Phase One when you are frightened of some of your feelings and of the potential consequences of admitting them to yourself. When that happens, your psychological defenses, discussed in Chapter 5, go into operation to protect you from your feelings. While your defenses operate at an unconscious level, there are still many ways in which you can distort your feelings at a level that is close to consciousness.

For example, if you are a bit frightened of your anger, you may pretend instead that you are just a little annoyed. Or you may convince yourself that the hurt against you was no big deal, when in fact it was. If you are afraid of admitting your guilt, you may try to assure yourself that someone else made you act that way or that you didn't intend to let things get so out of hand.

If you want to reconcile with the person you are estranged from and find forgiveness, you must get a clearer sense of your truest feelings. Not only do you need the information about your feelings, it is essential that you develop a willingness to focus on yourself, to examine what your role in the estrangement has been, if you are to accurately and fairly appraise the relationship in question. *People who can't settle their problems with others are people who rarely self-focus and instead project blame onto others.* By honestly self-focusing, without losing sight of the other person's role in the problems, you broaden your perspective. That will only improve your chances of finding forgiveness.

Of course, you may be better able to identify your feelings only *after* you have proceeded through some of the other phases of forgiveness. Each phase has something to offer that can help you to learn more about yourself. But begin being honest with yourself now. It gets easier.

Distorting Sadness

Sadness comes about almost immediately after you have been deeply hurt. You may also feel sad when you recognize that you, too, have been hurtful.

Sadness reflects your awareness of loss. Due to the betrayal, something was lost in the relationship. Maybe what was lost was the faith in your partner (or in yourself) to be perfect. Perhaps it was the innocence of the relationship and the magic of a promising future. Maybe you feel you have lost love or hope. Maybe you lost esteem as you recognized that you were taken advantage of, tricked, or lied to. All of those feelings can be hard to face, so you may distort any sadness you feel to protect you from your sense of loss.

Sometimes, what people really lose when they have been deeply hurt is the childhood fantasy that life is always wonderful and that love can prevent all hurt. Colleen's fantasy was that people who loved her possessed no faults.

"I always told people that I don't believe in knights in shining armor. In fact, it annoyed me when I overheard other women talk glowingly about finding the perfect man, the perfect lover. They were so naive. But I must have had my head in the clouds too, because since Joe had an affair, I've been devastated. I feel as if I've lost everything. I must have been giving lip service to the idea that no man is perfect, because I really believed that Joe would never hurt me. I thought he was as close to perfect as you could get."

Her eyes began to fill, and she turned from me, vainly fighting her sense of loss. A moment later, she could hold back no more and began to weep. She wept heavily and from deep within, sending her mind tumbling back through time and old memories. When her tears seemed spent, she calmed herself and spoke of a different loss.

"I was thinking of my father. He was a good man. Do you know that I've revered him all these years? Talk about perfect; I've held him up as the perfect father." She smiled away, as if looking at him, until she became more serious. "He died when I was fifteen. Nobody really knows how much I miss him."

"You lost your father too soon," I offered.

"And now I've lost my husband as well. My perfect husband," she said, shaking her head.

"Do you know what your father's faults were?" I asked.

"You mean other than dying too soon?" she said, sadly. "No. I can't think of what his faults might have been. But you're suggesting that he did have them, right? That is what you're getting at, isn't it?" She paused to think. "No. If I ever did know them, I don't anymore."

"I know your husband, Joe, has hurt you a great deal," I said. "Still, it must be more difficult to cope with your husband's faults when you regard your father as faultless."

"You don't think I'm being fair to Joe?" she accused.

"I don't know, Colleen. Actually, I'm wondering if you are being fair to yourself. I'm hoping you will sort out your feelings about Joe and your dad so you can see where things stand."

In fact, Colleen hadn't lost her husband. Not yet. But she associated the early loss of a "perfect" father with her husband's infidelity. Her grief over her father's death had been cushioned by putting her father on a pedestal, keeping him alive as the ideal man. But that made it more difficult when she had to deal with her husband's faults.

As therapy continued, Colleen was able to view her husband and father in different lights, as men with shortcomings. Certainly, the matter of Joe's affair had to be addressed squarely, but she was able to do that without being weakened by the memory of a more distant loss. Colleen even spoke with her mother to try to gain a more realistic picture of the man her father was.

"Talking with your mother can be very helpful, Colleen," I said. "Assuming your mother doesn't have him on a pedestal, too. No one is perfect. I want you to remember that. Your dad seemed like a wonderful person. If he really was that good and happy, then he was someone who knew his feelings and wasn't frightened of admitting them. He was able to accept himself as a man with limitations and weaknesses, and that self-acceptance enabled him to care for you. If you hold back on being aware of your feelings, you can't own them. You then question who you really are and hold back some from others."

I felt as if I were making a speech, talking a bit too long. But Colleen heard my words. I sensed that she would understand them more in time.

When Colleen was able to feel the sadness from her husband's infidelity, she felt sad at the loss of her father, too. He was dead, and she finally accepted that. Her sense of loss was freeing, however. She could now cope with what was happening in her marriage by not holding her husband to any unrealistic standard of perfection.

Distorting Anger

Sadness and loss are only the beginning of feelings

that are stimulated when there has been a deep hurt. Anger is felt as well.

Why might you be frightened of admitting to your-self that you are angry, really angry, when someone you love and trust betrays you? And if you were hurtful and now feel guilty or ashamed, why might you ignore the anger that lies behind your feelings of guilt? (After all, if you weren't angry in the first place, you probably wouldn't have been hurtful.)

The bottom line is that you are worried about oth-ers seeing you as you really are. Maybe as a child you felt embarrassed to express your feelings. Maybe you expected others to understand you without you hav-ing to let them in on your emotions. Now you don't want to rock the boat by behaving differently. You are afraid people will reject you or dislike you when you reveal yourself to them. You feel it is not only unsafe to feel angry, but condemnable, too. So you distort your anger, failing to acknowledge it even to yourself.

Maybe you are the kind of person who depends far too much on others. If so, you won't want to upset matters by stirring up angry feelings, even if they are justified. As a dependent person, you are afraid of failing. Your esteem is fragile, so to protect it, you avoid taking risks that might enhance your esteem if you were successful. You deposit too much power over your life in other people's hands so they can take the responsibility for what happens to you. Now when you are angry at them, you can't acknowledge it. That could lead to a disruption in your life that you don't want to risk.

Pauline is the kind of person who depends too much on others. She lets her husband make major decisions because she doesn't want to take responsibility if things go wrong. She'll complain to her mother about her husband and to her father about her mother. She says she doesn't enjoy working, so she hasn't looked for a job in years. Actually, she's frightened of failing on a job, but she thinks no one else knows that. She's afraid to take risks but ironically is taking the biggest risk of her life. By depending too much on others, she has awarded them power over her life. Now, when she feels angry at them, she can't risk being up-front about her feelings. People might leave her if she does. But then again, is it them she is angry at, or is it herself? By distorting her feelings, she has made everything confusing.

Intense neediness can block anyone's awareness of anger. Young children, who are very needy, may eventually deny their anger if family rules forbid such feelings. Adolescents in love for the first time may downplay the faults of their romantic partner (and, therefore, their anger at those faults) because the need to feel in love, and accepted, is so strong.

Some people are frightened of their anger because they feel they will lose control of it once they admit to it. People who episodically get out of control with their anger are usually people who have kept it in check too often. They don't try to resolve problems because they don't want to start a dialogue that may spark their anger. So they gloss over hurts and keep their feelings inside until they can't hold back anymore. They then lose faith in themselves as others become angry at them. Not wanting to make matters worse, they hold feelings back further, and the cycle continues.

Distorting Guilt and Shame

If you are guilty of causing deep hurts, why might you be frightened of admitting that guilt to yourself? Why would you want to overlook your shame? As discussed in Chapter 8, guilt and shame are painful feelings. No one likes to feel them. Feeling guilty and ashamed carries with it the expectation of being caught or eventually found out, and ultimately condemned and rejected. To experience those feelings is to fear a loss of love.

When you secretly dislike yourself or doubt your worth, you will be frightened of your guilt and shame because they reveal your shortcomings. Therefore, you deny or distort those feelings. But by convincing yourself of your innocence, you never test out the expectation that others would abandon you if they found out about your guilt. You go on in life with the perpetual fear of being who you are.

Dorothy was sixty-seven. Her husband was seventy-four. She'd been seriously depressed for two years. When she talked, she focused on how difficult her days were. It hurt to walk with the arthritis. It was hard to read, since her eyesight seemed to be deteriorating. She and her husband had little in common. And her daughter? She refused to discuss her. Still, each week she asked me to do something to help her.

"You always avoid discussing your daughter," I said. "You haven't seen her now in, let's see, fifteen years." Her face darkened. It was much easier for her when all we talked about was her arthritis. I could almost hear her heart throbbing.

"I guess that's right," she tried to say nonchalantly. She was frightened now. Too frightened. Should I back off?

"This seems to scare you so much," I said. "I can't help but believe it will continue to haunt you until you do something about it."

"Do something about what?" she said, sidestepping not only her hurt feelings but her guilt.

"You're estranged from your daughter. Actually from your husband, too. Your daughter has tried to reach you three times in the past five years, and you haven't responded. You're depressed now, your health isn't that great, you don't speak much with your husband, and you're lonely."

"I know, I know," she said. "You're not telling me anything I don't already know."

"How can I help you to look more closely at the one thing you aren't facing?" I asked. She waited for me to finish. "Dorothy, I know how your daughter has hurt you over the years with her defiant attitude. I know how your husband has hurt you by seeming to care more about his job and his friends than about you. But you've hurt them, too, and you aren't dealing cleanly with them now. You focus only on their guilt but rarely on yours. I think that your depression is a message to them. I think it's your way of telling them how much they've hurt you. But I also think you feel guilty about it. You know you've rebuked your daughter. You know you've moved away from your husband, emotionally speaking. And that guilt is making you depressed, too. When do you want to be more up-front with everybody?"

"It isn't easy," she answered. "And with my arthritis the way it is, you can't imagine how difficult it is getting out of bed in the morning . . ."

It was sad. It was frustrating. She wasn't about to face her guilt feelings, to examine what was keeping her from her daughter. And that was the prime reason for her depression. And the longer she avoided it, the guiltier she felt. And the guiltier she felt, the more frightened she was of trying to improve. Making improvements now would only spotlight her shortcomings. It would reveal how little she had done so far in attempting to heal her relationships.

So she hid from herself. She hid behind her arthritis and anything else that would distract her from the truth of her situation.

When you distort the pain that comes along after a deep hurt, be it sadness, anger, shame or guilt, you are not accepting yourself or the other person. When you do not acknowledge your anger at having been hurt, you are not accepting the other person's faults. When you do not acknowledge your guilt at having been hurtful, you may be underestimating the other person's strengths by convincing yourself that he or she couldn't possibly forgive you for what you've done. When you cannot accept people as they are, you reduce your opportunity to experience love and forgiveness with them.

When you cannot acknowledge your pain, be it sadness, anger, or guilt, you distance yourself from others. You must. It isn't possible to deny or distort one feeling without affecting other feelings. How can you feel true happiness when inside is anger and sadness at having been betrayed? How can you be playful and spontaneous when spontaneity threatens the control you must have over your feelings?

When you can't admit your truest feelings, you are defeating yourself. You never know when it is time to fight in a relationship or when it is time to give up the fight. Neither do you know for sure when your anger is ever depleted and your guilt ever removed. You can never be certain when the relationship is healed because a vital source of information, your feelings, is lost.

You are just like the paralyzed person who, having lost all sensation in his legs, fails to notice when one leg is badly cut or burned. More damage is done because of that numbness to pain.

AWARENESS EXERCISES

The following exercises can help you to clarify vague feelings or to stimulate feelings that have been dulled by distortions. If you attempt these exercises for only one week, you will likely see an improvement in your awareness of feelings.

Exercise #1

Make a pact with yourself that at least a dozen times during the day, you will carefully attend to aspects of your life. Listen to the tones and qualities of a child's voice. What subtle shade of blue or gray is the sky right now? Study the exquisite shape and fragrance of flowers inside your house or out in a garden. What is the sensation right now of socks on your feet? Close your eyes and notice your breathing. The list is endless. The point is that with each observation, you can tug out a feeling if you try. Your task is not to explore these feelings but just to acknowledge them.

What memories do you associate with the creaking noises your house may be making right now? Look at the dog bounding across the yard or the child peering in the storefront window. What memories and feelings does that conjure up for you?

The easier it is for you to introduce yourself to your feelings, the less frightened you will be of them.

Exercise #2

This exercise is a variation of a technique discussed in Harold Bloomfield's wonderful book, *Making Peace with Your Parents*.

Imagine that the person you need to forgive—your

husband, wife, or parent (or even yourself)—is sitting directly across from you right now. Say the words *I forgive you.* Notice the thoughts you had that immediately followed those words. You may have told yourself such things as, "This is silly," or, "He doesn't deserve forgiveness," or, "I'll just be hurt all over again." Whatever your thoughts were, they led to a feeling.

Again, repeat the words *I forgive you.* Notice once more the thoughts and feelings that emerge as you speak. If your feelings are rather global emotions of hurt or anger, examine the thoughts that preceded them more closely. Those thoughts will reveal the more important issues for you, and may help to further clarify what your specific feelings are and what they are about.

For example, Mary repeated the phrase five times. The first time she said, "I forgive you," she immediately felt angry and then sad. She hadn't realized that certain thoughts actually preceded those feelings until she took a few moments to examine her thinking. Then she became aware that right after she had said, "I forgive you," she thought, "I'm always the one giving in; he never changes." That was then followed by feelings of anger and sadness. Clearly, an issue for Mary in her marriage is her perception that she always accommodates her husband, while he "never changes."

She repeated the forgiveness phrase and still felt sad and angry but less so. Again she spoke the phrase. Again the intensity of her feelings diminished. When she reexamined her thoughts, they had also changed: "I know he has made some changes. I don't always give in. I guess it bothers me that he doesn't realize what an effort it is to get over my anger. He's able to put everything in the past and start over. I'm not there yet."

After only three attempts at the forgiveness phrase, Mary had focused more clearly on what was bothering her. Because her husband was so quick to put their problems in the past, she felt he was insensitive to her feelings.

Twice more she repeated the phrase. Each time, her anger and hurt lessened a bit. She now felt more clearheaded about what issue she needed to discuss with her husband, *and* she was much less emotional about it.

As you progress along each phase of forgiveness, repeat this last exercise. It will give you information on how much you've progressed and what areas you still need to work on.

Denying Anger: The Story of Christine

Christine, twenty-four, came for therapy with her fiancé Tim, also twenty-four. Before she would set a wedding date, Christine wanted Tim to stop his infrequent but periodic physical abuse of her. At first glance, it seemed that Christine was indeed able to acknowledge to herself (and others) that Tim's abuse of her was deeply felt and unacceptable. But a more complicated picture emerged.

Christine revealed that until she was sixteen, her father, an alcoholic, beat her with some regularity. Her mother tried meekly to protect Christine but was never successful. Christine viewed her mother as loving and strong. "I respect her for staying true to my father despite his problems."

The father stopped drinking after Christine turned sixteen, and he never beat her again. He then became more involved with religion. Christine described her relationship with her parents as "close and loving." However, she had periodic bouts of guilt and anxiety, "even over small things." For instance, last week she turned down a dinner invitation from her parents and afterward felt tremendous guilt.

"How did you cope with being beaten as a child?" I asked.

"As I look back now, it doesn't seem so bad. I'm sure I was scared, and I was glad when it stopped, but I really don't have any bad feelings left over. A little anger sometimes, but not much."

"You were able to resolve something that painful?" I wondered aloud.

"I just try to forget, that's all. I've forgiven my father, and it's all over with."

"Does he know you've forgiven him?" I asked.

"Yes. I mean, I'm sure he must. We don't discuss it, so I'm sure he must think I'm over it all."

In fact, Christine never confronted her father about his abuse of her. She never told him she was hurt and angry, let alone tell him she forgave him. She and her mother had an unspoken agreement to never mention what went on during Christine's first sixteen years.

Christine really hadn't acknowledged to herself the full extent of her pain. As a child, she didn't want to face the idea that her father might not love her, so she saw love and abuse as intertwined.

Actually, she was angry with both parents. She was angry at her mother for being ineffective at protecting her, although such feelings were hidden. Now, as an adult with a growing sense of independence, she was willing to face the deeper truths about her feelings.

From that willingness, she was able to see that her strong guilt feelings were really an anxiety about the anger she felt. The anger should have been directed at her parents, but she hadn't done that. So now, when she turned down a dinner invitation from them, she felt guilty because her underlying anger was sparked. Declining an invitation was her small way of opposing her parents and expressing anger at them. But she couldn't consciously admit she was angry, because she didn't want to risk upsetting the family stability. So she turned her anger against herself and felt guilty. She convinced herself she was the one doing something bad, not her parents.

In time, Christine understood that she really hadn't forgiven her parents. In fact, her involvement with an abusive boyfriend was evidence that her feelings of hurt were never really settled. But for the first time, she was on the road to forgiveness. Her first step was being able to acknowledge her full pain.

The price you pay for holding back a hurt is to reexperience the hurt, again and again, until you finally admit to it and make matters right.

REMORSE

Feeling remorse is an important part of this first phase of finding forgiveness. Remorse can come about only after you acknowledge your guilt. It signifies that you feel bad about your role in the estrangement and that you wish to have a more caring relationship.

Remorse goes beyond the feeling of regret. Whereas you may feel blameworthy when you regret your actions, remorse goes one step further and points you in the direction of reconciliation. Regret points nowhere. When you're remorseful, you want to *do something constructive* to begin the healing process. You don't hold onto remorse for long, but are driven to rectify your mistakes. You can hold onto regrets forever.

When you clutch feelings of regret, you move toward self-pity. At that point, you have strayed from the path of reconciliation. You are more concerned with *your* feelings than with the feelings of the person you hurt.

If you admit you were hurtful but feel no remorse, then the relationship has little meaning for you. You've stayed in the relationship unconcerned about the welfare of the other person, preoccupied only with trying to get what you can. You have regarded the other person as a thing, not a human being.

When you feel no remorse, you have no respect for the person you've hurt. Should that person forgive you anyway, you'll regard him or her as weak or blind, rather than face the possibility that someone could care about you in spite of yourself.

If you are open to the feeling of remorse but seem to get stuck in self-pity, then you are frightened of being rejected. You hope that others will recognize your fears and have sympathy and understanding for you. You hope that such an understanding will be all that's necessary to make the relationship right again. But it really won't. At least not for long. When you are stuck in your feelings of regret, you are also frightened of embarking on a road to productive change, which is what remorse would compel you to do.

Recall the story of Christine. Her father stopped beating her eight years ago. Yet once in a while he would wail how he expected to suffer the rest of his days from the guilt he feels for having been so cruel. What may have at one time been genuine remorse on his part evolved into self-pity and self-condemnation, a defense designed to protect him from the possible onslaught of those he hurt. His regret gave the impression that he was remorseful, but he was too frightened to be remorseful. His self-blame served to block any real healing and reconciliation. His self-criticisms made it hard for Christine to ever confront him about his past. With nothing really resolved between them, his fears persisted, and he sank deeper into regret.

Captured by the tentacles of anxiety that had overgrown in nine years, the man was in a pathetic state. He fooled himself into believing that his self-flagellations would assuage his guilt and relieve his unresolved fears. But he was mistaken. He was still hurting his family by not allowing them to be honest with him, so his guilt continued.

Don't be like Christine's father and let remorse settle so long that it becomes fright and self-pity. As soon as your remorse points you in a direction of change, begin your journey. Admit your guilt, first to yourself and then to those you've hurt. And work on changing your style of relating so that you won't be as hurtful again.

Remorse is more than an admission of guilt. It is a beckoning within to reunite in love with the people you've been distant from all this time.

Before you proceed with Phase Two, consider the following questions:

- Have you begun to identify your feelings more clearly?
- When you think about the problems in the relationship, can you spend at least as much time focusing on your role in the problems as you spend blaming?
- Are you able to understand what you lost when you were hurt? Love? Esteem? Power? Control?
- Have you examined whether you've felt this way before and with whom?
- Can you admit your guilt for things you did that were hurtful? Can you nurture remorse?

Remember, you may not get as clear a picture as you'd like about your feelings. If you've made an effort to do so but still feel you are missing something, proceeding with Phase Two may help. Sometimes, the experience of each phase sheds more light on all that you need to know.

You've begun to sort through your feelings. Now it is time to share them.

Chapter Twelve

Phase Two: Confessing and Confronting

"I have hurt you. I am sorry."

With such words, if said with honesty, humility, and a heartfelt caring for the other person, begins the more complicated but crucial second phase on your journey to reconcile and know forgiveness.

Whether you are the forgiver who needs to confront the other person about the hurts against you, or the one who seeks forgiveness and who needs to confess to the pain you've caused, there is no avoiding this phase if there is to be a full healing of the relationship.

If you are anxious at the prospect of confessing or confronting, such discomfort is normal. Your anxiety is a signal that what you are about to do seems risky. And it probably is. You are worried about how the other person will react to your message. Most likely you are frightened that the person will react negatively and that a deeper estrangement will result.

I can't tell you that such a fear is groundless. Indeed,

some marriages continue only because there is a tacit agreement between partners to ignore certain problems. What I *can* tell you, though, is that everything that is vital in life requires taking a risk. There are no sure things. And there is no way around that fact of life.

CONFESSING AND APOLOGIZING

By confessing, you put into words your recognition of an estrangement, and you admit responsibility for any hurts you caused. You own up to your guilt and the fact that you violated a relationship you were committed to. You convey your remorse. And even if you did what you did in retaliation for hurts against you, you accept that you nevertheless *chose* to act in the manner you did. In other words, you stop blaming your partner for acts that you committed. By confessing, you outwardly express the guilt and remorse you acknowledged to yourself in Phase One.

Confession may pacify or appease the person you hurt, but it does not by itself reconcile the relationship. Confession cannot heal, but it may soothe. Your confession is the first step of an outward one-on-one exchange with the person you hurt that will hopefully bring about forgiveness and reunion.

In its most sincere and least complicated form, confession comes from love. It is from your love of yourself and the other person that you wish the pain to be healed. And it is from a genuine self-acceptance that you are able to contend openly with your faults instead of having to deny or distort them in some fashion. It matters to you that someone you care about is in pain as a result of your shortcomings.

When you confess, there is a surrender. You no longer fight to pretend that you are innocent of

wrongdoing. You admit your guilt. You make no excuses, and you don't try to get the other person to feel
sorry for you. You give up fighting on the side of
defensiveness and false pride, and you surrender to
the freedom that love and honesty provide you.

Even so, it is also true that for most of us a good
deal of the time, fear is a motivation behind our
willingness to confess. We may fear being rejected or
condemned if we don't admit our guilt. We may fear
loss of love or personal esteem. Sometimes we fear
having to confess, so we hold out, hoping to get away
with what we did. And only when we are confronted
about our actions do we finally own up to them.

When marriage is involved, we are fooling ourselves if we believe we can hold back from owning up
to most of our serious mistakes and not see the relationship suffer. It is understandable that we may want
to hold back out of fear, but that fear then becomes a
wedge between ourselves and our husband or wife. It
keeps us estranged to some degree.

On the other hand, if we know that by confessing
our faults we will cause much hurt, then it may be the
more loving thing to say nothing. If our openness and
honesty harms others while making us feel unburdened, we are still causing pain. There is no easy
answer, for example, to the question: "Should I confess to my spouse that I once had an affair?" What
would the benefit of revealing it be, now that the
affair is over? Releasing your guilt feelings is not
justification enough if your partner will be terribly
hurt by the admission.

INAPPROPRIATE MEANS OF CONFESSION

Despite the importance of confessing as a means to
bring about reconciliation and forgiveness, there are

times when it is done in a manner that avoids real
honesty or culpability. Such inappropriate means of
confession can become a stumbling block to forgiveness rather than a passageway.

Confessing Innocence

"I think he's making a big deal out of very little,"
Martha complained about her husband. "He knows
that my work schedule is not carved in stone and that
sometimes I have to work overtime. I tell him not to
be upset that I'm late, and he says that I should at least
call him and tell him when I won't be home on time.
It's only an hour or two. What's the big deal? So I told
him I was sorry but that *I really didn't know I was
upsetting him that much by not calling.*"

Sometimes people confess and apologize while at
the same time proclaiming their innocence by stating
that they were unaware of how they had been hurtful. That may be true. However, if you make such a
confession of innocence more than once, it raises the
question as to whether you're concerned enough
about the relationship to become more aware of how
you affect people. You have a duty to be more self-
aware. You may not intend to be hurtful (but then
again, is there an underlying anger you haven't dealt
with yet?). But sometimes your "harmless teasing" or
"forgetfulness" can really be a thorn in someone's
side.

Another version of this type of confession is when
you admit being hurtful but then abdicate any responsibility for what you did. You may blame others for
provoking you, or you may explain away your actions
as due to a headache or a poor night's sleep. Or you
may nonchalantly dismiss what you did with a statement like, "I've always been that way. I can't help it. I

guess it's a habit by now." We are all vulnerable to such distorted reasoning, but we can help it, if it matters to us to make the effort.

While there are many influences on your behavior, confessing your innocence will not begin the process of healing after there has been a deep pain. Regardless of how your actions came about (unless someone put a gun to your head), those actions were hurtful, and you need to accept responsibility for doing something about that. Otherwise, you are discounting the other person's feelings of hurt, and he or she might rightly question the extent of your remorse.

Confessing to Attract Sympathy

Some people will loudly admit to their hurtfulness in hopes that others will feel sorry for them. They may even plead for some kind of punishment; after all, "I deserve it."

Anyone who confesses to attract sympathy is really quite desperate. Rejection is feared to be imminent.

If you confess to attract sympathy, then others may feel sorry for you at first. And if they have some unresolved fears about expressing anger, then you may succeed at holding them at bay. But eventually, such a style of confessing won't protect you. The relationship will suffer because of the dishonesty, and others will become angry with you. They may want little to do with you.

An insincere confession is inevitably seen for what it is.

Confessing to Appear Virtuous

"I even went and told her I was sorry. I admitted I was wrong, but what did she do? She said, 'Words mean nothing,' and got up and left. Well, I've done my part.

I said I was wrong. Now it's up to her. If we don't get back together, it won't be because I wasn't man enough to admit my mistakes."

The man who spoke those words was actually frightened of an ongoing dialogue with his wife to deal with their problems. He feared that a dialogue would lead to more accusations. And while he knew in his heart that he had hurt her deeply, he was still angry about how she had hurt him. And he didn't want to accept responsibility for any future problems. So when he finally confessed and his wife remained angry, he used her reaction as the excuse he needed to absolve himself of any responsibility. He also used his confession as a device to appear virtuous, to look like a person devoted to the notion of honesty and reconciliation when in fact he was frightened of the entire process. He just wanted a way out of feeling guilty.

A confession is not just a string of words. The man in this example did actually confess and apologize, but it was a hollow confession. The spirit of a genuine admission of guilt is the basic attitude of humility and a desire to reconcile, not to hurt. When one confesses in order to place oneself on a pedestal of virtue, then the true meaning of confession has been lost.

Superficial Confession

Finally, a subtle but common form of confession that impedes the reconciliation process occurs when you admit to having committed certain acts but you fail to confess to the underlying attitude that prompted your behavior. In essence, you overlook or deemphasize the meaning behind your hurtful acts. You admit your guilt, but you overlook other, more important areas of guilt. A common example of a superficial confession is apologizing for being late when deep down you were late because you were angry at the person you were supposed to meet.

Often, the reaction of the person to this confession of yours is one of believing that something is missing, that somehow you are only skimming the surface of your feelings. The person senses a hostility or fear in you that prompts him or her not to wholly accept your confession at face value. Guardedness and resentment can then build on both sides.

Carla is twenty-nine and episodically abuses alcohol. When drunk, she becomes angry and sometimes assaults her husband, Rudy. She apologizes later. But she never confesses to the underlying rage at her husband, which she feels whenever she perceives him as trying to control her.

"Yesterday he said to me, 'Let's go out to dinner tonight.' I was furious with him for saying that, but I couldn't tell him I was so angry. It was the way he said it that bothered me. He didn't *ask* me if I wanted to go out. He said, 'Let's go out.' I felt it was a command, not a request."

Whether Rudy was commanding her is not the issue. Carla had an underlying rage at him that she wasn't telling him about. Part of the reason she drank was to express anger at him. She couldn't be more direct about her feelings. Her husband, uneasy about facing her anger, always attributed her hostile outbursts to the drinking. "It isn't Carla doing that to me, it's the wine." However, her apologies to him did not sound sincere, since each of them sensed there was a lot more going on with her feelings that she wasn't being up-front about.

As Carla learned, her rage at Rudy was really a fury at her father that was displaced onto her husband. Her father, an alcoholic, was a controlling man. Even by being passive and helpless (when he was drunk), he exerted powerful control over family members who couldn't be themselves while he was drinking.

Repairs in the relationship were easier to make when Carla reacted to Rudy as himself, not as a representation of her father. But that didn't happen until she went beyond apologizing for her drinking and admitted there was a deeper meaning to her actions. Rudy, always reluctant to face her anger, was finally able to hear her out when she was upset with him, because she was being more honest and not overdoing her anger anymore.

Perhaps the most important aspect about confessing that bears repeating is that confession, by itself, does not heal. It doesn't mark the final phase of the return to a more loving relationship. Rather, it is among the first breaths of a relationship newborn.

Know that your confession must come not only from love but from humility. It is a humbling of yourself that, far from lowering your dignity, displays it; far from demeaning your worth, reveals it.

CONFRONTING

If you have been deeply hurt, perhaps betrayed, and you wish the relationship to be healed, you must confront the other person with your feelings of hurt and anger. You must also let the person know that your prime motive for the confrontation is to heal the relationship. While it is conceivable that you can find *forgiveness* without an honest confrontation, a true *reconciliation* will almost certainly be stifled without one. Often, the relationship is left a bit scarred when there is a holding back of feelings, and it may not survive many future problems.

Confronting is rarely easy or comfortable. But

nothing worthwhile comes easily. You must confront with humility and not arrogance. That is why Phase One asks you to examine your feelings closely. Only if you take the time to really identify your feelings and attitudes about what happened, and get a clearer sense of why you reacted the way you did, are you ready to confront with honesty and love. To confront too soon, without such self-scrutiny, is to risk acting in a way that will complicate matters.

Your purpose in confronting is not merely to communicate your feelings, but also to set an example for how you want the healed relationship to be. And *how* you confront the other person is just as important as *what* you say.

If your confrontation is a weapon of vengeance, then the other person will indeed know how angry you are. But the reconciliation process will get sidetracked or stalled. No one likes to be attacked. You and the other person each have dignity. Speak to that person in a manner that respects the dignity you each possess.

Conversely, if your confrontation is weak and incomplete because you don't want to stir up any more trouble, then any reconciliation will be founded on fear.

Be direct. Be open. Your feelings really do matter. It's OK to convey your anger, but do your best to convey that you really care about reconciling, too. Own your feelings. They are yours. No one forced them on you. And accept your share of responsibility for how your confrontation can affect the healing process.

BUT BEFORE YOU DO THAT . . .

Before you confront, take some time to experience the

feelings you acknowledged in Phase One. Experience the anger, embarrassment, guilt, shame, helplessness, fear, loneliness, sadness—all the emotions that the hurts have brought about. Now ask yourself these questions:

- Have I ever felt this way before?
- When was the first time I felt that way?
- How old was I?
- Who hurt me, or whom did I hurt?
- Did I ever really get over that hurtful time?
- If so, can I do something now that I did before to help me settle matters and heal the relationship?
- If not, is the residue affecting the way I am handling things now?
- Am I overreacting or underreacting to what's happening now because of what happened to me in the past?
- Does the person who hurt me (or whom I hurt) remind me of someone who hurt me before?
- Are there facts I could uncover, people I could talk to, that would help me to better understand the influences on the person who hurt me?
- Without trying to *excuse* the person who hurt me, is there some information that would help me to better *understand* him or her?

These questions may deliver you into an important corridor of your feelings. By answering them, you may discover that your understanding of the current problem is changed, likely for the better. If you are reacting to current problems in a manner that resembles some past hurtful event, you are probably operating at a disadvantage. And you may be blaming the person who you are now estranged from for more than is due.

"Our relationship has been up and down for a year now," Tony said to me about his four years with Monica. "Now Monica tells me she's not sure if she wants to marry me because I've switched jobs twice in six months. 'You don't know what you want in life,' she tells me."

"You sound angry," I said.

"I am angry. I know what I'm doing in life. I know what I'm capable of. She has no faith in me."

"What do you intend to do?" I asked.

"All I can do is tell her that I think she's out of line. If she wants to leave me, fine. But I can't stay with someone who has no faith in me."

Tony was about to confront Monica with his feelings. I asked him instead to sift through some questions first.

"Tony, you're angry and it sounds to me that on the one hand you want to prove something to Monica, but on the other hand you resent having to do that. Is that right?"

"Yes. Absolutely. Who does she think she is?"

"It makes you feel bad that she doubts you. But if you are honest with yourself, Tony, could it be that you feel bad because you wonder whether she might be right? At least somewhat?"

"You mean am I upset with her for not having faith in me because I doubt myself, too? Well, anything is possible but . . ."

"If it's possible, Tony," I interjected, "then I'd like you to take a few moments and really examine whether there is some truth to what I'm suggesting. What doubts do you have about yourself?"

He paused and appeared downcast. "You know I have switched jobs twice this year, but I've had five jobs in two years. I get dissatisfied quickly with the work. I'm not so sure I doubt my abilities though."

"Does your resentment at Monica for doubting you remind you of any past experience?" I asked.

"In college I started my own computer business. I earned more than enough to pay all my college expenses. But no one gave me credit. They thought that my partner was the brains of the whole thing. I was furious about that. I wanted to prove to them that I had talent, too, but no matter what I did, I never got the credit I deserved. So I dropped the business."

Lodged in his memory were a series of other events, all with the same theme: making an effort at something and never feeling successful in others' eyes, always secretly doubting his abilities and undermining his accomplishments. Tony labored through old memories and came to rest on one particular keepsake from his childhood.

"I was playing ball with my dad. I was about eight. He was teaching me how to bat, but I wasn't getting it. He got more impatient with me. I can see him leaning over me, yelling, criticizing. Finally he called me an asshole. Can you imagine what it's like for a father to call his kid that?"

"I'm sorry you went through that, Tony."

"Yeah. Me too," he said softly.

Tony was learning some important things. He really did doubt his abilities. His esteem was fragile. He understood that his anger with Monica resulted in part from his anger at his father. He learned that while he wanted to prove to his father that he was a capable son, he resented having to do that. And he also feared failing. That was one reason he left five jobs in two years. He was afraid of staying on a job and being unsuccessful, so he left before any real judgment could be made about his abilities.

Tony decided to confront his father about his unresolved feelings before making any rash decisions

about his relationship with Monica. "She's been right
all along. And she's stood by me. I may not square
things with my father by talking to him, but I want
him to hear what I have to say. At least I'll have the
satisfaction of knowing I'm doing the right thing for
myself. And it might just help me and Monica, too."

"Your anger at your dad is legitimate, Tony," I said.
"But my guess is there is a lot about him you don't
know. Talk to him about your feelings. But consider
that it is in everyone's best interests to also try to learn
more about him, too."

In many cases, it is a good idea to reestablish some
degree of togetherness, partnership, or intimacy with
the other person (spouse or parent) before you confront. An enjoyable weekend away from the kids may
serve as a foundation for an honest discussion with a
spouse later on. Partners who have returned to living
together after a separation, for example, may do well
to reestablish some sense of order in the household
before they discuss primary issues. Consequently,
returning to the routine of doing chores, going shopping together, having dinner together, or going to
school functions that the kids are involved in will
make the difficult task of working on the problems a
little easier.

Consider the case of Butch. Butch never got along
with his mother. He regarded her as critical and
controlling, and he was glad to be married and away
from her. But rather than work on his feelings, he
pretended his relationship with her was sound while
he told his wife, Sandy, to deal with her most of the
time. Predictably, the mother was critical of Sandy,
accusing her of alienating her son from her and doing
a lousy job of raising her grandson, too. When Sandy
complained to Butch, he got angry that she couldn't
get along better with his mother. After many intense

marital therapy sessions, Sandy made it clear that she no longer intended to be pulled apart by Butch and his mother. And Butch and Sandy realized that it was his responsibility, not Sandy's, to work on his relationship with his mother.

But before Butch could confront his mother with his feelings, he needed to reestablish a more involved relationship with her. Basically, he needed to spend more time with her to desensitize his emotional reactivity to her. If he were too uncomfortable just being in her presence, he'd never successfully confront her with his feelings. Therefore, over a period of six weeks, Butch spoke to his mother on the phone more often and made numerous brief visits. He agreed to my suggestion not to discuss any hot topics with her and instead spoke to her about everyday events that were less emotionally laden. He also made a point of praising Sandy in his mother's presence. From time to time, he listened while the woman spoke of her younger days. He began to view her not as a powerful tyrant, but as the more human, vulnerable woman she was. Six weeks later, Butch felt more at ease with his mother and began speaking with her more intimately about their own relationship.

It wasn't easy. Butch never was a "talker." But with coaching from me, he one day told his mother how much more he was enjoying his visits with her. He explained how in the past it had made him uncomfortable when she would criticize him or Sandy and how much he appreciated it when she spoke more kindly of them. His mother was a bit rattled by his confrontation but did hear him out. Butch continued to talk with her more often about routine events (so did Sandy), and he continued to speak well of Sandy to his mother. They never became as close to each other as some people might have, but there was a marked reduction in tension when they got together and a marked increase in contentment.

THE VALUE OF CONFRONTING

It Communicates Trust and a Desire for Growth

When your effort to reconcile is sincere, then your decision to confront the person who hurt you demonstrates a degree of faith and trust in that person to care about what you have to say. True, that person might not care about your feelings, and your openness will then not improve the odds of a reconciliation. But if the other person wants a reconciliation, too, he or she will appreciate your faith and willingness to trust.

Confronting another person is also a sign of your faith in yourself. After all, you will have to cope with the consequences of your openness.

Your courage in confronting is a measure of your caring that the relationship be guided not by fear, but by the secureness that an honest, compassionate expression of your feelings brings. It is your way of telling your spouse or parent that you want the relationship to be freeing and growing instead of confining and stagnating.

There is no growth in a relationship when you hold back feelings as a way to keep the peace.

It Helps You to Let Go of the Hurt You May Still Be Holding

Very likely, some of the pain you feel (be it hurt, resentment, embarrassment, and so on) has been inside you. The longer you held it in, the more damage it probably caused, perhaps even to innocent bystanders.

Anger held in intensifies. Then you either feel like a pressure cooker ready to explode, or you turn the anger against yourself and feel guilty and depressed. Far from letting go of your hurt, you've tied yourself to it.

One of the cleanest ways to let go of your anger is to express it directly at the source of the hurt. Especially if you express it honestly and straightforwardly with compassion and no dramatics, you'll notice an almost immediate reduction in your pain. And if you can say all you have to with an attitude of concern for the relationship, you'll feel even better.

It Provides Feedback

Your spouse who hurt you needs to know exactly what he or she did that caused problems and what your feelings about it are. Don't pretend that your partner should already know your feelings without having to be told. Even if the person has been living with you for years, you are setting both of you up for more hurt when you believe that he should read your mind. And you are putting off a potentially constructive dialogue by waiting for him to come to you first.

People who feel uneasy about expressing their anger may hold back confronting because they don't believe their anger is justified. They need more of an excuse to express their anger. So they sit and act hurt, and when the hurtful person doesn't notice that and apologize, the excuse to lash out is provided.

If you need an excuse to express legitimate anger, you'll eventually find one. But the person you are confronting will feel set up and trapped. He or she won't like it, and the two of you will have that much more to argue about.

Someone's ignorance of your feelings is not necessarily an indication of their lack of love for you, especially when you don't provide feedback on your feelings. It is a sign of love and concern to point out how you feel. And your feedback gives you an opportunity to clarify feelings that may still be unclear to you. Especially if you are someone who keeps feelings bottled up, you may need to sort through them before you understand them better. That sorting-through process is made easier when you start expressing yourself.

ATTACKING VERSUS CONFRONTING

When you've been deeply hurt, it is understandable that your anger can get the better of you. You may retaliate. Then your confrontation will be seen by your spouse for what it really is: an attack.

Perhaps your spouse will be feeling some remorse for having hurt you. That way, if you are hostile and attacking, he or she may let you say your peace without taking offense. Then the two of you can get on with some constructive dialogue.

But what if your spouse isn't remorseful? Or what if he or she still has mixed feelings about what happened between you two? Maybe your spouse feels hurt and unsettled by some things you once did. If so, the likelihood is that your hostile confrontation will not lend itself to a reasonable working through of your problems. Your spouse, whom you are attacking, may get very defensive, and understandably so. As a result, the legitimate aspects of what you have to say get lost as your spouse protects him- or herself from your verbal barrage. Owning up to one's guilt can be hard enough without also having to defend against a hostile attack. Unfortunately, interactions marked by hostile confrontations can become a routine way of dealing with problems.

"Peter, what the hell did you want me to do?" Emma said with disdain. "Sit there and tell our son, 'Oh, it's fine that you want to quit college,' when I happen to think he's making the biggest mistake of his life?"

"I didn't say that you should agree with him," Peter said, snarling. "All that I wanted you to do was . . ."

"Oh, all that *you* wanted *me* to do?" Emma interrupted. "If you wanted me to do something, why didn't you speak up then and there? I asked you to talk to your son and tell him he was making a mistake, and then you yelled at me, as if I were being unreasonable speaking to him the way I was."

"You were being unreasonable, and I resented being put on the spot. For God's sake, Emma, I just walked in the house after working all day, and you wanted me to immediately reprimand Tommy for his decision. He's old enough to do what he wants."

"You never support my opinions," Emma accused. "In fact, I think you do what you can to undermine what I want done. Just once I wish you'd be on my side."

"Do you realize how often you ask me to choose between you and one of the kids? That's no choice, Emma."

Arguments like that were routine for Peter and Emma. Each one would be hostile and accusing, and no issue was ever discussed fully. They would skip from complaint to complaint, using the other's attacking style as the excuse to do the same in return. Disgust and resentment would mount to the point where neither one could say or do anything without the other one finding something to be critical about.

If you are being confronted in an attacking manner, you do have choices other than retaliation. If you were hurtful to the one confronting you, and as long as you aren't being abused, you can hear him or her out. Later on, you will have time to give your side of the story if you think you are being unfairly accused.

For example, Emma and Peter could have transformed their argument into a constructive discussion if only they'd have been willing to hear their partner out and own up to any complaints against them that had merit.

When Peter told Emma she was unreasonable to complain about their son the moment Peter returned home from work, Emma might have said, "*You're right*, Peter. I did hit you with this problem right as you opened the door. Not a wonderful way to greet you, I know. I guess this problem with Tommy has really upset me."

When Emma accused Peter of always undermining her and never taking her side, Peter might have said, "*You're right*, Emma. Sometimes I don't take your side. I know we both want what's best for Tommy, so let's sit down and figure out what we need to do. OK?"

The fact that Peter might have been out of line to brand Emma as "unreasonable," or the fact that Emma was probably exaggerating when she accused Peter of "never" taking her side, misses the point. By attacking and counterattacking, they each viewed one another as the enemy rather than as partners with a vested interest in making matters work out.

It takes two people to resolve a conflict. Choose to be one of those two. You are not responsible for the way the other person decides to confront you, but you can choose to listen to what is being told to you—even if you don't like what you hear.

CONFRONTING HALFWAY

To lead to healing, your confrontation needs to be complete. Yet people often start with an honest confrontation, only to stop short and leave matters unfinished because of anxiety. Sometimes they want to leave well enough alone. (But if the relationship is so fragile as to fall apart should a discussion continue, is that something you want to preserve?) Some people express only part of what is on their minds as a test to see if it is safe to continue later on.

The bottom line is that if you hold back and confront only halfway, you are leaving problems unresolved and therefore increasing the odds that matters will get worse. When that happens, you may conclude that your "openness" was destructive or useless, when in fact you never gave it an honest try.

You don't have to confront your partner with all your feelings at one sitting, as long as you make it clear that you have more to say. "Let's talk again, Ruth. This really helps me when we clear the air like this." If you begin the process of expressing your feelings, you must do so with the intention of seeing it through.

Stopping short in a confrontation can be just as problematic as saying nothing at all. Michelle had a hard time saying what was on her mind. So did her fiancé, Kyle. Michelle was married twice before and spoke about her divorces using clichés to protect her from the pain.

"People are people," she would say. "They come and go and do their own thing eventually. What's finished is finished. No sense dragging out the past."

Her relationship with Kyle seemed fine until he gave her an engagement ring. Then she lost interest in him sexually. At first Kyle tried to be understanding.

Then he just got angry. She accused him of being insensitive. She teased him about men she worked with who she knew were attracted to her. When Kyle wanted an explanation of what she might be implying, she got indignant at the suggestion that she couldn't be trusted. She accused him of being jealous and immature.

By the time they entered therapy, their relationship had fallen apart. She was depressed and cynical. He was angry, but serious about keeping the two of them together. He'd occasionally back away from discussions, avoiding problematic issues, only to become more anxious and frustrated. She saw his frustration as evidence of his unwillingness to be tolerant of her need to have matters dropped for a while.

"I give up," Michelle said one evening.

"What, again?" Kyle said sarcastically.

"See what I mean?" Michelle said, looking at me. "I can't tell him anything without getting back some kind of smart-ass answer."

Kyle sighed loudly. "This is the third time in three weeks you've given up. I don't know what to believe anymore. I feel that if I look at you cross-eyed, you're going to use that as the excuse to end the relationship."

"I really wish you would try to understand my feelings for a change, Kyle."

"All right, all right, I'll listen," Kyle said. "Tell me about your feelings."

"Forget it," she concluded. "Talking about our problems won't work. It never has."

Their conversations typically went on like that, in fits and starts, without succeeding in resolving any issue. They both felt cynical and exasperated. They were open, but they only got so far in a discussion before it broke down.

If your interactions are similar to Michelle's and Kyle's, *what* you are saying is no longer as important as *how* you are saying it. Forget about the hurt and anger for a moment. Focus on how you are complicating the discussion. If you aren't sure where to begin to make repairs in your style of talking, listen instead. Look the other person in the eye, and listen as well as you can.

Maybe the other person is accusing unfairly. Listen anyway.

Maybe the other person doesn't deserve your consideration. Listen anyway.

Maybe you've heard it all before. Listen anyway. You owe it to yourself (and to the relationship), don't you?

THE FEAR OF HURTING ANOTHER'S FEELINGS

One common reason people give for avoiding a confrontation is the concern about hurting the feelings of the person being confronted. This concern is especially true when the relationship has been going on for years after the original hurts happened, and nothing was ever said about the problems.

"I can't tell her how I feel," Joyce said in dismay. "My mother is eighty-four years old. I've held it in for thirty-three years. Why bring it up now? It would hurt her so much. Our relationship is fine now. Why stir things up unnecessarily?"

Joyce's concern had some merit. If in fact her relationship with her mother was a caring, loving one, it is possible that the old hurts have been let go. It is hard to forgive and feel forgiven in silence, but it can happen. It just takes a long time before you can really be sure.

But in Joyce's case, her statements about her relationship with her mother contrasted with those made
in earlier sessions.

"I hate to admit it," Joyce said weeks before, "but I
do hold my mother accountable for why my life has
been so unhappy. She has good points, and she can be
loving, really. But while growing up, all I heard was
criticism. It wasn't always harsh, and there wasn't
much yelling. But it was constant, like one wave rolling in after another. She'd just put me down and act
disappointed with me. I wanted her to appreciate me,
but I was never sure she did. I always had doubts. I
still do."

One of the reasons Joyce came for therapy was to
deal with her twenty-year-old daughter, Shelley. Shelley was becoming so obstinate and rebellious that
neither Joyce nor her husband Howard could effectively deal with her. But it soon became apparent that
Shelley's disrespect for her mother reflected Howard's
disrespect for Joyce, too. Each was critical of Joyce,
Howard complaining that she was an ineffective
homemaker and disciplinarian. Joyce admitted she
was unassertive and had spent her life trying to please
others. It was that way about her that she says was
cultivated by her years with her mother. And that is
why she blamed her mother for her current problems.

"Mom had this perfectionistic quality about her,"
Joyce said. "Nothing I did was quite good enough.
Everything had to be just right. Appearance was ev-
erything."

"When your mother dies, Joyce, will you have any
regrets?" I asked one day.

"I'll always regret that she couldn't have been more
supportive and less critical of me," Joyce answered.

"I'm not talking about regretting things that your
mother did or didn't do. Is there anything you will

regret about your actions and your side of the relationship with your mother?" I inquired.

It was hard for Joyce to speak. She had placed the
responsibility for her life for so long in her mother's
hands (by blaming her) that she rarely considered how
she affected her own life. She shifted in her chair.

"I feel guilty, sometimes, about being so angry with
her. But I know I'm being too hard on myself. I always
have been," she said.

"Maybe not so hard," I said gently. "In fact, I think
you have been letting yourself off the hook too easily
on some things." Joyce looked uneasy, as if she were
afraid I might tell her something she already sensed
about herself. I continued. "I know that much of your
anger toward your mother is legitimate, but I can't
help wonder that by blaming your mother entirely for
your problems, you are holding her accountable for
too much. Where does your responsibility for your
own life fit in?"

Joyce began to realize that she found it safer to
regard her mother as the cause of her problems instead of looking at her own shortcomings. She felt
guilty about being angry with her mother, not because she was too hard on herself, but because *she was
guilty*. Rather than confront her mother years ago
over her hurt at being criticized, Joyce retaliated in
more subtle ways. She constructed a wall between
herself and her mother without ever saying why. She
kept the pretense that she felt close to her mother
when in fact she was keeping an emotional distance.
Joyce was guilty of maintaining an estrangement with
her mother (her mother was guilty of that, too) without ever trying to see if their problems could be
resolved.

Of course, being assertive with her mother years
ago would have been risky. Her mother might have

criticized her even more or rejected her outright. Fearful, Joyce decided not to take the risk.

"I'm still not sure it's a good idea to talk to my mother about how she hurt me," Joyce said two months later. "I really don't want to hurt her feelings. Not now. Not anymore."

"It really isn't an easy decision to make," I said. It depends on what you hope to accomplish by it all. Just expressing your anger after thirty years does seem unfair. But if you wish to feel closer to your mother and better about your relationship with her, it is important to express your feelings—but with some compassion.

"Tell her you want to love her even more than you already do," I continued. "Tell her you want to feel her love for you. Tell her you regret never doing anything about improving your relationship with her until now. Don't blame her for your current problems with Howard and Shelley. They are not her fault. You are human and have doubts and fears. So does your family. It is due to those fears that you haven't been able to make your life happy for you. But maybe if you start to face some of those fears, such as your fear of speaking your feelings, you can make some improvements.

Joyce did want to feel closer to her mother, and she did speak with her. In the end, she found it possible to forgive her mother for having been so critical.

"Do you know what she said to me by the time I finished talking?" Joyce reported one day. "She said, 'I wish you had told me this before, Joyce. I really do. I am so sorry. This should have been settled long ago.' I didn't know whether to laugh or cry, but I ended up crying. She did, too. I know I did the right thing by having a heart-to-heart talk with her. Then again, maybe the real hurt was that I held all this against her for so many years. I'm glad it's over."

You can never be certain you won't hurt the feelings of the person you confront. But if you are worried about it, chances are it reflects the fact that you haven't sorted out your role in the estrangement yet. The key to deciding whether it is time to confront depends upon your degree of self-focus. If you haven't examined your role in either the cause or the maintenance of the estrangement, then you will blame the other person for too much. Your fear then of hurting that person's feelings is real. If you blame and criticize without identifying your role in the problem, you will hurt the person's feelings.

Your feelings are important. So important that you owe it to yourself and the people you care about to express those feelings, especially when you are feeling hurt or love. But take the time to examine your feelings and your role in the estrangement so that your openness will be a healing experience.

It is when you hold back your feelings that you do damage to them. You also damage yourself and your relationships. That is probably why you have some concern about hurting the feelings of the person you've needed to confront about your anger. Your fear of hurting that person's feelings stems from the guilt you feel for having already hurt that person. You've been hurtful by withholding your feelings for too long when there were times when expressing them could have made all the difference.

Every moment you hold back from sharing your important feelings is one more moment of estrangement.

Before you go on to Phase Three, consider the following questions:

• Can you state your feelings with a minimum of

blame and criticism? Have you considered, once
again, your role in the estrangement?

- Is your confession completely honest, with a goal to
reconcile and not just to attract sympathy or appear
virtuous?
- Are you prepared to remain in a dialogue and not
confront only halfway?
- Are you prepared to learn more about the person
who hurt you and understand as well as possible
what that person has had to struggle with?
- Are you desperately afraid? Are your emotions hot?
If so, don't confess yet.

Let there be no more holding back. Confess if you
are guilty. Own up to your faults, and apologize for
any way that you've been hurtful. Confront the person who hurt you with your sadness and anger. Don't
wait until your anger turns into bitterness or guilt,
because then matters will be too confusing. Just be
honest. Now. And come from love. It's time, and you
really do deserve to be happier than you have been.

Chapter Thirteen

Phase Three: The Dialogue to Understanding

"You've got to help us with this, Paul," Chet said to me. "No matter how hard we try, we can't seem to talk too long about our problems before we get into a fight. Peggy starts it. She gets sarcastic—you know how she can get this snotty tone of voice—and then I get angry."

"If I get sarcastic," Peggy chimed in, "it's because you bring up the same old crap time and again. I'm tired of it."

"See what I mean about the tone of her voice?" Chet complained, eager for me to chastise his wife.

"Wait a minute," I said, feeling a bit like a camp counselor trying to break up a fight. "You each blame one another for turning a discussion into an argument, but what just happened here? Chet, you sure know how to push Peggy's buttons. What did you just do that might have helped her decide to refer to your concerns as 'crap'?"

"Well, I guess I got her going by saying she has a

snotty tone of voice and by accusing her of starting all the fights," Chet admitted. Peggy nodded her head in vigorous approval.

"See, it was his fault," Peggy charged.

"Hold on, Peg," I said. "You know how to push Chet's buttons, too. What did you do that helped Chet to decide to criticize your tone of voice?"

She sighed in frustration. "On the way here, I told him he was wasting his time coming to see you because he never listens to what you say. He hates it when I accuse him of being insincere."

Chet gave me a knowing glance.

"Chet, did you do anything on the way here that may have prompted Peg to question your sincerity?" I probed.

"Yeah," he said, with a provocative smile. "I saw this gorgeous woman while we were driving, so I stared at her. Gave her the once-over. Peg gets jealous when I do that."

I looked at Peg, and she guessed what I was about to say. "You want to know if I did anything that made Chet want to make me jealous, right?" she asked. "I don't think he liked it when I told him he was too fat."

"Let me stop the questioning here," I said. "Do you two see what I'm getting at? Do you understand how you each are responsible for turning your discussions into fights and how you each like to blame the other for it? You both know too well how to provoke one another. Do you want to learn to stop doing that and have a constructive dialogue, or would you prefer I keep my nose out of your business?"

It can be hard to hang in there and talk with your spouse about all that needs fixing in the relationship.

Your task at this third phase in the process of reconciliation and forgiveness is to undertake a dialogue with your husband or wife, a dialogue where a constructive exchange of personal thoughts and feelings occurs.

You've already either admitted your guilt and apologized or confronted your spouse with your hurt and angry feelings. Now you need to go one step further and discuss your concerns more fully. And you need to take time to hear what your spouse has to say. Phase Three is a natural extension of Phase Two. I chose to artificially separate them because distinctive complications arise at each phase. Many people, for example, can begin expressing their feelings as indicated in Phase Two, but they stop there. They find it too hard to carry on a more extensive dialogue as Phase Three requires.

An important reason for having a dialogue is to try to gain a better understanding of how and why the hurts came about. *You may not be able to reach a full understanding, however.* And any understanding you do reach will not change the facts of what happened. Ideally, you will come away with a broader, more helpful perspective. The better you understand yourself and your spouse, the more you'll be able to contend with problems in the relationship.

Keep in mind that the dialogue to understanding is not a search for excuses. You do not forgive because you discover "reasons" for what happened. You forgive because you decide it is time to let go of the bitterness and guilt. It is helpful when you learn some of the factors that contributed to the problems in the relationship, because you then have a clearer sense of what needs to be changed so the same problems don't arise again. But forgiveness must be decided on, whether you know all the "reasons" or not.

When you stay in a dialogue, you increase the probability that your resentment and guilt will be resolved (although such feelings tend to increase before they diminish). It is when you stop short in the dialogue that those feelings, or their remnants, remain. You then become uneasy in the relationship, often wondering how and when you'll be hurt next.

This third phase may well be the most difficult for you. While your tasks in the first two phases were to sort out and express your feelings, now you must be even more intimate with someone who might be more defensive than you. Some people get hurt and angry after being confronted, no matter how legitimate the complaint.

The dialogue is never predictable. It can be brief or long and involved, perhaps drawn out over many exchanges before there is some kind of resolution. Your spouse may tell you things you aren't prepared to hear.

It is common for the person who is confronting to receive a barrage of accusations in return. Both sides can feel betrayed and misunderstood. Your apologies may not be accepted, at least not right away. Out of anger or fear, either side can walk away and forget the whole relationship.

Yet, by staying with the dialogue until you reach an understanding, you will discover that there was more going on with each of you than you knew. And you may rediscover just how much you mean to each other.

THE SEARCH FOR SOME MEANING

There are many questions that, when answered, will help you both to find some meaning behind the hurtful acts:

- Just what was it that happened to bring about the estrangement?

- Was it one isolated act of betrayal, or was there a series of hurts on both sides?
- What was accomplished as a result of the acts? Vengeance? Self-protection? Selfishness? Control? Helpfulness?
- What was the felt pain, and what gave it its sting? Was it a shattered trust? A loss of personal esteem? Was it the realization that once again you used poor judgment and set yourself up to be hurt?
- Did you feel abandoned? Taken advantage of? Did you doubt your worth? Did you feel a loss of control over matters? Did you feel helpless? Humiliated? Or ashamed?
- Could you have been overreacting to the hurt because it connected with other past hurts that you haven't yet resolved?
- What have been some of the struggles that the person who hurt you has had to endure?

The reason for looking at these areas is to gain a better understanding of your vulnerabilities and your partner's. If you don't know your weaknesses, then you can't accept them, change them, or protect them very well. If you don't know your spouse's vulnerabilities, then you won't fully appreciate the meaning behind some of his or her actions.

It is also useful to determine whether a hurtful act nevertheless had a positive effect. It may seem strange at first, but family therapy recognizes that some actions, even hurtful, objectionable actions, serve a noble purpose. A troublemaking son, for example, not only can cause marital problems but can *distract* the couple from fighting. A woman with low sexual desire may be at times protecting her husband from his fears of intimacy. An irresponsible twenty-five-year-old, still living at home, may provide his parents with the feeling of still being needed. One woman, kicked out of her home at age eighteen, vowed never to do that to her children. Her thirty-year-old, drug-abusing daughter still lives with her, even though the home is always in chaos. Just who is helping whom in that family? Is the father passive and unassertive because he is a "wimp" or because he knows how important it is to his wife to do things differently from the way her parents did things? The longer a problem remains unchanged, the more likely it is that the problem may be serving a noble function for someone in the family.

The search for meaning by way of a dialogue is not an inquisition. No one is the interrogator, ready to condemn and pass judgment. The dialogue isn't undertaken with a haughty or belligerent attitude or to prove that you are right and the other person is wrong. It is a dialogue done to bring about reparation and healing. It is a dialogue where the real value of the relationship is not pushed aside temporarily, but revealed.

Some people search for meaning with the question, "How could you have done that *to me?*" That question can be a trap because the person asking it is taking matters too personally. In effect, the person is really saying, "If you loved me, you wouldn't have done what you did." The trap, of course, is that there often is no way to respond to such a question or comment without appearing, at worst, as if you do not love the person you hurt. There then may be no further search for meaning, or attempt at reconciliation, because it is believed that true love is absent.

Some people enter into a dialogue in order to prove that they (or even the other person) are innocent. They look for reasonable excuses to explain away the hurtful acts. Such people are misguided. It is rare that hurtful acts come about by accident. We are all very human and fall prey to our jealousies, weaknesses, and insecurities. But that doesn't make us innocent. The person who hurt you probably did so with some intent. Accept that. Now comes the real work of trying to be forgiving.

MAKING A PLAN OF ACTION

In your dialogue with your spouse, it is helpful and often necessary to come up with a plan of action designed to reduce the likelihood of the same problems recurring. The plan you make is based on your level of understanding of the problems.

In a plan of action, it is usually not enough to vow, "I will never betray you like that again," or, "I will stop being hurtful and inconsiderate." Such promises are well and good. But if you don't address some of the underlying reasons why you were inconsiderate to begin with, your plan may fall short.

A good plan of action not only reduces or eliminates problem behavior, but increases desirable behavior. That is the most important ingredient in the plan. For example, if you plan to reduce the amount of criticizing you do, it is a good idea to increase the amount of praising you do. If you vow to not take your spouse for granted, why not at the same time agree to go on more frequent trips together, without the children?

Kurt and Christine argued about disciplining Kurt's children. Kurt felt that Christine, who was the children's adoptive mother, was too strict. Kurt would interrupt her disciplinary efforts to "set her straight." Unfortunately, such attempts to solve the problem only perpetuated it. The children, aware that

Kurt was scrutinizing the situation, picked up on the tension between the two parents and acted out even more. Thus, they actually reinforced Kurt's tendency to interfere. And Christine, anxious and angry at being judged by Kurt, had even less patience with the children, which again reinforced Kurt's behavior. Their plan of action was this: Under no circumstances would Kurt interfere with Christine's discipline efforts. And each of them would tell each other what he or she liked about how the other one disciplined the children.

Mort and Cindy had parent problems. Specifically, Cindy felt obliged to visit her parents once a month but always hated it. She was never herself in their presence and tended to be irritable and insensitive to Mort on those days. He'd react angrily and claim he wasn't going with her to visit her parents. She'd accuse him of disliking her parents and would refuse to go without him.

Their plan of action was for Cindy to desensitize herself to the anxiety of being with her parents by calling and visiting them more often but for less time. She was to visit during the week, sometimes with Mort and sometimes without. Her goal was to learn to reduce her irritability when with them. And Mort was to agree not to condemn her for being irritable when she was with her parents, knowing that it takes time to accomplish such a goal.

The Dialogue to Understanding Involves Listening

During the dialogue, you must be able to truly listen to all that is being communicated if you are to be more understanding of yourself and the other person. Listening requires that for a short time you put aside your feelings about the matter at hand and concern yourself instead with the thoughts and feelings of the other person. You may disagree with or dislike what you hear, but that isn't the concern at this time. The concern is not to defend yourself, to be right, or to be understood. It is to listen fully to what the other person has to say (and how it is said) so that you can understand.

When you actively listen, you demonstrate that you care about what is being told to you. You then make it easier for the other person to say all that is important to say. And you improve your chances of having the other person's attention when it is your turn to speak.

When you feel as if the dialogue is getting nowhere, you would do well to spend more time listening.

One frustrated husband interrupted his wife by saying incredulously, "How could you say that?!" The point was not how his wife could say such a thing but that she indeed had said it. Wrong or right, the woman expressed her feelings, and her husband went quickly from listening to judging and self-defense.

It is tempting to stray from the task of listening, but you must not. You won't be able to listen well if you are rehearsing your reply while your spouse is still talking. Though you may be eager to state your feelings, you must allow time to hear what is being told to you, or else you will proceed with the added burden of your ignorance.

Understanding Is Not Always Logical

If you enter into a dialogue expecting that logic will resolve matters, you will be sorely disappointed. Strong emotions prompt people to behave in ways that are not always practical, and you must contend with the emotional side to the problem.

The person who grips onto logic may often end up

trying to persuade the other person not to feel so hurt because there are logical explanations for why things happened. ("Don't be so upset, honey. Even though I'm yelling at you, it's not you I'm mad at. It's my boss.") That is like telling someone you just hit with your car, "Don't feel hurt; it was just an accident."

When you only try to make logical sense out of why you were hurtful, you end up discounting the other person's feelings. You may use sentences that begin with the injunction "You should . . ." as you try to instruct the other person on the illogic of his or her ways. And if you are the guilty party, sooner or later you'll have to admit that you did what you did out of fear or some personal weakness and that's all. It is not your mother's fault, your spouse's fault, or anyone's fault but your own. By appealing to logic you are just trying to not be held accountable.

But you are accountable (not bad, not unlovable . . .). Express your sorrow for what you did, and begin healing the relationship.

Understanding Requires Patience

To achieve understanding, you need to be patient with yourself and the other person in your dialogue. You won't resolve matters quickly.

When you are patient, you are not merely tolerant of a long wait. Patience comes from the security of investing your energy into an endeavor that feels right. You have a peace of mind that comes from knowing you are moving in the right direction.

When you doubt that you are in the right place, it's hard to feel patient. You want the whole thing to be over with so you can see where you stand. But you can't rush through the dialogue to understanding.

When you are patient, you're free to experience each moment. You are free to listen and therefore take on a more productive role in the dialogue process.

When you are impatient, you focus on what may be up ahead, failing to take in what is happening now. You can't listen well, which creates opportunities for greater misunderstanding. Misunderstanding leads to more impatience.

If you find you are impatient in the dialogue, check to see if you've been taking what is being said too personally. When you take things too personally, you are still angry and hurting from some past event. But you held back from fully dealing with that old hurt. Now it's getting to you, making you feel uneasy and on guard, perhaps ashamed. That anxiety leads to impatience.

If you find that you are impatient in the dialogue process, say so. The other person's frustration with your impatience may be eased when you are up-front about it. And maybe the two of you have gone off track in your discussion so there is good reason to feel impatient. In any event, keep talking and listening even if you can't get a handle on why you are impatient. You'll learn soon enough what it is all about, if it is important.

Understanding Is Incomplete

You probably will never fully understand why events happened the way they did. If you enter into the dialogue with the full intention of extracting every bit of the "truth," you will trip yourself up. You'll always feel frustrated and suspicious so long as you haven't "gotten to the bottom of this." You will be limited in your understanding due to whatever psychological defenses are distorting your perceptions. You'll be limited by the extent of your knowledge of human nature and by what your spouse is able to reveal to you.

Seek to understand all you can at a given time, and

then move ahead. If you missed something that really was important, it will be revealed later.

When you feel less angry and frightened, that is a good indication that your level of understanding is adequate. If you have made a plan of action that appears reasonable and workable, then you have understood much.

If you still want to understand more, then get on with the relationship. Don't leave it in neutral. You'll learn more by living and experiencing the relationship than you will just by talking about it.

Understanding Leads to Acceptance

The more you understand your shortcomings and those of the other person, the greater the likelihood you will be more accepting of each other. It is ignorance and denial of one's own faults that make it hard to accept the faults of others. The inability to view things from the other person's perspective also impedes your ability to be accepting.

Victoria believed herself to be sensitive to the feelings of her husband, Michael. She disliked the way he disciplined their son and regarded Michael as being too critical and "nitpicky" when it came to parenting. Yet, she believed she dealt with Michael on that issue with honesty and a consideration for his feelings.

It was only after she experienced herself lecturing to Michael about his critical style with their son that she moved to a deeper awareness of herself and her husband. She realized how easy it was to be both critical and yet unaware of how she was coming across to others. She began to wonder if her frustration with Michael paralleled his frustration with their son. For the first time, she empathized with Michael. As she became more accepting of him, the two of them had a constructive dialogue on the parenting issue.

Acceptance is a confirmation of humanness. It is a recognition of the imperfections we all possess. You can be accepting of another and still want changes to be made. To be accepting doesn't mean you must tolerate another's actions. It is a willingness to see things as they really are (which usually means a realistic awareness of that other person's endearing qualities, too).

You can be more accepting of the realities of your situation. Taking the time to talk with the other person can help bring that about. The person who is accepting of reality truly understands that while all is not perfect, all is not lost.

WHEN THE DIALOGUE BREAKS DOWN

When a dialogue breaks down, restarting it is accomplished by focusing on one of three areas. First, the dialogue broke down because the couple simply didn't know how to keep it from stalling out or how to begin it again. Second, it broke down because each person's feelings about the controversial issue were more mixed than they believed. Third, it broke down because *emotional triangles* were complicating matters.

How to Begin Again

The simple truth: It takes two of you to turn the dialogue into a mess, but it only takes one of you to begin putting the dialogue back on track. It takes two of you to keep it there.

Hostile accusations, defensiveness, going off on tangents, and an unwillingness to listen can turn a dialogue into an escalating exchange of verbal gunfire.

"Now isn't the time to talk about it, Roger. Can't you see I've got my hands full with the kids?"

"Now is never the time, Eileen. When was the last time you made room for me? I swear, sometimes you disgust me the way you only think about yourself."

"Why the hell should I make room for you, anyway?" Eileen shot back. "What have you done for me? Not a damn thing, and that goes for the bedroom, too."

"That's right, Eileen, always bring that up," Roger shouted. "Listen, if you want me out of the house, just say so. But don't expect me back."

Roger and Eileen were off and running. That kind of escalating, poisonous conversation is what W. Robert Beavers, a noted family therapist, refers to as a "spin-out." It can be most difficult to stop, once it gets going. When that happens, a helpful technique recommended by Beavers is to ask yourself these questions:

• What am I trying to do?
• How am I trying to do it?

If you are honest with yourself, you will see that most often you are really trying to understand or be understood. But the way that you are doing it is counterproductive.

If what you are really trying to do is to be vengeful, put an end to the dialogue, or give the *appearance* that you are trying to work on the problems, then you are doing a good job by "spinning out."

Spin-outs are exhausting, dismaying, and damaging. But they don't have to continue. First, you must recognize when they are happening. Couples often get caught up in them without really being conscious of them. You must *want* to notice when it happens. One of you then, at least, can take responsibility for your own actions and choose to not escalate a spin-out once it gets going. Will that someone be you?

If you and your partner are unable to catch yourselves in a spin-out despite efforts to be more self-
aware, do the following exercise: Plan, with your
partner, to get caught up in a hostile spin-out. In
other words, make a conscious effort to have a deadly
argument. Don't try to be calm, sensitive, or understanding. As crazy as it seems, you won't be able to do
this task more than a few times without becoming
acutely aware of how the spin-outs get started. Then
the next time a real argument happens, you'll be
conscious of any spin-out the moment it occurs.

There is another vital question to ask yourself
when you don't like what your spouse just told you
and the dialogue is beginning to break down: *Is there
any merit at all to what was just told to me?*

So often, the legitimate aspects of what your spouse
has to say go unexamined because you're angry with
how he or she said it. How it was said is one issue.
What was said is an entirely different, *but relevant*,
matter. Probably your spouse exaggerated your faults
and minimized his or her own, but *is there any merit at
all* to what he or she told you?

When spin-outs happen, when the dialogue breaks
down, both of you are avoiding some truths about
yourselves.

But what if one of you wants to talk about your
problems, and the other one doesn't? How do you
enter into a dialogue with someone who hides from
you or refuses to have a conversation?

There are two approaches. First, you must make a
concerted effort to talk with your spouse and keep
trying. Don't let the other person's anger or fear be
your excuse to give up something that is important to
you. *But don't be pushy.* Give your spouse time to gear
up for a talk, but don't pursue forever.

Frequently, couples get into a subtle game where

one keeps pursuing and the other distances. "I keep after him to just talk to me, to open up, for God's sake. But he's a goddamned closed book!" a wife says with exasperation.

"What can I say except she's all over me? She never leaves me alone to think or relax. Yes, I know I back away from her, but if I gave in to her, I'd never have space for myself," the husband responds.

Don't keep pursuing a distancer. If you've made it clear that talking about the problem is important to you, *and if you've left the door open*, stop pursuing and get on with other matters. If the other person has absolutely no interest in talking with you, stopping your pursuit won't make a difference. But if you and the other person were caught up in an unconscious game of "catch me if you can," the distancer may get interested in a dialogue once you stop pursuing.

The second approach is a natural extension of the first. If you've kept the door open for a dialogue but still your spouse hasn't come knocking, you might want to say to your spouse that you think it's important to do exactly what he or she is doing. Say that you want your spouse to stay distant, not because you don't want him or her close, but because you realize that since your spouse has kept distant for so long, it must be very important to him or her to be that way. Explain that you don't like it but that it's not your place to change it. Say that, while your door is open, you now realize that you have other things to do with your time besides waiting for him or her.

This approach may sound silly or manipulative, but it is worth considering. However, you must be sincere. You should not merely *act* sincere; you must *be* sincere. And that includes sincerity in your statement that it really must be important for him or her to keep at a distance. The truth is that it is indeed very important for your spouse to behave the way he or she does. Don't consider doing it unless you are absolutely certain that you would tolerate your spouse's distancing from you. Don't consider doing it unless you are absolutely certain you will build up other areas of your life to make up for what you are missing. This is no game.

As long as you are sincere, you really can't lose. If your partner has mixed feelings about talking through problems with you, this stance will probably provoke him or her to take you more seriously. Thus, your spouse will likely stop distancing from you and begin approaching you. On the other hand, if your spouse maintains a psychological (or physical) distance from you, he or she is now doing it at your request and with your blessing. That will take some of the sting out of it for you.

An example will clarify this approach. Angela came to me in despair over her husband's behavior. Married for seven years and still living in an apartment in his parents' house with their three children, Angela was afraid that Doug was having an affair. Doug was going out nights without her and sometimes wouldn't return for a day or two after. Whenever she asked him where he had gone, he'd respond with a curt, "Mind your own business." When she argued with him about his behavior, he'd accuse her of trying to control him, "just like my mother," and then stay out even later that evening.

Angela had tried everything, from being patient and understanding to confronting him and challenging him. Nothing worked.

What was important here, too, was that Angela truly believed her husband was troubled by many day-to-day stresses. She knew he was overworked. She knew he wasn't appreciated by his employer even though he worked hard. She knew he received only intrusions and criticism from his parents, who called frequently to check up on their "irresponsible" son. She knew he loved his children, although he tended to be much too strict with them, almost as if he were making up for his absences by being the kind of father he thought he was supposed to be, that is, a disciplinarian.

"So what usually happens on nights when you think he's planning to go out?" I asked her.

"Sometimes I ask him when he'll be back; sometimes I yell at him; sometimes I ignore him and feel hurt. It doesn't matter, though. He usually yells at me, accuses me of being controlling and inconsiderate, and then he leaves." She appeared downcast.

I explained the procedure to her whereby she should tell Doug to spend more time away from home. Her initial reaction was typical. "You're kidding! Why would I want to do a thing like that?"

"Well, one good reason is that everything else you've done hasn't worked. A more important reason is that you've admitted how in one way you feel sorry for him. You believe he is under stress and does deserve some free time. He thinks you're being controlling and uncaring. If you told him it was important to you that he spend more time away from home to relax, and you were sincere about it, he'd have to regard you as being more considerate, right? You can tell him the truth. Tell him that you wish he would spend more time at home and that you worry he is having an affair, but that he must make up his own mind. Tell him you'd worry that he'd resent you if he stayed home more often."

Angela did as I recommended. The first week, Doug went out as usual, but there were no arguments. In fact, he was stunned and perplexed by her change of heart. The next week, he stayed home all but one night. And that night he came home early. On week three, Doug made weekend reservations at a resort for Angela and himself. And in between bouts of romance, they talked much more openly about their relationship than they had ever done before.

It can be frustrating and painful if you want more intimacy with your spouse and he or she wants more distance. Paradoxically, if you let your spouse know what you'd like to happen but still *lovingly* give your spouse what he or she is asking (that is, don't give your spouse what he or she wants with an "I'm fed up" attitude), the likelihood is that your spouse will respond to your needs.

Finally, keep these thoughts in mind as you prepare to have a dialogue with your spouse or some other person:

- Ninety to 95 percent of the time, people are doing the best that they can. Really.
- Your spouse has basically the same needs as you: to love and be loved, to feel good about oneself, and to have some mastery in life. Most people like to be appreciated, too.
- Hurtful acts against you, or withdrawal from you, is a form of protection for the other person. For some reason, your spouse is feeling threatened by talking to you. Probably, being pushy won't work. Neither will angrily giving your spouse what he or she *says* is wanted.
- If you find yourself yelling and accusing, you've missed something. The other person is feeling a certain way, but you don't understand it yet. You are also "talking down" to that person, treating him or her like a child. If you want a healthy, adult relationship, talk as an adult.
- It is better to talk more about what you need and

are afraid of than about what your spouse "should do."

- Sometimes when people are angry, they are also feeling helpless. Sometimes when people feel help-less, they'll do *anything* to feel more in charge again.
- If you already realize that the other person's bad qualities are just like your mother's or your father's or those of some other important person in your life, ask yourself if you see that person as unique. The dialogue to understanding is an opportunity to give up some of the fixed, rigid perceptions you may have about others. In all likelihood, you see the other person in only one or two dimensions. But the person is three-dimensional, full of facets you have yet to appreciate.
- Don't try to change the other person. Take respon-sibility only for yourself.

Analyzing Mixed Feelings

"You've never given your father a chance to redeem himself, Brian," Paula accused her son. "He hasn't had a drink in twenty years, but you still hold his drinking against him. You always have."

"You don't even want to consider my feelings on this," Brian answered hotly. "You always stand up for him and tell me I'm too unforgiving. Dad was brutal in those days, but you don't want to look at that. You want to pretend he was a victim."

"He hasn't treated me badly in quite some time," Paula said defensively. "He has his good side, but you don't want to see it."

Paula and her son had fought about this issue for most of their adult lives. Paula was also furious with Brian because she always tended to be the one who would drop everything and help her now-disabled husband when he needed assistance. "Brian never lends a hand. It's always up to me," Paula said with disgust.

Why is their battle still raging? What keeps them from seeing some merit in the other's position? While there are perhaps numerous good answers to those questions, a real trouble spot for Paula and Brian has to do with the notion of *ambivalence*, the experience of having strong mixed feelings about an issue.

In truth, Paula and Brian each have ambivalent feelings about the man. Paula is aware of her positive feelings, but she experiences the negative feelings not as coming from within her but from without: that is, as coming solely from Brian. She doesn't hate her husband; Brian does. Or so she believes. Brian, on the other hand, is aware of his negative feelings toward his father but experiences the positive feelings not as coming from within him but from Paula.

Together, Paula and Brian can avoid dealing with their personal mixed feelings by fighting each other. As long as she battles with Brian instead of with herself, Paula never has to contend with the fact that she too feels anger toward her husband. Brian never has to contend with the fact that, despite his fury, he loves his father and wants to be loved. That would be too difficult to sort out for himself. Instead, his positive feelings are played up by Paula.

And Paula and Brian reinforce each other's positions. When Paula puts her husband on a pedestal, Brian is compelled to knock him off. When Brian condemns his father, Paula is compelled to exonerate the man. The never-ending battle between them masks what is really a battle within each of them.

The solution to such a problem is for each one to recognize and own his or her personal feelings. Then each must resolve the inner ambivalence in some way, taking responsibility for the consequences.

Thus, Paula must acknowledge that she too was hurt by her husband and accept that. Pretending is not the solution. She can't let go of the hurt until she at least acknowledges it. Then she must decide whether she wants to talk to her husband and settle her feelings about him. Her dedication to him over the years was probably overdone. In part she may have compensated for Brian's underinvolvement. But she also was compensating for her bitterness toward her husband, which she didn't consciously acknowledge but which she felt guilty about anyway.

Brian has to search his feelings and find the love he holds for his father. One way to begin is to spend time with his father. Learn about the man and his younger days. How did he feel about *his* father? Then Brian must reconcile his feelings. He must take responsibility for the fact that he has distanced himself over the years from his father, in large part because he was denying his feelings of love for the man.

Another common example of how ambivalence gets played out *between* people instead of *within* is demonstrated when parents argue about how to discipline a problem child. If the child's problem is chronic, usually one parent becomes harsh while the other protects the child somewhat. Inwardly, each parent fears one day being criticized for being an inadequate or bad parent. Both parents doubt their abilities. But rather than work on their own insecurities, they project their doubts onto their spouse. The parents then blame one another for the child's behavior problems, with accusations that the other parent is either too strict or too lenient.

Analyzing Emotional Triangles

It's a fact: when the tension between two people gets

too high and they fear matters will get out of hand if toxic issues are pursued, a third party (either a person or an issue) enters the situation to distract, defocus, and defuse the potentially explosive situation. The appearance of this third person creates an emotional triangle. The result is that problems don't get resolved, they just get reshelved, put on hold because at least one of the two people loses the motivation to focus on the real problems between them.

The emotional triangles that develop with a warring or quietly dissatisfied couple typically fall into one of the following categories:

- One spouse has an affair. Finding a warm, passionate confidante diminishes both marital frustration and the motivation to resolve marital problems. The marriage stabilizes at a level that isn't very good but isn't very bad either.
- One spouse gets overinvolved with the children, or one child acts out in a way that forces parental attention onto that child and away from the marital distress.
- One spouse gets overinvolved with work (or a cause such as Alcoholics Anonymous).
- One spouse spends more time with his or her parents, either complaining about the marriage or assisting the parents through their own current crises.

Alyssa, twenty, was an only child. An older brother died at birth. Overprotected as a child, she met and married Phil, a successful businessman set in his ways. He was thirty.

To Alyssa, Phil was strong, decisive, and warm. To Phil, Alyssa was sweet, outgoing, and somehow pleasingly fragile. To Alyssa's parents, Phil was their son resurrected. Life was wonderful for six months. Then

Alyssa viewed Phil's decisiveness and strength as a tightening vise that restricted her freedom. She felt controlled. And Phil seemed to turn his warmth on and off like a faucet. He was warm when he was in charge and cold when Alyssa stood her ground on issues.

To Phil, Alyssa's outgoingness had transformed into more frequent evenings out with her friends, which he interpreted as rejection of him and a desire for more excitement in her life. "Now she insists we learn how to ski," Phil lamented. "I hate skiing. When is she going to grow up?"

When they first came to see me after two years of marriage, their beliefs about each other had hardened. Both said that the other person was no longer the person they married. Both said the other had to change. They had tried everything to improve their marriage. Nothing worked. What they didn't realize was that emotional triangles had formed which kept them stuck. What were those triangles?

- *Triangle One:* Phil, Alyssa, Alyssa's parents. As problems mounted in the marriage, Alyssa naturally sought advice from her parents. Unfortunately, Alyssa invested more energy talking to her parents *about* Phil than she invested in talking *with* Phil. Talking with them, over time, gave her the feeling that she was "working" on her problems when in fact she was avoiding dealing with Phil. Phil sometimes resented his in-laws' "intrusions," but at other times he welcomed them. In truth, Phil was reluctant to face some of his own insecurities and found it easier to blame the marital "stuckness" on his in-laws than on anything to do with himself.
- *Triangle Two:* Alyssa, her mother, her father. Al-

though it was rarely admitted, let alone discussed, Alyssa's parents' marriage was always troubled. Her father was demanding and harsh. Her mother deferred to him but then took her anger out by ignoring him and getting overinvolved with Alyssa. Alyssa was the glue that kept them together. When she married Phil, her parents were left without the focus they needed to stabilize their marriage. By going to her parents for advice, Alyssa was once again providing them with the opportunity to be distracted from their own problems.

- *Triangle Three:* Phil, Alyssa, Phil's family. As close as Alyssa's family is, Phil's family is distant. While his father tried to hold the reins of power in the household by being cold and dictatorial, members learned to get closeness and satisfaction from people and events outside the family circle. Phil was both attracted and repelled by Alyssa's close involvement with her family. At one level he wanted to share in the closeness. At another level, he felt smothered and out of control by it. By staying married, he had the closeness he yearned for. But by having marital problems, he had the distance he needed. To "work" on the problems in any meaningful way risked losing the perfect balance established.

By becoming aware of the existence of the emotional triangles, Phil and Alyssa completed the first step in unfreezing their marriage. They then allowed themselves to have a dialogue with each other that was rarely interrupted by the force of those emotional triangles. It was not easy at all. But they persevered. And they were willing to take an honest look at their own insecurities that fed the emotion in those triangles.

FINAL GUIDING PRINCIPLES

If you put them into action, three key principles will create a positive atmosphere for a constructive, healthy, and loving dialogue.

Principle 1: Allow Yourself to Become a Nonanxious Presence

While you probably can never be completely free of anxiety during a dialogue, the less anxious you can be, the better. Of course, from time to time you will be anxious, and it is important to determine what that anxiety is about. As stated before, anxiety is a signal to you that something important is being threatened. Don't pretend you aren't anxious when you are. If you face your anxiety and deal with it directly, you will reduce or eliminate it.

The less anxious you are, the less defensive you'll become when your partner says things you don't like.

The less anxious you are, the less likely you are to say or do something hurtful during the dialogue.

Principle 2: Allow Emotional Reactivity in Your Spouse

Sometimes your spouse will shoot first and ask questions later. You may be verbally attacked during the dialogue. Your spouse may react hotly to things you have to say. Don't tolerate abuse, but at the same time it is important to give your spouse some room to maneuver. If you quickly take offense at his or her emotional reactivity, you'll end up arguing about *that* and will avoid more relevant issues.

As you become less anxious and allow for reactivity in your spouse, the initial reaction might be an escalation in his or her reactivity. Expect it. Plan on it (see Chapter 10). Devise ways to cope with it when it happens. If it doesn't occur, great. But the longer you've had problems between you, and the more frequently the two of you have exchanged verbal gunfire in the past, the greater the likelihood that an escalation will occur.

Principle 3: Extend Caring

Every opportunity you have to extend caring, do so. Don't be sickly sweet. Don't be patronizing. Just be aware of the countless times during the dialogue when you can show caring, and then do it. Apologize when you say something out of line. Hear your spouse out when you feel like interrupting. Let your spouse know your understanding of what he or she has told you so that he or she is aware you've listened. Point out what your spouse is doing that you appreciate. Give him or her the benefit of the doubt. Allow some freedom to make mistakes during the dialogue. End the discussion on a positive note. Emphasize what was helpful about the dialogue; deemphasize what you didn't like.

Some people feel that to extend such caring is to overlook the problems or the negative side of what is happening. That is true. However, without such caring, people tend to overlook the good things that are happening. They take for granted anything kind or considerate and home in on anything unkind or inconsiderate. Is that fair? Of course not.

Hopefully, you and your partner can get to a point where you don't have to overlook anything, good or bad, in the dialogue. But right now, it may be too easy for the dialogue to break down. You want to avoid that. If you are going to overemphasize aspects of the dialogue, why not overemphasize the positive? It really won't hurt and can only help.

Before proceeding with Phase Four, consider the following questions:

- Do you feel understood by your spouse?
- Does your spouse feel that you understand him or her?
- Are you able to focus more on what you need to do to improve the relationship rather than what the other person needs to do? Can your partner do the same?
- Do you recognize at least one important issue about which your fights reflect, in part, a conflict within yourself?
- Have you identified some emotional triangles that are keeping your marriage stuck?
- Have you made a plan of action that will diminish the likelihood that the same problems will recur?
- Will you allow for emotional reactivity in your spouse during the dialogue and increase the amount of caring that you show?

The dialogue to understanding is a crucial but often cumbersome phase in the forgiveness process. It requires time, patience, self-acceptance, and a willingness to listen. Now it is time to experience what you've wanted to experience all along: the healing of your relationship; a new, reinvented relationship; and the resolution of your pain by finding forgiveness and the love that sprays from its wake.

Chapter Fourteen

Phase Four: To Forgive and Make Reparation

"I was expecting that by the time we got this far in working out our problems, I could forgive him as easily as I slip on my coat," one woman said about her husband. "But it isn't quite like that. I'm still a little hurt. I still feel angry, at least somewhat. But what else is there to do now? Fight? Stay miserable? No. There is more for us than just that."

"Now I know what you mean when you say that forgiveness is a decision, that it doesn't just happen. I guess I was really hoping that you'd be able to *make* me be forgiving. I can see now that even though I'm not as hurt as I was, I still have to make a choice about whether or not to be forgiving. You don't make it easy on me, do you?"

There comes a time when you must forgive or be forgiven if you are to be reunited with the person you are estranged from. Even if the relationship cannot be

243

saved, you need to find forgiveness so you can be released from your pain of guilt or resentment.

Yet perhaps you don't fully understand why the hurts happened. Perhaps you are uncertain whether you'll be hurt again. All you know is that your desire to be reconciled is strong. You've confessed and felt remorse for any pain you've caused. You have confronted the other person about hurts against you. You have discussed the fears and concerns you each have, so as to understand each other better. And you've even made a plan to help reduce the likelihood of future acts of disloyalty or betrayal.

Your anger at having been hurt is lessened, although it hasn't been freed. You must now forgive the person who hurt you. And if you were hurtful, you must forgive yourself, too.

Your ability to forgive is a human quality, as human as your ability to cause pain. But as you now understand from reading this book, forgiveness is not always a simple act. It has at its source all of the human yearnings and fears, glories and frailties, passions and promises that well within everyone. It is made spectacular, however, when you become all that you are; when you accept your God-given gifts as challenges to soar, to experience life more fully, more vitally; when you realize that withholding forgiveness after a time is really your fear to be all of who you are. It is easier to stay hurt and angry, forever blaming and condemning, than to soar.

Yet, with all the power to heal possessed by the act of forgiveness, it remains a quiet and gentle act. You don't forgive in a boisterous manner that calls attention to yourself. You don't place yourself above the person you're forgiving. As great as the act of forgiveness is, its power to heal grows from your recognition that you are not above having to be forgiven.

Forgiveness is an act that comes more from love than from fear. Although fear is often present, it is secondary to the love you feel for the other person. Forgiveness stems from your deep understanding that the person you are estranged from is to be loved and accepted in spite of weaknesses. Especially if that person is yourself.

Forgiveness is the act that cleanses and unites. It asks the one forgiven to abandon the belief that he or she is unlovable.

WELCOMING FORGIVENESS

Some people believe that forgiveness must flow naturally and warmly from you, that to be genuine, it must be an effortless and instinctive next step. If you can welcome forgiveness with such grace, then you have accomplished much. But for most of us, forgiveness is found not by taking one final step, but by making one final, awkward leap.

If forgiveness is anything, it is a giant leap of faith. It is a decision to believe the best about people, and it is an extension of your love. It is a willingness to trust when that trust was previously betrayed. You risk being hurt again in order to grow in a relationship that is important to you.

It is not unusual to welcome forgiveness with some degree of uncertainty and hesitation. On the other hand, the love, warmth, and trust you feel when you do forgive may be more than words could describe.

If you have gone through all the other phases of forgiveness and have noticed a definite lessening of your pain, and if you feel genuinely more accepting of the faults you each possess, then it is time to forgive (if you haven't already done so).

THE WORDS OF FORGIVENESS

Forgive, but not silently. Tell the person you love that you are offering forgiveness. What's the point of keeping quiet about it? Our worst fears are that we will be deemed unlovable and that any love we have found will be taken from us. Express your love by stating the words of forgiveness. Don't keep people guessing. "I forgive you" is as important a phrase as "I love you."

Of course, words aren't everything. You need to show that you have forgiven. You do that by demonstrating you are no longer suffering from the hurts against you. You show that you no longer cringe at the memory of what happened. You no longer approach the person you've forgiven with animosity or guardedness.

"Yes, I still remember how he betrayed me," one woman said of her husband, "but I no longer hold it against him. I don't throw the past in his face when I'm angry with him, either. And he sees that. It helped me to decide not to remind him of how he hurt me. He'd always react angrily when I'd remind him of that, and then he wouldn't believe me when I finally would forgive him. It's hard enough to forgive someone without that person doubting your sincerity. But when I stopped bringing up the past, he started to believe that I really was sincere after all."

Forgiveness, whether you offer it or receive it, spills over into all you do, filling in the nooks and crannies and all the hidden places in your life. The relationship is renewed, reinvented, revitalized. It is young again. It invigorates and frees you to be what you have wanted to be all along. Yourself.

FORGIVENESS IS RARELY
DONE PERFECTLY

Your effort to forgive will have flaws. Paul Tillich has written compellingly that only God can be truly forgiving, while we can only approximate forgiveness. Other philosophers and theologians point out that if we are to be forgiven by God, we must be forgiving of others first, implying that we do possess the ability to forgive. Whether or not you agree with the scholars who see true forgiveness as beyond our human reach, the effort to forgive can be a struggle—particularly when the hurts are deep.

However, if the human act of forgiveness is inadequate, it is not so in its purpose of reuniting the estranged. Neither is it inadequate in its power to heal and to nurture love.

As Chapter 1 discussed, the phases of forgiveness are not invariant. You don't necessarily forgive only after you've confronted the person who hurt you. *Sometimes you can feel genuinely forgiving before all the phases are completed.* After all, these phases are not *the* way to forgive, but *a* way.

On the other hand, if you need to repeat some of the phases before you feel ready to offer or accept forgiveness, that doesn't mean your efforts have been inadequate. It means you still need to come to terms with your feelings before the relationship can be reconciled or the pain resolved.

Understand that once you forgive, you may discover that you did so prematurely. Your anger may still be stinging. So you may have to offer forgiveness again later. That is not ideal, but it may happen that way.

Similarly, if someone who you've hurt forgives you but then still continues to act hurt, don't hold it against that person and accuse him or her of insincerity. Instead, go to that person and try to understand what hurts still remain. Forgive the person who is struggling to forgive you.

FORGIVING YOURSELF

You must be forgiving of yourself. If you can't, you will be limited in your ability to forgive others. You will either take offenses against you too personally and refuse to forgive, or you will forgive too quickly for fear of being abandoned.

To forgive yourself, you need to recognize your faults and weaknesses, accept yourself as worthwhile in spite of them, and feel remorseful that your shortcomings have brought pain. Your remorse should be sincere but not something you wallow in. You must also desire to learn new ways to handle some old problems. You must love yourself. It can be most helpful to have faith in an all-loving God, too. If God loves you, you must be pretty special.

If you slip up in any of these steps to self-forgiveness, you will falter when you try to forgive someone else.

You will know that you've forgiven yourself when you can be open to your faults without great fear or self-condemnation. You will know that you've forgiven yourself when you no longer punish yourself by making the same mistakes over and over. You will know that you've forgiven yourself when you can tolerate being alone, when you can find tranquility and enjoyment even when you are by yourself. You will know that you've forgiven yourself when you aren't afraid to ask questions or ask for help when you need it. People who must constantly prove their worth to themselves by always being knowledgeable in others' eyes are afraid of who they really are.

When you forgive yourself, you will be enthusiastic about making positive changes and taking positive risks. The fearful claim "I can't" reveals a belief that you aren't forgivable if you make mistakes.

We all need self-forgiveness. Perhaps the one thing we've all been guilty of at one time or another is to use the deep pain someone has caused us as the excuse not to accept responsibility for our problems. While we may not be responsible for a tragic past or for the way our parents treated us as children, we are responsible to do something constructive about our problems now.

Self-forgiveness is an act of love. It doesn't allow you to overlook mistakes but compels you to face them. The way to change for the better is to become all that you are, which is what forgiveness frees you to do; rather than behave in a manner that is not true to your best self, which is what failing to forgive forces you to do.

MAKING REPARATION

When you've betrayed someone and you seek forgiveness, you may wish to amend the relationship by somehow "making it up" to the person you hurt.

But is it essential that some act of reparation occur in order for forgiveness to happen? No. Is it ever possible to pay back whatever was taken by an act of betrayal? Probably not. It is difficult, if not impossible, to place a price on the other person's trust and esteem, both of which can be affected by an act of betrayal or disloyalty.

Then can an act of reparation ever have a beneficial effect? Yes. Reparation has its place in the forgiveness process nonetheless, although it is not a necessary condition for forgiveness to occur.

If you were the one who was hurt, you can't demand some form of reparation before you can offer forgiveness. "You owe me" is not an attitude that goes along with forgiveness. In the same way, you can't be expected to automatically forgive the person who hurt you just because that person made some reparation.

In its most sincere form, reparation is an act of love whereby you care enough about the feelings of the other person to want to heal what was broken by your actions. The desire to make reparation stems from your remorse. You feel bad about what you've done, and your love compels you to do something to ease the other person's pain.

Types of Reparation

There are many ways to make amends, some ways being more helpful than others. The best distinguishing feature between helpful and less helpful acts of reparation is this: When your act of reparation is helpful, you feel good about yourself and the relationship. When your act of reparation is not helpful, you feel apprehensive and doubtful.

Another distinction: Good reparative acts demonstrate your willingness to change for the better. They reveal a caring attitude on your part. Bad reparative acts convey your doubts and fears about changing. Feelings of care for the other person are then obscured by your fears. So, for example, if your relationship has been scarred by your selfishness and lack of consideration, make reparation by giving something of yourself to others with no expectation of return. If you've been too critical, listen and praise. If your jealousy of others' achievements caused you to be hurtful, start making repairs by giving credit where credit is due.

Stopping your hurtful ways and making positive changes are the best forms of reparation and healing. And if you think that changing one's behavior isn't a sufficient sacrifice, you are wrong. Changing one's style of behaving can be a difficult chore indeed.

If you perform some act of reparation only to appease the other person, while at the same time you fail to make any constructive changes in your style of relating, your act of reparation won't be helpful. You may *feel* less guilty, but over time your same ways of hurting others will reappear and your attempt at reparation will be viewed as insincere.

You may be the kind of person who believes that an act of reparation necessarily involves a sacrifice beyond the "mere" changing of one's ways. Such an attitude probably won't lead to complications if the sacrifice is a token of one's love and desire for the relationship to be healed. Consequently, a flower or a small gift may be token enough.

But you need to know that healing comes not from the gift or sacrifice, it comes from the motivation behind the sacrifice. If the prime motivation is fear or manipulation, then complications can arise.

A reparative act that is symbolic of the renewed growth in the relationship is also appropriate. As such, planting a tree or small garden in honor of a pledge of commitment to the other person can be a fitting representation of growth and love. One couple renewed their marriage vows as their way of pledging their newfound faith in each other.

One man had been living in a psychiatric institution for over two decades. He had no family to speak of and would probably never live his life without some supervision. He was troubled for weeks over the memory of something he had done as a child. Evidently, he once found a small, wounded bird and instead of trying to help it or at least let it be, he killed the bird. Now, over forty years later, he was frightened and remorseful over what he had done.

Instead of trying to convince him that he shouldn't feel so guilty, since he was just a boy when he killed the bird, a wise counselor advised him on what to do to alleviate his guilt. "Feed the birds," she told him. "Every day for a week, I want you to go outside and feed the birds."

It was a wonderful task. Not only did it involve a bit of sacrifice (which was necessary because the man could see no other way of relieving his guilt), it required him to change the way in which he related to birds. He was no longer a killer of birds but one who helped them to survive.

Some people believe that they can get away with almost any type of abuse as long as they make up for it later on. Dan was like that. He was an abusive father who would shower his children with gifts in order to feel less guilty for having beaten them.

"What was I supposed to do?" said Dan Jr., now twenty-four and still reeling from his father's cruelty. "He made me feel like I was supposed to feel sorry for him. As if my feelings didn't matter. Once I threw a stuffed bear he gave me right into the fireplace. He was furious, and he made me go after it. My hands didn't get burned that badly, but he made me hold the bear close to me, real tight. The warmth from the fur only added to the burning sensation in my hands. I was supposed to love that bear and tolerate the pain."

Obviously, and quite tragically, Dan's efforts at reparation were terribly hurtful. His main concern was not for his children, but himself. It is not that way with a genuine act of reparation.

Ultimately, forms of reparation are primarily manifestations of caring, and secondarily they are ways to alleviate guilt feelings. Some people need to make a sacrifice to help get rid of their guilt. But that alone, without an honest effort to change one's hurtful ways, will not heal the wounded relationship.

The Story of Donna

Donna was forty-two years old. She had never married but hoped that her boyfriend of five years would one day propose to her. She still lived in her parents' house with her mother. Her father had died fifteen years before. Donna had no friends. She said she was too shy. She dressed and thought conservatively.

She had spent her entire life acting cautiously, afraid to be assertive or to stand out in a crowd. She had a job that she hated but would never risk leaving it for the uncertainty of a different job. Rather than try to meet new people or develop hobbies and interests, she waited for her boyfriend to call. Sometimes he did. When she was with him, she would get bored and frustrated, but he was all she had. She got depressed frequently and felt guilty a great deal, although she wasn't always clear why. She was quick to judge others and often regarded people as selfish and inconsiderate.

She came to my office one afternoon and began to cry. An uncle had died over the weekend. She felt guilty for not having visited him when he was in the hospital, although she could have easily done so.

"Why didn't you visit him?" I asked.

"Because I wanted to spend time with Tony instead. He didn't want to go to the hospital with me, so neither of us went."

"Couldn't you have gone without Tony?"

"Yes," she answered and began to cry again. "I was just being lazy. If I ever knew he was going to die, I would have visited him," she explained.

Donna went on to say how her grief and guilt had caused her to lose her appetite, and she found it hard to get to sleep. She wanted to feel better but didn't know how. "He's dead now. There's nothing I can do to make it up to him."

That represented a typical problem for Donna. For a variety of reasons, she never gave much of herself. She was always too frightened to get involved with others. Even with her mother and Tony, she was not one to share her feelings. Intimacy scared her. Much of her free time was spent fantasizing. There was the fantasy that Tony would marry her. There was the fantasy that her job was adequate and better than anything else that might be available. There was the fantasy that if she kept to herself, she wouldn't feel hurt by others.

Donna couldn't undo her failure to visit her uncle. Her choice was to stay feeling guilty and depressed or to make a constructive change in her life.

I suggested to Donna that she pay a visit to the hospital her uncle died in, and inquire about doing some volunteer work there. Donna was artistic when she put her mind to it. Perhaps she could make some drawings that might brighten up a patient's room? I further suggested that she make drawings especially for the patients who had few or no visitors.

Such a type of reparation had meaning not only because it required her to do the kind of thing she had failed to do when her uncle was alive, but it also required her to give of herself. Donna's life took a needed turn for the better when she eventually followed up on that suggestion.

In the fourth phase of finding forgiveness, you utter the words of forgiveness, or hear them spoken to you, and you consider making some kind of reparation if you were hurtful.

When forgiveness is accepted, the reunion is complete. What is left to do is to resolve any pain that lingers, to let go of the remnants of anger or guilt and feel warm again.

Chapter Fifteen

Phase Five: To Let Go and Forget

It may come with a sigh, a bittersweet remembrance of a pain that now subsides. Or it may come as a satisfying contentment, a breath that both soothes and invigorates. Eventually, it is a gladdening in your heart that comes with your finally letting go of the deep hurts that once kept you estranged. And it is a welcoming back of your ability to more fully give love again.

After you have forgiven the one who has hurt you, what remains to be done is to let go of the pain of anger and resentment. When you are the one forgiven, your task is to let go of the pain of guilt and shame.

Unlike the other four phases in the process of reconciliation and forgiveness, this phase need not be a struggle to complete. In fact, your experience of letting go may be gentle. For since you have already expressed your anger or your remorse, and especially if you've begun to make positive changes in your life, your hurt is now less stabbing. Your fears are less cumbersome. You are reawakened to experience your love (or at least a calming sense of caring) for the other person and the love that is there for you.

You may notice that remnants of the old hurts and fears remain, despite your genuine efforts to find forgiveness. That doesn't necessarily mean that you must retrace your steps on the journey. If you believe that your effort to forgive was sincere and thorough, then don't be disheartened at any lingering pain there might be. Remember, this can be a gentle phase. The struggle to resolve your anger or guilt is basically over. Notice any pain you feel for what it is, a residue of something passed. Do not fight it, resist it, or in any way try to change it. Instead, simply acknowledge it to yourself by saying, "This is just the memory of the old hurt that comes by now and again." Then get on with whatever you were doing before the memory intruded. Letting go can be as simple as that.

Another way to help let go of any unsettled pain is to repeat the phrase, "I forgive you," or, "I forgive myself," depending on what you need to have happen. As you may recall from Chapter 11, some thoughts will immediately follow such a phrase. For example, "I forgive you," may be followed by the thought, "But it still hurts too much." Or, "I forgive myself" may be followed by the thought, "But do I deserve it?" Keep repeating the forgiveness phrase many times in succession, and then pay attention to the troublesome thoughts that immediately follow it. You will discover that after several repetitions, the troublesome thoughts don't appear. Or, if they do appear, you'll notice that your emotional reaction to the thoughts is more neutral than it was before. By repeating this exercise several times a day, you can overcome any sensitivity you once had to finally letting go of the pain.

FORGETTING

After there is forgiveness, some forgetting follows. It is a mistaken belief that you must completely forget about the painful events for the forgiveness to be genuine and healing. Probably, you will always be able to recall what happened that led to the estrangement, but your memory will be less aching over time, and your recollections will occur less frequently.

In a way, the type of forgetting that takes place after forgiveness happens has similarities to the kind of forgetting that follows after the death of a loved one. There is less grief and anger as time passes, and the memories of the person or of the death are less intrusive. Instead, more pleasant memories replace the painful ones.

Another analogy is the forgetting that takes place when you move away from your home town. There is always something to recall, but the specifics fade. And as you make a new life for yourself, the thoughts of how things used to be seldom arise.

When you have truly forgiven, then you will rarely recall the hurt—not because you've forgotten, but because your energy is invested in more important things such as growing, giving, and loving.

WHEN THE GHOSTS REMAIN

You have tried to reconcile, tried to find forgiveness, tried to let go and forget, but you are still haunted. You clench your teeth, and stabbing within you is the memory of the hurt, and it cuts deeply still.

Part of the difficulty may have nothing to do with either your willingness to let go or with the severity of the hurt that tore apart the relationship. The difficulty may have to do with the nature of the forgiveness process.

The road you took when you set out on your journey to reconcile and forgive was not straight. It was like a steep mountain path that winds around upward toward the summit. At any given stop along the way, you saw that you had gone full circle although you'd moved to a higher level. The landscape you looked out on was the same one you saw earlier, but your perspective changed.

And so it is with forgiveness. After working hard toward a resolution, you discover that the hurts remain the same, but hopefully your perspective is different. And you still may have to go around again, repeating some of the phases, until you arrive at your destination.

Perhaps, the first time around, you didn't fully acknowledge your feelings and the nature of the pain. Maybe you held back some of the truth while confessing or confronting.

Perhaps you doubt that love can really burst forth after there has been a betrayal. Then examine whether you believe in an all-loving God, or a God who condemns, or in no God at all. If your ideas of God are ideas of damnation and nonforgiveness, you may struggle when it comes to the task of forgiving yourself and others. *Once you doubt that there can be such Great Love, you will hold back from loving greatly.* And you may hold on to guilt and resentment.

Some people make great strides in overcoming their bitterness but find the idea of offering forgiveness still a bit distasteful. Perhaps they should focus on *pardoning* the hurtful person before trying to find forgiveness. It may seem like a minor semantic distinction, but it is a useful one nevertheless.

When you pardon someone, that person is regarded as guilty but is freed from the obligation to pay for the crime. When you forgive someone, guilt is removed. To pardon someone allows you to maintain some degree of emotional distance from that person. When you find forgiveness, however, you also feel a deeper sense of caring for that person. You don't have to care as much when you pardon someone. You simply agree to free that person from any obligation to you. A final distinction is this: When you pardon someone, you are in a superior, one-up position. When you forgive, you regard the other person as being on a fairly equal level to you.

It can be frustrating when you think you've done all you can but still the resentment or guilt remains. But you are at a better place than when you began. Continue with the journey, and try to understand why you are still holding on to guilt and resentment.

Holding on to Guilt and Resentment

When you can't let go of the pain despite strong efforts to reconcile, when the acts of betrayal or disloyalty are branded and burning in your memory, it signifies that there is still some unfinished business. Two key and related emotions are involved: guilt and resentment. Each of these emotions ties you to the other person. You may be miles apart physically, but emotionally you are wrapped up with one another.

The unfinished business as it pertains to guilt is this: You feel that *you still owe something to the person you hurt.* There is a nagging within you to do something to pay back or appease the other person for what you did that was hurtful.

The unfinished business as it pertains to resentment is this: You feel that *the person who hurt you still owes you something.* You either expect something realistic such as an apology or unrealistic such as a new childhood.

If you still feel overwhelmed with guilt even though you owned up to your faults, felt remorse, and were forgiven by your spouse, then you are guilty. At least you are guilty of failing to accept the forgiveness offered to you. You are guilty of keeping yourself at arm's length from someone who has wanted you to be closer. Probably, you are also guilty of not trying to change your style of relating that you felt guilty about in the first place. Instead of investing your energy into improving your relationship, you depleted yourself with guilt. You gave people the impression that you want to change, but that was all you did.

If that is true of you, then you have to do something about it. Tell the person you hurt that you accept the offer of forgiveness (even though you don't feel quite deserving of it). Then demonstrate your love by making a plan of action to improve your esteem and your style of relating with others. Remember, your strengths are your sensitivity and your willingness to give of yourself. But your weaknesses are your oversensitivity and your tendency to treat yourself harshly so as to appease others. Use your strengths.

What if you were the one who was hurt, and in spite of your offer of forgiveness, you still feel very resentful? Your resentment means that you want the other person to feel guilty about something, and that person doesn't feel as bad as you'd like.

Two possibilities are open to you to deal with your

resentment. First, you can go back to the person and begin a new dialogue. Tell him or her that you are still resentful (even if you aren't sure why). It's possible that you are angry about an issue that wasn't addressed the first time around. Or maybe you resent what you perceive as the other person taking your concerns too lightly. Get it off your chest.

The second possibility open to you to let go of your resentment is a bit more complicated. It is based on the concept of *projection*, a defense mechanism whereby you project onto others the feelings or attitudes you possess but can't admit to. So, your lingering resentment (your wish for the other person to feel guilty) might really be your own guilt feelings projected onto that person. An example will clarify the point.

Having to care for his two children after a divorce, Elliot was anxious about his ability to be a single parent. He also felt very guilty that his children had to suffer from the effects of a failed marriage. (Elliot's parents divorced when he was eleven. He vowed to have the perfect marriage so his children wouldn't suffer the way he did.)

Finally, he met and married his second wife Madeline. From the start, Madeline had difficulty disciplining her step-children. Elliot, on the other hand, observed that his children obeyed him more readily. His esteem and confidence as a parent were raised, but at a cost. He began to criticize Madeline for her ineffectiveness with the children. When she accused him of being unsupportive of her discipline efforts, he resented what he perceived as her attempt to make him choose between loyalty to her or to his children. And his resentment increased over time.

What really was happening with Elliot was that his resentment of Madeline, that is, his expectation that she should feel guilty, stemmed from guilt he felt about himself but never resolved. He still felt guilty about his failed first marriage. He wondered if that failure would ultimately harm his children. Rather than make an honest appraisal of his role in the first marriage, rather than forgive himself for any past mistakes and recognize that he did the best he could, he focused on Madeline and her difficulties. He resented her and branded her as the guilty party, as the person who would be responsible if his children developed any emotional problems, because he was avoiding his own anxieties about his impact on his children.

By the time you feel resentful about something, you've waited too long to deal with the problem. You've either held back on some anger and not confronted the other person about it, or you haven't faced up to some guilt feelings which are now being unfairly projected onto someone else.

Don't wait any longer. Go to the other person, and discuss your feelings. Sort out where your own guilt may lie. Most people, if they are lucky, have only a handful of close, loving, meaningful relationships. Why risk having one less if you really can avoid it?

Letting Go of Resentment and Guilt: The Story of Matthew

Matthew came in for therapy because he believed that job stress was interfering with his home life. "For the past six months, I've been taking my anger out on my wife and kids. I feel terrible about that."

"How do you show that anger?" I asked.

"Mostly I just yell. But I'm very loud. I practically scream at the top of my lungs. I don't hit anyone, though. The only thing I hit is the walls. Yesterday I yanked the phone from the wall. That's when I decided I needed to talk about the job with someone."

Matt worked for a large construction company that was under new management. He felt that the new owners were ignorant of some procedures in construction work as evidenced by the passing out of assignments that were often too dangerous or lacking in adequate safety precautions.

"They don't care about us, although they say they do. But I can't complain. They're just looking for reasons to lay people off. I'm not going to put my head on the chopping block."

Matt then went on to describe himself as "busy, always on the go." He'd find work projects at home to fill in his spare time. He couldn't even watch television with his family without fidgeting with some appliance in need of repair. Such projects often kept him away from his family.

"But I do all these things for them," Matt argued. "My wife doesn't seem to understand that I do all these things for her and the kids."

While Matt's tendency to be industrious was admirable, he seemed to be neglecting his family in other ways. And they found it hard to complain to him about his work schedules because he always said he had their best interests in mind. They felt guilty, and no one in the household felt satisfied.

Something wasn't sounding right to me. Matt indicated that the real problem was his job stress, but it was apparent that family tension had been high before his job became too stressful.

"Tell me more about your temper," I said.

"I don't know what to do about it. Sometimes I get so angry with my kids that I have to go to the garage and work on the car or something. Keeping busy helps me to control my anger."

"It has been like this even before the new management took over on your job, hasn't it Matt?" I asked. "Controlling your anger has been a problem for years."

Matt nodded. He went on to say how after he is especially loud, he feels guilty. Sometimes he goes out and buys a present for whoever he yelled at. If the gifts aren't appreciated, he feels angrier.

Of course, Matt's gift buying could never succeed in relieving him of guilt, because that wasn't doing anything about his temper. He was still loud and abusive. And he was discounting his family's feelings when he expected them to accept his gifts joyfully at a time when they were still hurt by him.

Matt's long-time anger meant that something from his past was unresolved. He was unable to let go of something that had hurt him at one time.

"How was your relationship with your father?" I asked one day.

"I respected him," Matt answered.

"Which means what?"

"I did what he wanted me to do, whenever he wanted me to do it."

"You were obedient?" I said.

"I had to be, or else he'd turn into a maniac. He'd go wild, yelling and screaming and throwing things. He only hit me once, and that was enough. I didn't dare cross him."

Matt and his father were alike in other ways, too. The father worked long hours, "for the family's sake."

"But he wouldn't buy me any gifts. At least I do that," Matt said.

"I get the feeling, Matt, that you never wanted to be like your father, so you convinced yourself that by buying gifts to make up for your temper, you'd be different."

"Yes. You've got to believe me, I hate the way I am.

My father never cared how he acted, but I care about my family."

I believed Matt. But I also knew that his kind of problem was not easy to change. It would take some time. I was concerned about his family, too. I asked to see them on a regular basis. They needed to know that while change was possible, putting up with continued abuse was not something they had to endure. Since expressing feelings was never really allowed in the family, the first order of business was determining whether that rule could be broken. The family's anger at Matt was legitimate. But holding it in turned it into guilt. The family members began to believe that they were the cause of Matt's problems.

That was how it was with Matt and his father, too. Matt couldn't express anger to his father. Eventually it changed to guilt, as he believed he must be an unlovable son to receive such abuse.

Matt's perception that his bosses were insensitive to the workers' needs, and that to speak up about it would cost him his job, paralleled the way it was with him and his father. Because he hadn't found a good way to cope with his father, his ability to deal with authority figures was impaired.

There were a number of therapeutic strategies to help Matt. But one important part of our work together was teaching Matt how to talk with his father. At first we practiced, with Matt pretending to be his father and me pretending to be Matt. Then, since his own children felt toward Matt what he felt toward his father, I helped them to talk to Matt.

Finally, Matt was ready. He didn't go to his father to blame him, but to speak his mind, to understand his father better, if possible, and perhaps to become closer to the man. They'd been estranged for some time.

When he finally talked with his father, Matt didn't

downplay his feelings. He spoke of his resentment, but he also said he intended to resolve his anger. He spoke of caring for his father, too. And his intention was to spend more time with the man and learn more about how his father grew up, so that he could put his father's behavior in a more accurate context.

Matt's father found the discussion hard to endure. He became angry and defensive. Matt began to doubt himself. He felt like a bad person for showing his feelings to his father. But he stayed with it. The conversation didn't end positively; each one felt misunderstood and unappreciated. But they agreed to talk again later.

When I last saw Matt, he had spoken with his father on three occasions and felt forgiving of him. His guilt feelings disappeared, his temper outbursts ceased, and he was making plans for a part-time business of his own.

LETTING GO AND THE STAGES OF LIFE

Letting go puts you in a new place. You are no longer suffering over parts of your past but are able to live in the present and welcome prospects for the future. You are free to develop at whatever stage of life you are in, unburdened by guilt or resentment.

Much has been written in recent years about adult life stages. Those stages include leaving the parents' home; establishing new, intimate relationships; seeking a career; getting married; having and raising children; stabilizing a career; readjusting when the children leave home; and finally, dealing with widowhood, old age, and one's own mortality.

As it pertains to this book, your ability to forgive and your willingness to admit you need forgiving not only free you to more ably contend with each life stage, but by entering into any new stage you'll be tugged at to let go of any painful past so as to better deal with the present. In fact, some of the difficulties you have when trying to forgive may have much to do with the fact that you haven't yet experienced certain life stages. Many people, for example, who felt slighted by a parent are less judgmental when they themselves become parents.

Conversely, failing to forgive or be forgiven leaves a residue of resentment, guilt, and often self-denunciation that draws on your capacity to make the most of your current life situation. If you once failed to forgive, say, your parents for something, you could be at a disadvantage if the same issue arises in your dealings with your spouse or children. Old fears and resentments reemerge, distorting your perceptions and draining you of energy and conviction. That was the case with Matt when his unresolved feelings toward his father interfered with his role as husband and father. It is indeed an insightful and courageous person who can realize at such times that "I've been in this problem before," and set out to resolve the issue for good.

Arnold and Leslie weren't sure why they had chosen to get some marital counseling. After all, they'd been fighting for over twenty years. Their arguments weren't easy to listen to. They knew how to hurt each other and always went for the jugular. "We didn't used to fight as often as we do now," Leslie said. Neither of them knew what had changed.

With just a little exploration, it became clear what was going on. They were contending with two major transitions in life, and the added stress was snapping their marriage in two. The first transition was that all of their children were now living away from home. Dealing with the kids had always been a distraction from the pain of the marriage, particularly for Leslie.

The second transition affected Arnold more than Leslie. Arnold had left a highly stressful job as a broker on Wall Street for a less intense job with a smaller company north of New York City.

"My way of avoiding my problems with Leslie was to get hip-deep in my work. But I just couldn't take the pace anymore. I'm fifty-three years old, and I don't want to die of a heart attack at fifty-four. Anyway, with my new job, I have less work to do. I can't avoid the marriage the way I used to be able to."

It can be difficult enough for people when they change jobs or when their children grow up and leave home. It is so much more difficult when the job and the children have served the function of protecting a marriage from further destruction. Because of their inability to come to terms with their relationship problems years before, Arnold and Leslie were struggling in their effort to make a successful transition to a new phase of life.

Clark had difficulty with a different transition. Clark came for therapy because he was worried about his difficulty, at age twenty-six, in sustaining his relationships with women.

"The relationships always end the same way," he complained. "My girlfriends expect too much from me. They want me to drop everything on a moment's notice and be at their beck and call. I can do that up to a point, but then they resent it when I draw the line."

"What exactly do they expect from you?" I asked.

"To be patient with them, to give them the benefit of the doubt more often than they say I do. Whenever there is a problem with them, I do try to work it out, but sometimes I don't think they take the problem seriously enough. Then when I'm frustrated about that, they tell me I'm too impatient, that problems can't be solved overnight. So, I keep giving them opportunities, but nothing ever gets resolved. Then I say the relationship should end, and they start acting desperate. They say they can't live without me. I feel as if they are just testing my commitment to them by expecting me to put up with all their crap."

Clark's mother had died when he was seventeen. She was an alcoholic. On one of the few weekend nights she was sober, she had slammed her car head-on into a telephone pole.

"What was your relationship like with your mother?" I asked.

"I took care of her. I never knew just how bad her problem was, but some days she looked like hell. I'd fix her something to eat, and she'd make me promise not to tell Dad she'd been drinking."

"Did she ever take care of you?" I asked.

"I suppose when I was real little, she did the things mothers are supposed to do. But mostly I remember her being sick or drunk, staying in bed, or crying after an argument with my father. She wasn't able to do much more than that."

Clark's mother had expected a great deal from him. Too much, in fact. He was too young to be so responsible for her care and to be put in the no-win position of having to lie to his father to protect her. Clark resented his mother for the way she was, and yet he loved her, too. He also felt some guilt, wondering whether his occasional resistance to protecting his mother was an indication of his not being a good enough son. (Children of alcoholics often take on special roles in the family to help keep the household functioning. Clark was the overresponsible protector.)

"When you speak of your mother," I said, "there is not much anger in your tone. Have you forgiven her? Or is the memory simply too draining for you to feel much of anything?"

"I guess I have forgiven her," he said. "But I don't like to think about her. I never like myself after I think about my mother."

Clark hadn't really let go of his resentment. And he felt guilty, too. That was a shame but an all too common occurrence in alcoholic families. And it was clearly interfering with his ability to move forward into the stage of life where he could date and establish close, loving relationships with other women.

Clark decided he wanted to finish up the business with his mother. He chose to write her a letter, as if she were still alive. That specific approach to forgiveness is discussed more fully in Chapter 17. In the letter, he told his mother how hurt and angry he was over her drunkenness and her intense neediness of him. He said how he sometimes felt guilty, believing he wasn't helping her enough. He said he was having a difficult time accepting his girlfriends because his feelings from the past were interfering with his life now.

"And I want to be more forgiving of you, Mom," he wrote. "I don't want to blame you anymore. Yes, you hurt me, but I know it's up to me to get over everything. I'm sure you must have hated the way you were. It's sad that you didn't try to make your life happier. But I'm not like you. I want my life to be better than it has been. If there is truth to the idea of resting in peace, I hope that now you'll be able to."

Writing that letter went a long way toward helping Clark let go of his pain. Freed from the bondage of his childhood and adolescence, he was able to step more cleanly into his young-adult stage of life.

When you finally let go, when the guilt and resentment wither, I hope you'll feel content, happy, and hopeful. But you may feel a bit down and blue, at least initially. Saying good-bye to a part of your past isn't always easy, even when you are glad to be moving on.

Perhaps you may also be discovering that out of your own fears and weaknesses, you held on to your guilt and resentment longer than you needed to, thereby making your life more painful than was necessary. That can make you feel a bit sad.

You may also feel sad as you understand that what you are letting go of is not just a memory or a feeling, but a myth. You may have held the false belief that your mother or father or husband or wife was all-loving or all-hateful. Now you know better.

But let go anyway. And when you do, you will finally accept the truth that neither you nor anyone else is perfect. The people who hurt you did so not because you were unlovable, but because they had weaknesses. They had imperfections. They were angry; they felt threatened. And your imperfections will cause you to be hurtful at times, too.

Let go of all that is holding you back and keeping you unhappy and unproductive. No one is stopping you, and it really is time.

Chapter Sixteen

When Forgiveness Still Seems Unjust: The Hunger to Get Even

"He deserves to suffer after the way I suffered," Matty argued bitterly. "That's just how I feel. I know it's wrong to feel so hateful, but I can't help it. If he only knew how much he hurt me . . ."

Her words dropped off, and she hunched down in her chair, trying to muffle her feelings by burying her face in her scarf.

Two years had passed since her husband of nearly thirty years had left her for another woman. It was one year since her heart attack forced her to retire from her job as a sales representative. Now, at fifty-six and without children or nearby relatives, Matty was alone, lost, and wanting revenge.

"He was so callous," she continued. "He never bothered to tell me what was wrong with our marriage. He just emptied his bank account and left me a note. He knew I was in the hospital last year, too, but he never wrote or called. I'm so bitter. I want to get back at him."

Matty's feelings were normal. Everybody at one time or another wants to get even with whoever was hurtful. The desire for retribution can be intense as "justice" is sought.

But what role do retribution or punishment and the need to "see justice served" play in the process of reconciliation and forgiveness? Can vengeance, of any sort, ever promote a reconciliation? If not, what happens to justice if retribution is absent? Wouldn't forgiveness without some form of punishment only teach the hurtful person that he or she can get away with almost anything? The answer to these questions is based on psychological research and my own observations from clinical practice.

As a rule, if you wish to reconcile a relationship and steer it in a direction of love and growth, retribution or vengeance will complicate and hinder that prospect, if not destroy it completely. That being said, however, it is still vital for the healing of your relationship that you stand up for yourself, express your anger, and work on ways to *improve* the relationship rather than let it remain exactly as it has been. To not seek retribution in no way means you must keep your feelings hidden and your rights pushed aside.

Also, retribution or punishment must be distinguished from self-protection. If the person who hurt you continues to do so (even though there may have been a temporary pause when that person appeared to be apologetic and remorseful), then you may have no choice but to leave the relationship or at least set strict, protective limits on it. You will have to begin saying things like "I will not tolerate that kind of treatment anymore" and mean it. It may seem punishing to you to do that (particularly if you are someone who has been abused in the past and who pretends that the abusive person "is going to change this time"), but it is a necessary form of self-protection.

You are not here on this earth to save the person who is always hurting you by offering yourself up for sacrifice. People who love you don't hurt you that way. It is possible to be forgiving of the person who never ceases to hurt you, but it isn't necessary to remain in the relationship and forever put up with the abuse.

HOW VENGEANCE BLOCKS RECONCILIATION

Aggression Breeds Aggression

In all likelihood, your act of vengeance will only lead to more aggressiveness. Clinical research is clear: aggression breeds aggression.

When you think about it, why should retribution lead to reconciliation and growth? When you retaliate, you succeed only in bringing more negativity to an already bad situation. You put forth your weakest side precisely at the time when you need all of your strong points if the relationship and the pain are to be healed.

Once you do get even, there is now one more hurt to be worked through. It doesn't matter as much any more that you weren't the one who started the acts of harm. The pain that you cause by retaliating can just as powerfully erode the relationship as any pain you suffered.

Of course, by getting even you may feel as if some balance has been restored in the relationship. Each of you has suffered at the hands of the other. Each of you is guilty. Now you can go about trying to forgive one another, if you're still talking. Everything seems so perfectly balanced. While it is possible to reconcile under such conditions, the risks of doing lasting harm have increased markedly. Is that a chance you wish to take?

If you have a strong desire to get revenge, ask yourself these questions first:

- Am I someone who is used to getting the short end of the stick from people?
- Am I someone who tends to hold back angry feelings until I just can't take it anymore?
- Did I grow up in a competitive family where I always had to win in order to feel good about myself?
- Did I grow up in a family where some members were the "black sheep" or were emotionally cut off from other parts of the family?

If you answered yes to any of those questions, I urge you to wait before you decide to get even. Your decision to seek vengeance may be coming, in part, from some unresolved past events.

If you need to be more assertive, now is not the time to act aggressively. You *can* be assertive now. But there is a difference between assertiveness and aggression.

If you need to improve your esteem, do so in some way other than competing and sizing yourself up to the competition. Actually, you then have a better chance of improving your esteem within a healthy relationship. But your relationship may not get healthy if you retaliate.

If you've been hurt a lot before by others, if you were not given the kind of love or attention you deserved growing up, you may be taking out your anger on someone who doesn't deserve it all.

Think about it.

Vengeance Compels You to Keep Your Anger Alive

To justify, at least to yourself, that your act of vengeance was called for, you must keep your anger alive. Anger is the heartbeat of vengeance. When you retaliate, the release of anger and the sense that justice is being served may provide a temporary satisfaction. But discomfort can also result. That discomfort may be feelings of guilt that perhaps you went too far in getting even. The discomfort may be the fear that the other person will strike back in response to your retaliation. Or the discomfort may come as a sadness that the relationship has deteriorated to such a vindictive level.

So how do you deal with the guilt, fear, or sadness? By feeding your anger and keeping it alive. You may start to put yourself down harshly, turning your anger inward until you feel depressed. Or you may kindle an even deeper resentment against the person who hurt you.

The more you resent the person you retaliated against, the less guilty or frightened you will feel about how you were hurtful.

"I went to bed with another woman that same night Betty told me about her one-night stand," Trevor confided. "I was so enraged, so humiliated. I wanted to humiliate her just like she did to me." His face was grim as he continued. "Now that we're trying to set things straight I . . . I don't know anymore. I'm left with a kind of loss. My marriage vows *meant* something to me, they really did. And while Betty regrets breaking them, well, I broke them too. It doesn't make me feel much better trying to convince myself that it was her fault I did what I did. All I know is that on an impulse I went to bed with another woman, something I never believed I'd do. And I did it so easily. It scares me. It saddens me. And I don't like those feelings."

For a few months afterward, Trevor fluctuated between feeling enraged at Betty and feeling guilty over his own infidelity. Those emotions were more than discomforting. They almost led to the dissolution of his marriage.

"Not only has my whole perception of Betty changed, my perception of myself has changed. Who am I? I don't know anymore. And just to get this entire confusing mess over with, I almost feel like walking out for good. I'm so tired of fighting, of not trusting her, of feeling guilty."

Trevor kept alive his anger at Betty to justify his infidelity. Then he kept alive his anger at himself to appease his own guilty conscience. It was costing him his marriage.

DOES RETRIBUTION EVER LEAD TO HEALING?

Sometimes retribution leads to healing, but it's risky. Retribution allows you to relieve some of your anger, and that can be helpful. However, telling the person who hurt you that you are angry also lessens it, and with fewer complications.

In general, if the hurts are not numerous and long-standing, and if the two of you are not locked in a pattern of hurting each other periodically, an act of retribution may not hurt the relationship. In fact, it could be a springboard for change. It can serve as the "slap in the face" that stuns you both into realizing you have let matters get out of hand.

Yet you may wonder, "Doesn't holding back on vengeance just teach the hurtful person that he or she can get away with anything?" Some people think so. But as a result, their relationships are often filled with attacks and counterattacks.

Look at it this way. What is it saying about a person if the only thing that keeps him or her from hurting you is the fear of retribution? If a person's actions are restrained primarily by external forces (such as the threat of retaliation), then that person has no conscience to speak of. You want the people in your life not to hurt you, not because you may retaliate if they do, but because they care enough about you to do their best not to hurt you.

Don't expect guilt to be a driving force in people with little conscience. Their main concern is themselves, not the feelings of other people. They may *act* guilty, but it is a fleeting feeling for them. Retribution may keep them in line, for a while anyway. But is that the kind of give-and-take you really want in a relationship?

THE STRUGGLE TO GET EVEN: MATTY'S STORY

At the outset of this chapter, you met Matty. She wanted her husband to suffer for leaving her after thirty years of marriage. She wanted to get even, but she didn't know how. Matty came to my office one day and began with these words:

"I spoke with my sister-in-law last night. She told me that Johnny is in the hospital. He's been there for two weeks. He has liver cancer. The doctors say he can't survive, but he doesn't know that yet."

The bitterness was gone. She was subdued. Her face was drawn, her eyes moist.

"He's lost over thirty pounds," she continued. "He was always pudgy around the middle," she said, smiling slightly at the memory.

I spoke a few words that went unheard.

"He's all alone, you know," she began again. "That other woman left him when he got sick." She shook her head, stirring up bitter feelings. "I never believed she loved him. Not the way I loved him." She paused, and there was silence. "I told you that I wanted him to suffer for what he did to me. But I didn't want him to suffer this way, not this way . . ." she said, her voice aching, trailing off.

I brought up the idea of her visiting him. She couldn't imagine doing that. Not now. But over the next several weeks, she became depressed. She couldn't sleep. She'd feel angry and guilty and bad about herself. She felt jittery and was preoccupied, unable to concentrate.

"What are you hurt and frightened about, Matty?" I asked.

"I don't know," she answered quickly. "I just don't feel right. I'm not myself."

"Have you been thinking that Johnny will probably die soon?"

"Yes, I've thought about that. And I've thought about my wanting to hurt him and how he hurt me. Why did this whole thing have to happen?" she wondered aloud, the anger in her voice quickly giving way to sadness.

"There may not be much time, Matty," I said. "Will you have any regrets about things you have or have not done when Johnny finally does die?"

She stirred uneasily in her chair, unable to answer but clearly troubled by the question.

"You have some feelings you aren't fully dealing with," I continued. "When do you suppose the best time to deal with them will be?"

Matty started to cry. "I miss him, and he's hurting. I don't want him to die." And with words that were as true for her as they were for him, she concluded, "He's so alone. He doesn't deserve that. Nobody does."

"Matty," I said gently. "There is not much time left for you and Johnny. And you have so many important things to say, feelings to share. Could you go to him and let him know all you are feeling?"

Matty nodded, and later that day saw her husband for the first time in well over a year.

"He was so happy to see me," Matty said to me, smiling. "He stared at me the whole time and wouldn't let go of my hand. He didn't look well, but I couldn't tell him that. 'You haven't changed much,' I told him. 'Except you've finally lost some of the weight you've always wanted to lose.'

" 'You're just the same too, Matty,' he told me. And I knew from his eyes that he still loved me. 'Matty,' he said, 'can you ever forgive me? Please say that you can. I was wrong to leave you. I hurt you so much. Please forgive me.'

" 'Of course I forgive you, Johnny,' I told him. 'That's what wives are for.' He just held my hand as tight as he could and seemed so happy that I forgave him.

" 'You're right, Johnny. You did hurt me,' I said to him. 'For two years I've been so angry with you.'

" 'I don't blame you, Matty. I don't know why I left. It wasn't your fault. I was fooling myself. I thought there was something better, but, oh, how wrong I was. But we're back together now, if you'll have me.' "

For the next two weeks, Matty visited Johnny daily. They talked about what had happened between them, and shared fond memories. Johnny made some sketchy plans for their future while Matty stayed quiet over the fact that her husband would probably never leave the hospital.

"It's a blessing we've been able to see each other and overcome the hurt," Matty said to me, comforted by her thoughts of Johnny. "I combed his hair for him and kissed him. Last night we watched the stars through the window. We always liked the stars be-

cause it was on a starry night that Johnny proposed to
me."

She looked away from me. Her memories of the far
past weaved her a blanket of warmth, while the reality of the present loomed gray in her awareness.

"He told me how he loved me," she began. "I never
thought I'd hear him say those words again after we'd
been apart for so long. 'I love you, too, Johnny,' I told
him. He reached for my fingers and held my hand
until he couldn't anymore." Her eyes glistened. "I'm
glad he wasn't suffering at the end." She put a cloth to
her eyes before continuing. "And I'm glad I did what I
did. There was more to Johnny, more to our relationship, than what happened two years ago when he left
me. I'm happy I was here when he came back."

Was it just the fact that Johnny was suffering that
made it easier for Matty to reconcile with him? Or
was there more to it? If Johnny had not been sick with
cancer, would Matty have been able to resolve her
feelings about him and perhaps even reunite with him
eventually?

Those questions can never be answered. What is
known is that Matty's wish for vengeance was normal. If it had been a stronger wish, she might never
have visited him in the hospital. If it had been a
weaker wish, she might have sought him out sooner.

Was "justice" served in Matty's story? If you ask
Matty, she says yes, but it wasn't served by Johnny
having to die.

"The best thing was that he wanted me to forgive
him and I did. That made everything well again. And
it's only right, you know. He was wrong to have done
what he did, but he wasn't a bad person. He deserved
to be forgiven. Most everybody does."

When vengeance is yours, when the other person

pays dearly for the betrayal or cruelty against you, when your cry for "justice" has been answered, you may discover that you are still left wanting, that your wounds are not yet healed.

Perhaps it is those who have forgiven a deep hurt, or who have been forgiven, that fully understand how justice, rather than being overlooked when there is forgiveness, is instead revealed.

Chapter Seventeen

When Others Are Forever Gone: Forgiveness Without Reunion

You were too late. You kept putting off what you knew your heart beckoned you to do. You avoided revealing the truth of your feelings, and then it was too late. Now the person you need to talk to, to be open with, the one person you need to apologize to or set straight about all that has been hurting—that person is gone.

Perhaps that person is dead. Maybe the person is alive but no longer wants you to be a part of his or her life. Husbands and wives often want little to do with each other after a divorce. Parents and their adult children can cut themselves off emotionally from one another, severing blood ties. Someone once said that you can never divorce yourself from your parents or your children. But people seem to succeed in that every day.

And now you find yourself more alone and left with an aching inside that you cannot ignore. You suffer not only from the effects of the original hurt—be it your anger, guilt, or depression—but the hurt is now compounded by the reality that true reunion is impossible. That person is forever gone, and you are left with regrets.

Forgiveness is still possible if you really want it. Even if you did everything you could to salvage and rebuild the relationship but were left rejected time and again, forgiveness is still possible. Indeed, forgiveness is necessary, if you really want it.

When others are forever gone from your life, you can let go of the residue of pain by forgiving them and, if need be, forgiving yourself. Of course, there can be no physical reunion, and that may leave you with a hunger that can't be fully satisfied. It simply feels best when forgiveness reunites you with the person you've been estranged from. However, while you may be left wanting, your act of forgiveness will leave you deeply content and at peace with yourself, as well as rejuvenated and eager to get on with living.

WHOM DO I REALLY NEED TO FORGIVE?: CLEARING UP ANY CONFUSION

First you thought it was only your husband or wife who hurt you badly. That was the person who needed your forgiveness. Then you realized that you played a role in the estrangement. Maybe you were hurt more than you were hurtful. Maybe not. But you understood that you needed to be forgiven, too.

Then it became more confusing. There had been other hurts, some long past. Old lovers, old friends, and even your aging parents. You thought you'd overcome those hurts. Some of them you did overcome. But now you see that when your partner hurt you deeply, it affected you profoundly, because you'd been hurt like that before. And it all started coming back to you. But the truth is that if you can't heal your old wounds, the cuts will open more quickly the next time someone hurts you. Then who is responsible for your pain?

There is a phenomenon that occurs with frequency in troubled marriages. When people feel they've been hurt deeply by a parent and have yet to heal their pain, their marriages become the stage on which they try to work through the old, unsettled issues. It is the same script, only the players are different. Maybe they find themselves married to someone who more and more begins to resemble the hurtful parent. Maybe they discover how they are treating their spouse the same way Mom and Dad treated each other. Maybe they marry someone they know will be offensive to their parents. They use their spouse as a weapon against them.

A woman, abused by an alcoholic father, marries a man who is an alcoholic, or who becomes one. Or he gambles. Or he beats her, too.

A man who felt smothered and controlled by his mother marries a woman he adores because she's so lively and sentimental. A few years later, he regards her not as lively but impulsive, not as sentimental, but as overemotional, and as controlling in her efforts to get him to open up.

A woman vows never to act the way her mother acted. But her daughter now has so many of her mother's traits that all they do is battle.

A man vows never to act the way his father acted. But his wife is becoming so much like his mother, it's all he can do to keep himself from being the man his father was.

When a parent hurts you, you feel angry, betrayed, and fearful. And you are ambivalent. Part of you says it's OK to be angry; part of you says you can't because you love (and fear) your parents. Part of you says you didn't deserve to be treated the way you were; part of you isn't so sure.

You can never eliminate your ambivalence, because no one is perfect. But you can resolve your ambivalence. You can allow yourself to have mixed feelings without having to be confused by them. Or afraid of them. You can emphasize what is good about the other person, set protective limits if you have to, and remind yourself that while the ones who've hurt you are far from perfect, they are far from evil.

If you don't resolve your ambivalent feelings about your parents, you run the risk of unsettling your marriage. If you see your father as all bad, you may idealize your husband. But because he's not perfect, he'll eventually let you down (and even hurt you on purpose), and you'll convince yourself he's just like your father: untrustworthy and unforgivable. If you see your mother as completely good and without any weaknesses, you may hold your wife up to a standard she could never meet. (And even if she could meet it, you wouldn't let her, out of loyalty to your mother.)

If you were treated unfairly by your parents and haven't resolved your ambivalence, you may expect your spouse and children to make up for what you never got. You'll have low tolerance for their selfishness. You'll feel very unappreciated. And you may battle with them over issues that really should be addressed with your parents.

If you were treated unfairly by your parents and never resolved your ambivalence, you may work hard to be extra fair and loving toward your children and spouse. To give them what you never received. Unfortunately, you'll make so many sacrifices that you'll end up depleted. Your family will feel guilty. They'll try to pay you back for the good you've done, but you won't allow them to do much more than a little bit. Then you'll redouble your efforts at sacrificing for them, and they'll feel even guiltier as you grow more tired and unhappy without knowing why.

When your ambivalence toward your parents remains unsettled, you'll seek a spouse who will help you to either recreate those unworked relationship patterns, or to reverse those patterns. Regardless, the risks then run high for a marriage to fail, all because the players on the current stage are not the players from the original drama.

The influences your parents have on your life continue long after you've left home.

HOW TO FORGIVE WHEN THERE CAN BE NO REUNION

The essential difference between the phases of forgiveness described in Chapters 11 through 15 and the phases when no reunion is possible is the lack of opportunity to have an ongoing dialogue with the other person. Whereas a dialogue to understanding would ordinarily help you to see some reasons for what happened between you two, empathize with the other person, and feel understood, you are now left to speculate. When the other person is unavailable, there are always questions that will go unanswered.

Dolores had been raped by her father when she was a teenager. When she wished to finally forgive the man decades after his death, she sought out distant relatives who once knew her father. She asked them questions about him, about his original family, his upbringing, his values in life, and so on. By talking with them, she gained a better understanding of the kind of man her father had been.

Nevertheless, because her father was dead, his voice

went unheard. She was ultimately left by herself to resolve a most painful past.

"He was a shell of a man, I found out. You know, as I spoke to my relatives, I had such mixed feelings. Part of me wanted to hear from others that he was a horrible man, as if I needed reassurance about my feelings of hate for him. But another part of me wanted to find something, some piece of his existence that told me he felt sorry for what he did. I wanted to feel sorry for him, too. You know, he never showed remorse, and that's been the hardest thing for me to deal with. So I just needed to hear something that told me he suffered in his life so I could feel sorry for him. I knew if I felt sorry for him, I could forgive him more easily."

"What did you finally understand about him?" I asked.

"Actually, I understood more about myself. I found out that I was searching for some justification to forgive him. I was staying hurt and angry inside while I worked overtime trying to find some salvageable part of his life that would make it easier for me to forgive him. 'Look what you're doing!' I told myself. 'You're staying miserable, and you're doubting your value as a person while you search through your father's life. Stop it! Give it up! Who are you trying to kid?' "

Dolores looked hard out the window. Usually, everything about her was hard. Her expressions, the tone of her voice, her opinion of herself, her opinion of her far-away, grown-up children. She breathed in deeply, but as she let it out, a softness emerged, her sad eyes lightened.

"I don't know why he did what he did to me," she said, with a contentment that comes from true acceptance. "I don't intend to keep asking why, to keep looking for answers anymore. I realize that he must have felt miserable about himself his entire life, although he probably never admitted it to himself. And I know I wasn't at fault. I know I wasn't wrong. And I didn't deserve his abuse.

"There comes the time when you just have to forgive," she continued. "After a while, looking for reasons to forgive just keeps you from forgiving."

She looked at me and smiled a half-smile. I smiled back, knowing that she, like so many of the people I work with, was truly remarkable.

Phases of Forgiveness

When the other person is forever gone, you have three phases of forgiveness to go through.

Phase One

First, you need to identify as fully as possible all of your feelings about the estrangement. If you were hurt, you must acknowledge the intensity of your anger and sadness. You must see whether the hurt left you feeling anxious, guilty, depressed, doubtful, helpless, suspicious, envious, or lonely. Did you lose esteem? Power? A sense of being loved?

And if you caused harm, then you must own up to your guilt. Also, if you could have done something about healing the relationship sooner but did not do so out of anger, fear, or ignorance, admit it. Don't bludgeon yourself for such weaknesses. That does no good.

If you are guilty, then nurture your remorse. Remember, remorse is regret coupled with a strong desire to change for the better. In Phase One, you not only admit to feeling bad about ways in which you were hurtful, but you set out to make improvements.

Phase Two

The next phase is crucial, for it includes the act of forgiveness. Here, through the use of symbolism and maybe ritual, you express your feelings as if the other person were able to hear and understand you.

A good way to achieve this is to write a letter to that person. The format is straightforward. If you were the one who was deeply hurt, then put into the letter all you recall that was hurtful. Write about your sadness and bitterness. Let the person know about your rage at having been betrayed. Be truthful. Don't soften your account in any way. And if you were guilty of being hurtful, admit your guilt. Apologize with sincerity. Don't make excuses for what you did.

At the end of the letter, write of forgiveness. Tell the person who hurt you that you will be forgiving, even if it is hard to feel forgiving at the moment. If you are the guilty one, write of your remorse. Say you forgive yourself for how your actions ultimately hurt you (kept you from being your best self).

After the letter is completed, go one step further. Perform some ritual that involves the letter. David Viscott, in his book *The Viscott Method*, recommends taking the letter to the grave site, if the person is deceased, reading the letter aloud, and then burying it. I strongly encourage such a ritual.

If that isn't possible, go to a place that has special meaning for you and the other person, and read the letter there. Once again, you could bury the letter or burn it ceremoniously. Maybe you could go to a room in your home and take with you something that reminds you of that person, such as a photograph or family heirloom. Undisturbed, you could read the letter aloud, perhaps even light a candle, and burn the letter when you've finished.

Speaking aloud to an empty chair, pretending that the person is sitting beside you, can also be a powerful method of expressing feelings. Many find it useful to also exchange seats and pretend to respond to what was just said aloud. By taking the role of the other person and having to defend against any accusations, many people are able to increase their level of empathy, something that often precedes forgiveness.

You could plant a tree, not in memory of the hurt, but as a living memorial of your goodness and whatever was good about the other person. It would be a memorial that honors growth, honesty, and love. At that site you could read the letter.

The importance of performing such a ritual can't be overstated. It allows you an opportunity to perform some *outward action* in an effort to heal. So much of the forgiveness process is an inner experience that it becomes important, particularly when the other person isn't there to talk to, to include some outward expression of your feelings in the process. You can forgive and feel forgiven without such actions, but the process is less difficult and more satisfying when you include them.

I've known numerous people who say that such rituals are unnecessary. They say they don't need to write a letter because they already know too well their thoughts on the matter. They regard going to a grave site or speaking to an empty chair as a waste of time. But their anger and guilt continues, and their current relationships often suffer from the effects of their unresolved feelings.

By writing a letter, you not only convey your feelings, you legitimize them. You dignify them. In all probability, you'll further clarify them. You held back feelings before when the other person was still a part of your life. Don't make that same mistake now.

Also, the relief you will feel when you write the letter and read it aloud will be evidence that you can indeed let go of your pain; that you can forgive and be forgiven.

The experience of a ritual is also important in that it provides you with a memorable starting point of when you began to change your life around. There is the point when you can say firmly, "That part of my life is over. The pain is fading. My life is here, now, and it is ahead of me."

Phase Three

The final phase involves letting go of the residue of guilt and resentment. You begin to take full responsibility for the way your life is, no longer blaming others for your unhappiness.

In the letting-go phase, you will experience some degree of grief. After all, the bitterness or guilt you held on to kept you from saying good-bye. Now it is time to do just that. And you must grieve for the good part of the spouse (or parent, child, sibling, or friend) that is gone and was overlooked when you focused only on the pain.

You grieve over the fact that the other person failed to treat you in a manner you deserved. You grieve for any part of your life that was wasted. But it is a grief that comes from acceptance. You finally accept that things were the way they were. You give up the fight to pretend otherwise. And you understand that no amount of bitterness, resentment, guilt, or depression will change what happened.

THE STORY OF SAMUEL

Samuel began therapy after depression had gotten the better of him. Retired from his career as a pilot after twenty years due to a disabling kidney condition, at forty-seven Sam was lost.

"I just feel bad about myself. I don't like myself anymore. Maybe I never did. I don't know what it is, but I can't get comfortable with people the way I used to. Nobody cares. People only think of themselves. Makes you want to give up trying."

Sam went on to describe a life with no intimacy. After his divorce fifteen years ago, he had had only casual, unsustaining affairs until he met Marilyn. But that marriage had begun to hurt, too. She was living away from him in a new apartment, telling him he'd better "grow up." His parents were dead. His only child, a son from his first marriage, was a thousand miles away. Further away emotionally.

"Steve's a good boy. When he graduates, he'll be an engineer," Sam said with restrained pride.

"Sounds as if you miss your son," I said.

"Yeah, well, no . . . I mean, I'm used to it. It's been almost five years since I last saw him," he said, and added with a grin, "I hope he has better luck with women than I've had. It's not easy finding the right woman these days."

"Do you love Steve?" I asked, steering him back on the topic. Sam was very good at evading some issues.

"Love? Yes, of course I do."

"Does he know that?"

"I always buy him things, even when I can't afford it. I'm not the man my father was. He promised me a car when I turned eighteen, but he was full of lies. You'd better believe I bought Steve a car when he was eighteen."

"How is it that you haven't seen Steve in over five years?" I asked, wondering if perhaps I was pushing a topic that was too much to deal with at the moment.

Sam stirred uneasily. "If you want to know the truth, Steve feels funny about me. I think he's embarrassed or disappointed in me."

"Why would he be that way?" I asked.

"I'm not sure," Sam said. "I worked so hard not to

be like my father. I've told you before how bad he was. He was brutal. I remember when he was sick, dying actually. I was nineteen. My mother made him some soup, and I brought it to him in his bed. He didn't talk to me. He didn't smile. He told me to get the hell out. This is hard to understand, but I worried about him. His illness scared me. I wanted to give him a hug. But I just stood there, frozen, not sure what to do, and he started yelling at me again. Then he threw the bowl of soup at me. It burned my face, and he was scream- ing . . ."

"You must have felt so hurt," I offered, feeling that my words were inadequate.

"And I hated him for it. I hated him for everything he did. You asked me once if I could ever forgive him. I don't think I ever could. It's too hard."

"I can see how hard it would be to forgive him, Sam, and maybe you never will. But I'm concerned about you, not him. If you find you can't forgive him, what will that leave you with?" I asked.

"I'm left with memories. Anger, hatred, all of those, I guess," he answered.

"Do you deserve that? I mean, just because your father treated you so horrendously, are you now sup- posed to spend the rest of your life alone and angry?" Sam didn't speak. "Tell me, Sam, you and Steve are so far apart; how did you disappoint or embarrass him? You never did answer that question."

"That's just it. I'm not sure. He must have under- stood why I left him and his mother and how I didn't have a lot of visitation rights. I know I wasn't around when I could have been, but my schedule was too hectic. I was flying planes across the country."

"If Steve felt disappointed, Sam, was he wanting something from you that he wasn't getting?" I won- dered aloud.

"My time? Is that it? Is he still mad at me because I

wasn't available to him as a father should be?" Sam asked with concern.

"I don't know. You'll have to ask him that. Do you think you could do that?" I suggested.

"No. He might tell me something I don't want to hear, like maybe he couldn't care less about me right now."

"You wonder whether he still loves you," I commented.

"Yeah," he answered sullenly.

"Sam, you mentioned before how you wanted to hug your father but never could. Did Steve ever hug you?"

Sam closed his eyes. I watched his face crumple into his hands. "No. I wouldn't let him. Not when he was older anyway."

"Why not, Sam?" I asked softly.

"I didn't want him to get too . . . to expect too much from me. I knew I wouldn't always be around for him, so I wanted him to learn to get by on his own. Without his father."

"Do you think that might have hurt him?" I asked gently.

"Probably. Yes, I'm sure it must have," he replied.

"Maybe you even wonder if Steve could ever find it in his heart to forgive you, Sam."

Sam stood up abruptly and left the room. I didn't know whether I should go after him, but I chose not to. Maybe I was expecting too much from him right now. He returned a few minutes later, composed and somber.

"I'm afraid," he said. "My son doesn't understand me, and I'm not sure he ever will. I don't think he'll ever forgive me, although I didn't want to hurt him. But why should I talk to him? It will only stir things up. I could lose everything. Damn it!" he shouted, pounding his fist on the table. "This never would have happened if it weren't for my father. It's not fair."

Sam was at a crossroads in life. Of that he was becoming painfully aware. He could leave matters be, never feeling content or fully loved, but safe in the hopeful fantasy that his son might care for him. Or he could talk with his son and risk finding out for sure whether Steve did love him and want a relationship with him.

That is a choice you may be facing, and it can be agonizing. Most of the time, people should eventually take those kind of risks. But then, it is easy for me to say, "Take the chance," when it isn't my life.

"Sam, I know you were deeply hurt by your father. And you probably are right; things might be different today if he hadn't been so unloving. You blame your father, but he is gone. It is up to you to do something about your life now. I can hear that you're frightened of talking to Steve. I have an idea of something you can do that may ease your worries about facing him. I think it can be helpful, although nothing is certain. It's up to you. Would you like to try?"

"What's your idea?" Sam asked.

"Would you like to see if you can forgive your father?" I asked. "Maybe, if you can do that even just a little, you can begin to believe that you, too, are forgivable. At least you can forgive yourself. Maybe it will give you some strength to work on your marriage. You know, as much as you have hurt your son, you are not the man your father was."

Sam waited a week before he gave me his answer. "I'd like to try," he said. "I want to forgive my father. How can I do it?"

Phase One: Acknowledging Pain and Nurturing Remorse

In the first phase of forgiving his father, Sam admit-

ted all of his hurt, sadness, and anger at having been
rejected and abused. He acknowledged how over the
years, he had wondered if perhaps he was an unworthy son. He admitted to himself that he had
thought poorly of himself and that he had been afraid
to get too close to others.

He also admitted guilt. Sam was guilty of blaming
his father for why his life was so unhappy while not
doing anything to change his life for the better, until
now. It was easier for him to blame his father than to
accept responsibility for doing something constructive to solve his problems. That way, when things
went wrong, he could salvage whatever self-esteem
remained by convincing himself it was his father's
fault, not his.

But by blaming his father, Sam gave up power over
his life. That only left him feeling more helpless and
depressed. It was time to take responsibility and put
matters in a clearer perspective.

Phase Two: Confronting, Confessing, Forgiving

It took Sam nearly three months to find the courage
to begin the second phase. But finally, he wrote a
letter to his dead father and let loose a torrent of
anger and painful memories.

". . . And do you remember, Dad, when you threw
the bowl of soup at me? Do you have any idea how
that hurt me? My God, you were on your death bed,
and you still hated me. I began to hate myself after
that, Dad. But you didn't care. It was agony, telling
myself I was no good as a son and never having a
chance to redeem myself because you died. How could
you have been so cruel? And the beatings you gave
me. They were the only things you gave me. I wanted
a father, and you wouldn't be one for me. You weren't
human. You were an animal. You cared about nobody

but yourself. Do you know how many times I cried alone in my room because of you? Do you know it's impossible for me to cry now? I didn't ask for much. But I want you to know that I am better than you ever gave me credit for. I don't want to give you the satisfaction of me being miserable for the rest of my life."

Sam also admitted in the letter that by harboring such anger and self-hate most of his adult life, he had distanced himself from the people he most wanted to be close to.

"I blamed you for everything. The divorce, the separation, the fact that my son wants little to do with me. But I'm beginning to realize that there came a point in my life when it was really more my fault than yours. I just didn't want to admit it. Am I sorry for blaming you when I should have been looking more honestly at me? Yes, but only because it screwed up my life. I'm not sorry for telling people how you screwed up my life. You got off easy.

"I suppose you want to know whether I love you, Dad. It's hard to say, but I don't think so. Not anymore. In a way, I wish I could. I loved you when I was nineteen, holding that bowl of soup out for you. I would have given anything then for you to have loved me back.

"I can't love you the way I want to, but I can forgive you. Somehow, I don't feel as hurt right now. It's probably temporary. Forgiving you is more than you deserve. I hope you realize that. But I do forgive you.

"I've said all I can. Goodbye, Dad. Your son, Samuel."

Sam then drove for three hours to his father's grave. At the site, he read aloud the letter and buried it near the headstone. He came to see me two days later.

"It still hurts some," he said. "But I feel better. Maybe in time I'll feel even more forgiving."

Phase Three: Letting Go

Sam needed to continue to let go of his pain. He accomplished that in two ways. The first way was a more passive process whereby his anger and guilt diminished over time as a result of his having offered forgiveness to his father. By regarding his feelings as legitimate and himself as worthwhile, despite his weaknesses and his father's treatment of him, he relinquished the frightened side of himself and allowed his best self to stand tall. He surrendered to the reality of all that once was and no longer tried to fight to preserve the undermining beliefs that his father *should* have acted differently and that his own worthwhileness was in doubt.

And Sam began to grieve. He grieved for a father whose memory he was laying peacefully to rest. He grieved for that portion of his childhood that was lost to fear and abuse. And he grieved for the part of his adult life that was spent feeding his anger and self-doubt, making him more guarded, depressed, and lonely.

This grief, though, wasn't unending anguish or self-pity. He was letting go of his pain, letting go of his anger and his fears. He was beginning to forgive himself.

The second part of the letting-go process was more active. His old hurts were still being kept alive to some extent because he was not yet making necessary changes in his style of relating with others. Because he kept distant and guarded from people, his anger, depression, and self-doubts could not wither away. So Sam decided to start being more open with others. Especially, he wanted to talk with Steve.

"I wrote this letter to Steve," Sam began one day. "I'd like you to read it before I mail it to him."

"Dear Steve," the letter began. "I have some very

important things to tell you. I want you to know that I realize I haven't been much of a father to you. My father wasn't much of one either, so I should have understood before now just how much I've hurt you. I didn't mean to hurt you. And I'm not trying to make excuses. I just want you to know that my intention wasn't to hurt you. I simply couldn't allow myself to get close to you. I bought you a lot of presents to make up for it, and I know that presents are not everything. The truth of it was that I thought you'd love me more if I bought you things. That was wrong of me. If that hurt you in any way, please know that I am sorry.

"I want to make it all up to you, but I don't know how. And I don't know if you want me anyway. I've thought a lot about how our relationship has been, and I want it to be better. If you think it would be possible to forgive me for how I've hurt you, I'd welcome you. I want you to know that I'll make myself available to you if you want to talk. I don't want us to be distant, but I realize you may not want to know me any better than you already do. I'm here if you want me. I understand if you don't.

"I love you, Steve. Believe me when I tell you that. Maybe you feel that if I really loved you, I would have been around for you more often than I was. It's true I wasn't there for you like a father should be, but it wasn't because I didn't love you. Don't ever doubt that.

"Take whatever time you need, son. I'll be thinking of you. Love, Dad."

I looked up from reading it. Sam didn't wait to hear my reaction.

"Do you think he'll write back?" Sam asked.

"I hope so, Sam. He has quite a father, you know."

"Yeah, hard to believe, ain't it?" Sam said, cracking a broad smile. "I'm not completely sure what forgive-

ness is," he continued, "but I think I've forgiven my
father. I don't know if it's sincere enough, yet. Maybe
I'm feeling that way about him because I want Steve to
feel forgiving of me."

He thought a while and added, "If forgiveness includes feeling sorry for someone, well, I do feel sorry
for my father. What a life he must have lived. So
angry, so miserable. He hated himself, I'm sure."

Sam turned from his memories and faced the present. "It's time that I go now," he said, looking at his
watch.

"OK, Sam," I said. "I'm glad you stopped by. Take
care and have a good night."

Sam stood up and paused by the door, as if waiting
for me to say something else.

"Well," he finally said to me. "Can you give me back
my letter, please? I'd really like to mail it today."

I smiled, a bit embarrassed, and handed him back
his letter. He winked at me as he stepped out the door.
A burly man at six-foot-five, he carefully tucked the
small envelope into his coat pocket, and made his way
out on the street toward the post office.

Chapter Eighteen

Final Reflections:
Of Ships and Old Photographs

I had thought of beginning this chapter with the words *give it time* as my reminder to you that the process of reconciling and forgiving is not always easy and that it can take time.

But then I remembered something.

On January 28, 1986, a space shuttle exploded, splitting open the sky and delivering the spirits of seven men and women swiftly and forever into God's arms and into our hearts and minds. The people of the world sank into grief, prayer, and quiet reflection. A great ship of our time had been pulverized, its pieces scattered across the sea.

Give it time, I nearly told you. As if there will always be another tomorrow.

But then again, none of us can expect to live our lives as fully as we might if we knew there would be no tomorrow. And your effort to forgive and accept forgiveness, however genuine and sincere, can take time. We are human, after all.

Do give it time. Whatever time it takes for you to be freed from guilt and resentment, to be reunited in love with the people you've been distant from. My hope is, however, that you do not waste many moments, that you do not hesitate long when you could be moving forward, that you do not pretend that forgiveness is just a pipe dream or an injustice when tugging inside you is the belief that it really is within your grasp. If only you might reach for it.

I watched, a bit saddened, as a man left my office.

"By the way," he called out, turning to me as he reached the door. "Wish me a happy birthday. I'm fifty-one today."

A decent man, but a man resolute on keeping alive his anger at his twenty-six-year-old daughter. There had been a series of hurts on each side, mostly beginning after his divorce. His daughter thought he was being unfair to her mother. He thought his daughter was being unfair to him. It doesn't matter anymore now. He'll go home to find a birthday card from her, polite but empty of love, and he will feel angry when she doesn't bother to call.

It is the same story, always the same. "She'll regret it one day when I'm dead," he had complained. True. She probably will.

But his words were disturbing. He said them as if he were aware of his mortality, yet he conducted his relationship with his daughter as if he'd always have another chance, another tomorrow when he could resolve matters. He seemed to be waiting for something, too. Perhaps he waited for her to make the first move, to apologize. Perhaps for her to hug his neck and say, "Dad, I really do love you." The man waited. And it was sad because he was all alone.

"Happy birthday," I said, smiling. "Listen, why don't you do something special for yourself today like . . ."

"No. I'm not going to call her," he interrupted, guessing what I was about to say.

"Am I that predictable?" I asked. "Or had you been thinking about calling her, too?"

"Maybe a little of both," he answered. He had a slight, uncomfortable grin.

"You know," I said, "I was also going to say that instead of complaining to her just yet, you could tell her that you called because you'd been thinking a lot about the time when she was seven and you were pushing her on the swing and the two of you couldn't stop laughing. Remember?"

"Of course I do. But that was before. . . . Don't think you can get me with sentiment," he said grimly, looking uncomfortable again. He stood there a moment, as if he weren't quite ready to leave. I wasn't sure what more to say. "Gotta go check the mail," he finally said. "I'll see you next week."

The heavy door closed tightly after him. The room was silent.

"Hey, happy birthday!" I called out, reminding him a bit late. I was sure he didn't hear me.

Think about these things.

I hope that after having read this book, you at least come away with a growing belief that you are worthwhile and lovable. I want you to feel that there is hope, even though the prospects for your future make you somewhat anxious. I want you to know that you can heed the call inside you, that beckoning within to do something about your long-standing hurts. You can forgive and be forgiven. You can heal your wounded relationships. And you can reinvent those relationships into something spectacular.

Forgiveness is the key. Forgiveness finds you when you are lost, fills you when you are empty. When it happens, it doesn't merely influence you, it affects you profoundly.

As a sudden birth of a mountain, sprawling and spiring, would leave you shaken and in awe, so does forgiveness capture you. Yet it is also gentle, caressing you like wind upon a field of wheat. And it reawakens you to all that you are, all that you can become, should you accept it and make it your own.

There was a knock on the door, quite unexpected.

"Sorry to disturb you," he said. "But I think I may have dropped my wallet when I was here. Have you seen it?"

"Wouldn't want to lose your wallet, especially on your fifty-first birthday," I said. He located it quickly, hidden underneath the cushion of the chair he'd been sitting in. But he wasn't ready to leave just yet.

"You know who this is?" he asked, pointing to an old, creased photograph that had been tucked inside his wallet, and his heart, for years.

"She's precious," I said, looking at a picture of a girl six or seven years old. The woman next to her, probably the mother, seemed vibrant then. I imagined him asking them to pose, her asking him to get it "just right." Bygone days. "Thanks for showing it to me," I said.

"I'm still not going to call her," he insisted. "I don't care what you say. I've tried before. It wouldn't work now anyway."

He looked hard at me, expecting me to challenge him.

"No, it may not work now," I said. "But then

again . . ." I stopped myself. We had been at this impasse before. I looked him in the eye and sighed. "You don't have an easy choice to make, I know," I said.

He nodded, turned around, and ambled out the door for the second time that morning.

"Hey," I called out. "Happy birthday." The door shut tightly after him.

Maybe that time he heard me.

Bibliography

Ashbrook, James B. "Paul Tillich Converses with Psychotherapists." *Journal of Religion and Health*, 1972, *11(1)*, 40–72.

Bloomfield, Harold. *Making Peace with Your Parents.* New York: Ballantine Books, 1985.

Boszormenyi-Nagy, Ivan, and Geraldine Sparks. *Invisible Loyalties.* New York: Brunner/Mazel, 1984.

Bowen, Murray. *Family Therapy in Clinical Practice.* New York: Jason Aranson, Inc., 1978.

Buber, Martin. *The Knowledge of Man.* New York: Harper & Row, 1965.

———. *I and Thou.* New York: Scribner & Sons, 1958.

Buscaglia, Leo. *Learning to Love.* New York: Ballantine, 1984.

Chartier, Myron R. "Parenting: A Theological Model." *Journal of Psychology and Theology*, 1978, *6(1)*, 54–61.

Close, H. T. "Forgiveness and Responsibility: A Case Study." *Pastoral Psychology,* 1970, 21, 19–25.

Donnely, Doris. *Learning to Forgive.* New York: Macmillan Publishing Co., 1979.

Fisher, Sebern F. "Identity of Two: The Phenomenology of Shame in Borderline Development and Treatment." *Psychotherapy,* 1985, 22, 101–09.

Forward, Susan. *Men Who Hate Women and the Women Who Love Them.* New York: Bantam, 1986.

Fraiberg, Selma. *The Magic Years.* New York: Charles Scribner & Sons, 1959.

Frankl, Victor. *Man's Search for Meaning: An Introduction to Logotherapy.* Boston: Beacon Press, 1968.

Friedman, Maurice. *The Healing Dialogue in Psychotherapy.* New York: Jason Aronson, Inc., 1985.

Guerin, Philip J., Leo F. Fay, Susan L. Burden, and Judith G. Kautto. *The Evaluation and Treatment of Marital Conflict: A Four Stage Approach.* New York: Basic Books, 1987.

Hart, O. VanDer. *Rituals in Psychotherapy: Transition and Continuity.* New York: Irvington Press, 1983.

Hoffman, Lynn. *Foundations of Family Therapy.* New York: Basic Books, Inc., 1981.

Hunter, R. C. "Forgiveness, Retaliation, and Paranoid Reactions." *Canadian Psychiatric Association Journal,* 1978, 23(3), 167–73.

Jampolsky, Gerald G. *Goodbye to Guilt: Releasing Fear Through Forgiveness.* New York: Bantam Books, 1985.

————. *Love Is Letting Go of Fear*. New York: Bantam Books, New York, 1979.

Jessee, Edgar H., and Luciano L'Abate. "Paradoxical Treatment of Depression in Married Couples." In Luciano L'Abate (ed.) *The Handbook of Family Psychology and Therapy*, Volume 2. Homewood, Ill.: The Dorsey Press, 1985.

May, Rollo. *Man's Search for Himself*. New York: Dell, York, 1953.

Pattison, E. M. "The Development of Moral Values in Children." *Pastoral Psychology*, 1969, *20(191)*, 14–30.

————. "Ego-Morality: An Emerging Psychotherapeutic Concept." *Psychoanalytic Review*, 1968, *55(29)*, 187–222.

————. "Social and Psychological Aspects of Religion in Psychotherapy." *Journal of Nervous and Mental Disorders*, 1966, *141*, 586–97.

————. "On the Failure to Forgive or Be Forgiven." *American Journal of Psychotherapy*, 1965, *19*, 106–13.

Peck, M. Scott. *The Road Less Traveled*. New York: Simon & Schuster, 1978.

Ramsay, R. W. "Behavioral Approaches to Bereavement." *Behavior, Research, and Therapy*, 1979, *15*, 131–35.

Rando, Therese A. "Creating Therapeutic Rituals in the Psychotherapy of the Bereaved." *Behavior, Research, and Therapy*, 1985, *22*, 224–36.

Sager, Clifford J. *Marriage Contracts and Couple Therapy*. New York: Brunner/Mazel, 1976.

Sandler, Joseph (ed.). *Projective Identification, Projective Identification*. Madison, Conn.: International Universities Press, Inc., 1987.

Scott, Edward. "Combining the Roles of Priest and Physician: A Clinical Case." *Journal of Religion And Health*, 1979, *18*, 160–63.

Sexton, Ray O., and Richard C. Modack. "The Adam and Eve Syndrome." *Journal of Religion and Health*, 1978, *17*, 163–68.

Smedes, Lewis. *Forgive and Forget*. New York: Harper & Row, 1985.

Spidell, Steven. "Moral Development and the Forgiveness of Sin." *Journal of Psychology and Theology*, 1981, *9(2)*, 159–63.

Stern, E. Mark (ed.). *Psychotherapy and the Religiously Committed Patient*. New York: Hawthorne Press, 1985.

Strong, Stanley R. "Christian Counseling in Action." *Counseling and Values*, 1977, *21(2)*, 89–128.

Viscott, David. *The Viscott Method*. Boston: Houghton-Mifflin, 1984.

———. *Risking*. New York: Pocket Books, 1977.

———. *The Language Of Feelings*. New York: Pocket Books, 1976.

Wapnick, Kenneth. "Forgiveness: A Spiritual Psychotherapy." In E. Mark Stern (ed.), *Psychotherapy and the Religiously Committed Patient*. New York: Hawthorne Press, 1985.

Wegscheider, Sharon. *Another Chance.* PaloAlto, Calif.: Science and Behavior Books, 1981.

Wilson, W. P. "Utilization of Christian Beliefs in Psychotherapy." *Journal of Counseling and Theology,* 1974, 2(2), 125–31.

Yallom, Irvin. *Existential Psychotherapy.* New York: Basic Books, New York, 1980.

Zerin, Edward. "Finishing Unfinished Business: Applications of the Drama Triangle to Marital Therapy." *Transactional Analysis Journal,* 1983, 13, 155–57.